Financial valuation workbook

Step-by-Step Exercises to Help You Master Financial Valuation

JAMES R. HITCHNER

and

MICHAEL J. MARD

WILEY

John Wiley & Sons, Inc.

To my mother and father, Earle and Virginia Hitchner, and my sister, Deborah Hitchner, who left this world too early for me to get to know her.

To Pam, Seph, Joe and Shelley, Laura and Jacob, and my mom and dad, Geneva and Joe Mard. And to Derick, we miss you.

James R. Hitchner, CPA/ABV, ASA, The Financial Valuation Group, Financial Consulting Group, L.C. James R. Hitchner is the managing director of The Financial Valuation Group (FVG) in Atlanta, Georgia. FVG is a national financial advisory services firm specializing in valuation and litigation services and is a founding member of the Financial Consulting Group, L.C. (FCG). FCG is a national association of professional services firms dedicated to excellence in valuation, financial, and litigation consulting.

Mr. Hitchner has more than 24 years of professional experience, including 22 years in valuation services and two years in real estate development. He spent seven years with Phillips Hitchner Group and was partner-in-charge of valuation services for the Southern Region of Coopers & Lybrand (currently PricewaterhouseCoopers), where he spent more than nine years. He was also employed as a senior appraiser with the national appraisal firm American Appraisal Associates, in both the financial and industrial valuation groups.

He has been recognized as a qualified expert witness and has provided testimony on valuations in Florida, Georgia, Indiana, New Jersey, North Carolina, Ohio, Tennessee, and Virginia. In the valuation area he has co-authored 10 courses, taught over 35 courses, published over 30 articles, and has made over 80 conference presentations.

Mr. Hitchner is co-author of *Valuation for Financial Reporting: Intangible Assets, Goodwill, and Impairment Analysis—SFAS 141 and 142* and editor/co-author of *Financial Valuation: Applications and Models,* both published by John Wiley & Sons. He is also co-author of the American Institute of Certified Public Accountants (AICPA) three-part self-study videocourse series on SFAS 141 and 142 on business combinations, intangible assets, and goodwill impairment.

He is an inductee in the AICPA Business Valuation Hall of Fame and current member of the AICPA task force on Business Valuation Standards. Mr. Hitchner is past chairman of the Business Valuation Committee of the Georgia Society of CPAs and the ABV exam review course committee; past member of the AICPA Business Valuation Subcommittee and the AICPA ABV exam committee; and contributing editor of AICPA CPA Expert newsletter.

He has a Bachelor of Science degree in Engineering from the University of Pittsburgh and a Masters of Business Administration degree from Rider University. He holds the AICPA Accreditation in Business Valuation (ABV) specialty designation, and is an Accredited Senior Appraiser (ASA) with the American Society of Appraisers.

Michael J. Mard, CPA/ABV, ASA, The Financial Valuation Group, Financial Consulting Group, L.C.   Michael J. Mard is a managing director of The Financial Valuation Group (FVG) in Tampa, Florida. FVG is a national financial advisory firm specializing in valuation and litigation services. Mr. Mard was founding president of the Financial Consulting Group, a national association of professional service firms dedicated to excellence in valuation, litigation, and financial consulting.

Mr. Mard has been a full-time business appraiser and expert witness for over 19 years, specializing in intangible assets, specifically intellectual property. He has developed analyses that have been reviewed and accepted by the Securities and Exchange Commission (SEC), numerous accounting firms (including the Big Five), the Internal Revenue Service (IRS), and the courts. Mr. Mard has provided expert testimony in both Federal and state courts related to intangible assets, intellectual property, business damages, marital dissolution, shareholder disputes, and IRS matters.

Mr. Mard is lead co-author of *Valuation for Financial Reporting: Intangible Assets, Goodwill, and Impairment Analysis—SFAS 141 and 142* and co-author of *Financial Valuation: Applications and Models,* both published by John Wiley & Sons. He is co-author of the American Institute of Certified Public Accountants (AICPA) three-part self-study video course series on SFAS 141 and 142 on business combinations, intangible assets, and goodwill impairment. He also co-authored the *AICPA Consulting Services Practice Aid 99-2: Valuing Intellectual Property and Calculating Infringement Damages.* Mr. Mard has co-authored 20 courses and published over 60 articles. He has been a presenter, speaker, and instructor over 70 times.

Mr. Mard is very active at state and national levels with emphasis on business valuation standards and intellectual property valuations. He has served on numerous committees and task forces of the AICPA, Florida Institute of Certified Public Accountants, American Society of Appraisers, and the Financial Accounting Standards Board (FASB). Mr. Mard continues to serve on two FASB task forces: Disclosure About Intangible Assets and Business Combination/Purchase Method Procedures.

He has received the AICPA Business Valuation Volunteer of the Year Award and been inducted into the AICPA Business Valuation Hall of Fame. He has been published in the Marquis Who's Who in Finance Industry and the International Who's Who of Professionals. He has a Bachelor of Science degree in Accounting and a Masters of Accounting from the University of South Florida. He holds the AICPA Accreditation in Business Valuation (ABV) specialty designation, and is an Accredited Senior Appraiser (ASA) with the American Society of Appraisers.

acknowledgments

Several people were instrumental in preparing this book. Thank you Faye Danger and Deanna Muraki of The Financial Valuation Group in Tampa, Florida, and Terri Houston of Phillips Hitchner in Atlanta, Georgia. You were great.

We would also like to thank Jim Alerding, CPA/ABV, ASA, CVA, of Clifton Gunderson in Indianapolis, Indiana for helping with the case study, and all the authors of *Financial Valuation: Applications and Models* for submitting the ValTips in Chapter 3: Mel H. Abraham, CPA/ABV, ASA, CVA; R. James Alerding, CPA/ABV, ASA, CVA; Terry Jacoby Allen, CPA/ABV, ASA; Larry R. Cook, CPA/ABV, CBA; Michael A. Crain, CPA/ABV, ASA, CFE; Robert E. Duffy, CPA/ABV, ASA, CFA; Edward J. Dupke, CPA/ABV; Nancy J. Fannon, CPA/ABV, BVAL, MCBA; John R. Gilbert, CPA/ABV, ASA, CVA; Thomas E. Hilton, CPA/ABV, CVA; Steven D. Hyden, CPA, ASA; Gregory S. Koonsman, CFA; Eva M. Lang, CPA, ASA; Harold G Martin, Jr., CPA/ABV, ASA, CFE; Michael Mattson; Raymond E. Moran, ASA; Charles M. Phillips, CPA/ABV, CFE; James S. Rigby, Jr., CPA/ABV, ASA; Ronald L. Seigneur, CPA/ABV, CVA; Robin E. Taylor, CPA/ABV, CBA, CFE, CVA; Linda B. Trugman, CPA/ABV, ASA, CBA; Donald P. Wisehart CPA/ABV, CVA; and Mark L. Zyla, CPA/ABV, ASA, CFA.

contents

The Financial Valuation Workbook (FVW) contains both educational exercises that guide the reader through a complete business valuation and valuation tools that professionals can use in preparing business valuations. It is structured to be used on a stand-alone basis. It is also a companion text to *Financial Valuation: Applications and Models* (FV) (John Wiley & Sons), where the subject matter contained in the workbook is expanded upon. This workbook contains basic, intermediate, and advanced topics on valuing businesses conveyed in a series of easily understandable exercises with comprehensive answers.

FVW is targeted to the following professionals and groups who are typically exposed to financial valuation issues:

- Appraisers
- Appraisal Associations and Societies
- Actuaries
- Attorneys
- Bankers
- Business Brokers
- Business executives including CEOs, CFOs, and tax directors
- Business owners
- CPAs
- Estate and Gift Planners
- Financial Analysts
- Government agencies including the IRS, SEC, and DOL
- Insurance Agents
- Investment Advisors
- Investment Bankers
- Judges
- Pension Administrators
- Stockbrokers

FVW contains five chapters, each with a different purpose.

Chapter 1 contains more than 75 exercises that have been placed throughout excerpts of an actual business valuation report presenting numerous valuation topics, including rates of return, the capitalized cash flow method of the income approach, and the guideline company transaction and guideline public company methods of the market approach.

Chapter 2 contains comprehensive answers to the exercises in Chapter 1.

Chapter 3 includes over 350 ValTips that are extracted from the companion book FV. This summary of ValTips can serve professionals as a quick reference source of important concepts, application issues, and pitfalls to avoid.

Chapter 4 presents a Valuation Process Flowchart to allow professionals to follow a more structured process in applying and documenting the income approach.

Chapter 5 includes over 40 checklists that can be used by professionals in documenting their valuations. It can also be used by less experienced professionals as a guide in applying valuation concepts.

* * * * * * *

Financial valuations are very much affected by specific facts and circumstances. As such, the views expressed in these written materials do not necessarily reflect the professional opinions or positions that the authors would take in every business valuation assignment, or in providing business valuation services in connection with an actual litigation matter. Every situation is unique and differing facts and circumstances may result in variations of the applied methodologies.

Nothing contained in these written materials shall be construed to constitute the rendering of valuation advice; the rendering of a valuation opinion; the rendering of an opinion as to the propriety of taking a particular valuation position; or the rendering of any other professional opinion or service.

Business valuation services are necessarily fact-sensitive particularly in a litigation context. Therefore, the authors urge readers to apply their expertise to particular valuation fact patterns that they encounter, or to seek competent professional assistance as warranted in the circumstances.

* * * * * * *

Disclaimer Excluding Any Warranties: This book is designed to provide guidance to analysts, auditors, management, and other professionals, but is not to be used as a substitute for professional judgment. Procedures must be altered to fit each assignment. The reader takes sole responsibility for implementation of material from this book. The implied warranties of merchantability and fitness of purpose and all other warranties, whether expressed or implied, are excluded from this transaction, and shall not apply to this book. None of the authors, editors, reviewers, or publisher shall be liable for any indirect, special, or consequential damages.

Valuation Case Study Exercises

INTRODUCTION

The purpose of this chapter is to highlight and discuss important concepts in valuation through a series of exercises. These exercises have been intermittently placed in excerpts of a valuation report. You should attempt to complete these exercises as you read the report with reasoning and emphasis on an explanation of your conclusion. The authors' solutions to these exercises can be found in Chapter 2.

The following case presents selected excerpts from a business valuation report that, in its entirety, was in full compliance with the Uniform Standards of Professional Appraisal Practice. This report format is one of many that analysts can use in presenting business valuations. All schedules have been omitted as they are not necessary for the exercises. Some of the terms, numbers, sources, and other data have been changed for ease of presentation.

THE VALUATION REPORT

August 20, 2000

Mr. Tom Profit
LEGGO Construction, Inc.
123 Builders Drive
Anycity, Anystate 54321

Dear Mr. Profit:

The object of this valuation report is to estimate the fair market value of 100% of the common stock in LEGGO Construction, Inc. (LEGGO or the Company), on a nonmarketable, control interest basis, as of December 31, 1999, for management purposes and internal planning.

EXERCISE 1: The purpose of the valuation of LEGGO is to assist management in internal planning. What other purposes are there?

_____

_____

_____

_____

EXERCISE 2: Which of the following is the "as of" date for valuation?

a. Anytime within one year
b. "As of" a single point in time
c. "As of" a single point in time or six months later
d. Date that the report is signed

In our opinion, the fair market value of 100% of the common stock in LEGGO, on a nonmarketable, control interest basis, as of December 31, 1999, for management purposes, is (rounded):

FIVE MILLION EIGHT HUNDRED THOUSAND DOLLARS
$5,800,000

EXERCISE 3: Valuation conclusions can be presented as:

a. A range of values
b. A single value
c. An estimate of value
d. All of the above

EXERCISE 4: This valuation is being done on a nonmarketable, control interest basis. It is also on a control stand-alone basis. Name the four levels of value that are considered in a valuation.

1._____

2._____

3._____

4._____

The standard of value used in this appraisal report is fair market value. *Fair market value* is:

The price, expressed in terms of cash equivalents, at which property would change hands between a hypothetical willing and able buyer and a hypothetical willing and able seller, acting at arms length in an open and unrestricted market, when neither is under compulsion to buy or sell and when both have reasonable knowledge of the relevant facts.[1]

---

[1] International Glossary of Business Valuation Terms (The C.L.A.R.E.N.C.E. Glossary Project comprised of the following professional organizations: American Institute of Certified Public Accountants, American Society of Appraisers, Canadian Institute of Chartered Business Valuators, National Association of Certified Valuation Analysts, and The Institute of Business Appraisers, 2001).

EXERCISE 5: Which of these are standards of value?

a. Fair market value, fair value financial reporting, investment value
b. Fair value investment reporting, fair value state actions, intrinsic value
c. Investment value, intrinsic value, equal value
d. Fair market value, equal value, investment value

Valuation is based on relevant facts, elements of common sense, informed judgment, and reasonableness. Our scope was unrestricted and our methodology and analysis complied with the Uniform Standards of Professional Appraisal Practice. In addition, this valuation report and the values determined herein cannot be utilized or relied on for any purpose other than for internal management planning.

The enclosed narrative valuation report, as well as all documents and schedules in our files, constitute the basis on which our opinion of fair market value was determined. Statements of fact contained in this valuation report are, to the best of our knowledge and belief, true and correct. In the event that facts or other representations relied on in the attached valuation report are revised or otherwise changed, our opinion as to the fair market value of the common stock of the Company may require updating. However, Valking LLP has no obligation to update our opinion of the fair market value of the common stock of the Company for information that comes to our attention after the date of this report.

No partner or employee of Valking LLP has any current or contemplated future interest in the Company or any other interest that might tend to prevent them from making a fair and unbiased opinion of fair market value. Compensation to Valking LLP is not contingent on the opinions or conclusions reached in this valuation report.

We wish to express our appreciation to you and the management of the Company for your cooperation in making available to us financial data and other pertinent information necessary for the preparation of the report.

Very truly yours,

Valking LLP
Val Dude, CPA/ABV, ASA, CBA, CVA

INTRODUCTION

Description of the Assignment

Valking LLP was retained by Mr. Tom Profit to determine the fair market value of 100% of the common stock in LEGGO Construction, Inc. (LEGGO or the Company) on a nonmarketable, control interest basis, as of December 31, 1999, for management purposes.

Summary Description and Brief History of the Company

The Company was incorporated in 1978 in the state of Anystate. The Company is a closely held subcontractor whose revenues are predominantly earned from sewer and water-line construction, primarily in central Anystate. The Company's customers generally consist of area contractors, developers, and local governments. The Company is now legally structured as an S corporation.

EXERCISE 6:   Valuation of S corporations is one of the most controversial issues in business valuations today. The main issue is whether to and how to tax effect S corporation income. What four options are there in valuing S corporations?

1._____

2._____

3._____

4._____

The Company obtains most of its business through bidding competitively with general contractors. Management believes that customers contract with the Company due to its solid reputation and competitive bids; its customers have remained loyal. The two largest customers are XYZ General Contractors and the city of Anycity.

Employee relations have been harmonious with minimal turnover. All employees of the Company are unionized with the exception of several office workers. Currently, the economic climates in the market and industry are good. The Company has six competitors that are similar in size and nature.

Ownership and Capital Structure of the Company

The Company is legally structured as a closely held S corporation. As of the date of valuation, there were 5,000 shares of common stock outstanding, structured as follows:

Name	Shares Owned	Percentage of Ownership
Tom Profit	4,250	85%
Gary Profit	250	5%
Susan Profit	250	5%
Michelle Profit	250	5%
Total	5,000	100%

EXERCISE 7:   We are valuing a 100% controlling interest in LEGGO. The percentage of ownership of individual shareholders is not an issue here. However, assume we are valuing the 85% of Tom Profit as opposed to the 100% in LEGGO. The value of an 85% interest in LEGGO would be based on 85% of the 100% control value in LEGGO.

   a. True
   b. False

Standard of Value

The standard of value used in this report is fair market value. Fair market value is defined as:

> *The price, expressed in terms of cash equivalents, at which property would change hands between a hypothetical willing and able buyer and a hypothetical willing and able seller, acting at arms length in an open and unrestricted market, when neither is under compulsion to buy or sell and when both have reasonable knowledge of the relevant facts.*[2]

Among other factors, this valuation report considers elements of appraisal listed in the Internal Revenue Service's Revenue Ruling 59-60, which "outline[s] and review[s] in general the approach, methods, and factors to be considered in valuing shares of the capital stock of closely held corporations."[3] Specifically, Revenue Ruling 59-60 states that the following factors should be carefully considered in a valuation of closely held stock:

EXERCISE 8: Revenue Ruling 59-60 is only applicable to estate, gift, and income tax valuations.

    a. True
    b. False

---

1. *The nature of the business and history of the enterprise from its inception.* The Company was incorporated in 1975. It is engaged primarily as a sewage and water-line subcontractor. The Company has grown since its inception, and its customers have remained loyal.
2. *The economic outlook in general and condition and outlook of the specific industry in particular.* The consideration of the economic outlook on a national level, as well as on a regional and local level, is important in performing a valuation. How the economy is performing has a bearing in part on how the Company performs. Overall, the Company outlook is positive.
3. *The book value of the stock and the financial condition of the business.* The Company has a relatively strong balance sheet with a majority of its assets in three categories: cash, contract receivables, and fixed assets. The fixed assets consist primarily of construction equipment and vehicles.
4. *The earning capacity of the company.* The Company's compound growth rate in revenues from 1995 to 1999 was approximately 5%. The Company has demonstrated a good ability to generate profits.
5. *The dividend-paying capacity of the company.* The Company has made distributions equal to the amount of the shareholders' respective tax liabilities in the recent past and will likely continue this trend into the future.
6. *Whether the enterprise has goodwill or other intangible value.* It is generally acknowledged that goodwill is often measured by the earnings ability of an enterprise being valued. Goodwill can be broadly defined as characteristics that

---

[2] Ibid.
[3] Internal Revenue Service, Revenue Ruling 59-60, Section 1.

induce customers to continue to do business with the Company and to attract new customers.

7. *Sales of the stock and size of the block to be valued.* There have been no sales of stock of the Company that would provide an indication of value during the period being analyzed.

8. *The market prices of stock of corporations engaged in the same or a similar line of business having their stocks actively traded in a free and open market, either on an exchange or over the counter.* The market approach was considered in this valuation. A search for guideline companies that are similar in nature and size to the Company was performed.[4]

EXERCISE 9:   These are the only eight tenets of value in Revenue Ruling 59-60 that need to be considered.

   a. True
   b. False

Sources of Information

Sources of information used in this appraisal include:

1. Audited financial statements for the years ended March 31, 1995 through December 31, 1999
2. *Stocks, Bonds, Bills, and Inflation, 1999 Yearbook*, published by Ibbotson Associates
3. *The Federal Reserve Bank* for the 20-year maturity rate on 30-year bonds as of December 31, 1999
4. *1996-1999/2000 editions of Benchmark Statistics and Ratios* (fictitious)
5. *The National Economic Review*, published by Mercer Capital Management, Inc., for the fourth quarter of 1999
6. *The Beige Book* published by the Federal Reserve Bank as of December 8, 1999
7. *www.xls.com* web site for public company information
8. *www.hoovers.com* web site for public company information
9. *Pratt's Stats* Online Comparable Transactions Database
10. *IBA* Comparable Transactions Database

Valking LLP has relied on these sources, but has not provided attest services in regard to any of the sources. Val Dude, a financial analyst with Valking LLP interviewed management of the Company.

NATIONAL ECONOMIC OUTLOOK

In conjunction with the preparation of our opinion of fair market value, we have reviewed and analyzed the economic conditions as of December 31, 1999, the date

---

[4] Ibid, Section 4.

of valuation. This report includes summary discussions and analysis of the national economy for the fourth quarter of 1999. These discussions are based on a review of current economic statistics, articles in the financial press, and economic reviews found in current business periodicals. The purpose of the review is to provide a representative "consensus" review of the condition of the national economy and its general outlook at the end of the fourth quarter of 1999.

General Economic Overview

According to preliminary estimates released by the Department of Commerce's Bureau of Economic Analysis (BEA) real Gross Domestic Product (GDP), the output of goods and services produced by labor and property located in the United States, increased at an annualized rate of 5.8% during the fourth quarter of 1999. Revised growth in GDP for the third quarter of 1999 was 5.7%, which is higher than the preliminary estimated annualized growth rate of 4.8%. Increases in personal consumption expenditures, government spending, inventory investment, and exports were major contributors to the increase in GDP. These components were partially offset by an increase in imports. Annual growth in GDP for 1999 was 4.0%, modestly lower than the 4.3% growth rate reported for 1998. The U.S. economy is expected to continue expanding in the year 2000 at approximately a 3% to 4% growth rate.

The Composite Index of Leading Economic Indicators (the government's primary forecasting gauge) increased 0.4% in December after rising 0.1% in October and 0.3% in November. The composit index attempts to gauge economic activity six to nine months in advance. Multiple consecutive moves in the same direction are said to be indicative of the general direction of the economy. In December, nine of the ten leading economic indicators rose. The most significant increases were money supply, interest rate spread, manufacturers' new orders of nondefense capital goods, stock prices, and manufacturers' new orders of consumer goods and materials. During the six-month span through December, the leading index rose 0.9%, and seven of the ten components advanced. According to the Conference Board's report, "the leading indicators point to a continuation of the [economic] expansion during 2000."[5]

Stock markets ended the year at record levels. Broad market and blue chip stock indices turned in 20% to 25% annual gains, while the NASDAQ gained an unprecedented 85.6% during 1999. The Federal Reserve (the "Fed") increased the Federal funds rate in mid-November in an effort to slow economic growth and thus curb inflation. The Fed is attempting to cool the robust economic engine before it produces excessive inflationary pressure. Additional rate tightening is expected during the early part of 2000. Despite a midquarter respite in bond price declines, bond yields reached their highest levels of the year in December, with the 30-year Treasury bond averaging a yield to maturity of 6.35%.

Inflation results for 1999 reflect very low core price growth but high growth in energy prices. The Consumer Price Index (CPI) rose 2.7% for the year. Tight labor markets and strong economic activity may produce inflationary pressures, however, pricing data continue to suggest that gains in productivity and limited pricing

---

[5] *The National Economic Review,* published by Mercer Capital Management, Inc., for the fourth quarter of 1999.

power are keeping inflation in check. The inflation rate is expected to continue at approximately 2.5% to 3.0% in the first half of the year 2000, but increasing fuel prices are posing a significant threat to future price stability.

Consumer Spending and Inflation

According to the Bureau of Labor Statistics (BLS), the CPI was unchanged at 168.3 in December (CPI: all urban consumers, 1982-1984 = 100, before seasonal adjustment). Excluding food and energy, this rate increased at a seasonally adjusted 0.1% in December, following an increase of 0.2% in November. The seasonally adjusted annual rate of inflation for the fourth quarter was 2.2%, compared to 4.2%, 2.9%, and 1.5%, respectively, for the prior three quarters. The inflation rate for 1999 was 2.7%, higher than the 1.6% rate of 1998 which was the smallest annual increase since a 1.1% rise in 1986. The acceleration in 1999 was largely due to an upturn in petroleum-based energy prices. The energy index, which declined 8.8% in 1998, increased 13.4% in 1999. Following a 15.1% decline in 1998, petroleum-based energy costs increased 29.5% in 1999, the largest annual advance since 1990.

The Producer Price Index (PPI), generally recognized as predictive of near-term consumer inflation pressure, increased 0.3% in December (PPI for finished goods, seasonally adjusted) following a 0.2% increase in November and a 0.1% decline in October. For the year, the PPI increased 3.0% and reflected the dramatic impact of energy costs on producer costs. The PPI was flat in 1998, reflecting the aforementioned energy price declines. Core PPI in 1999 increased only 0.9% and mirrored the same underlying pattern in the CPI regarding productivity enhancements and limited wholesale pricing power.

According to the Census Bureau of the Commerce Department, the increase in retail sales for the October to November period was 1.1%, higher than the 0.9% originally reported. The advance estimate for December retail sales (adjusted for seasonal, holiday, and trading day differences) reflected an increase of 1.2% from November and a 9.7% increase over December 1998 sales. Total sales for 1999 were $3.0 trillion, 8.9% higher than 1998. Personal consumption spending represents approximately two-thirds of total economic activity and is generally the primary component of economic growth. Real personal consumption spending increased 5.3% in the fourth quarter, following a 4.9% increase in the third quarter. Durable goods purchases increased 11.8% in the fourth quarter after an increase of 7.7% in the third quarter of 1999.

The Financial Markets

Stock markets began the fourth quarter with a volatile October amid speculations of an interest rate increase. Equity markets plunged during the third week of October before rebounding on investor hopes that the U.S. economy was slowing. The National Association of Securities Dealers Automated Quotations (NASDAQ) showed breathtaking gains in November and December, while the Dow Jones Average (Dow) and Standard and Poor's (S&P) 500 faltered several times before finishing with a strong December. The Dow, the S&P 500, and the NASDAQ finished the year at record levels. For the Dow and the S&P 500, it was the fifth straight year of double-digit growth. However, blue chip stocks were overshadowed by the NASDAQ's phenomenal 85.6% growth for the year.

The Dow Jones Industrial Average (DJIA) closed the fourth quarter at 11497.12, an increase of 11% for the quarter. The DJIA gained 25.2% in 1999 after a 16% gain in 1998. The S&P 500 closed the quarter at 1469.25, a 14.5% increase for the fourth quarter, following much the same pattern as the Dow. The S&P 500 gained almost 20% in 1999 after a 27% gain in 1998. The NASDAQ composite index, generally consisting of smaller and more technology oriented issues, increased 48.2% during the quarter to close at 4069.31. The NASDAQ surpassed its almost 40% gain in 1998 with an 85.6% gain in 1999. More than half of the NASDAQ's 1999 gain came after the index crossed 3000 on November 3. The broad-market Wilshire 5000 index closed at 13812.67, reflecting a quarterly gain of 18%. The Wilshire 5000 gained 22% in 1999 following similar growth in 1998.

The monthly average yield to maturity on the 30-year Treasury bond during the fourth quarter of 1999 was 6.26%, 6.15%, and 6.35%, respectively, for October, November, and December. Bond prices are negatively correlated with their respective yields, which can shift abruptly on investor reactions to major variances in reported economic data versus market expectations (i.e., expected inflation, growth, monetary policy and other Fed action, etc.). With few exceptions, yields have generally risen throughout the year. Oddly, the November Fed rate hike did not result in a dramatic repricing, but in tandem with the Fed's lack of action at its later December meeting, bond prices fell abruptly in expectation of high growth and the possibility of impending action by the Fed to slow the economy.

Interest Rates

After leaving interest rates unchanged at its October 5 meeting, the Federal Reserve Open Markets Committee (FOMC) raised interest rates by a quarter of a percentage point at its November 16 meeting, the third increase in a three-month span. The change was made to "markedly diminish the risk of rising inflation going forward." Although the FOMC remained idle at its December 21 meeting, it remains concerned "with the possibility that over time increases in demand will continue to exceed the growth in potential supply." Such trends could foster inflationary imbalances that would undermine the economy's performance. Nonetheless, the FOMC decided to adopt a symmetric directive in order to indicate that the focus of policy in the inter-meeting period must be to ensure a smooth transition into the year 2000.[6]

EXERCISE 10: What types of industries would most likely be affected by anticipated changes in interest rates?

_____

_____

_____

_____

---

[6] Ibid.

Construction, Housing, and Real Estate

Home building is generally representative of overall economic activity because new home construction stimulates a broad range of industrial, commercial, and consumer spending and investment. According to the U.S. Commerce Department's Bureau of the Census, new privately owned housing starts were at a seasonally adjusted annualized rate of 1.712 million units in December, 7% above the revised November estimate of 1.598 million units, but 2% below the December 1998 rate. Single-family housing starts in December were 1.402 million, 8% higher than the November level of 1.299 million units. An estimated 1.663 million privately owned housing units were started in 1999, 3% above the 1998 figure of 1.617 million.

The seasonally adjusted annual rate of new housing building permits (considered the best indicator of future housing starts) was 1.611 million units in December, similar to the revised November rate of 1.612 million and 6% below the December 1998 estimate of 1.708 million.

Unemployment

According to the Labor Department's Bureau of Labor Statistics, unemployment levels during the fourth quarter remained historically low. The unemployment rate for October, November, and December was 4.1%, slightly lower than the September rate of 4.2%. This marked the 30th consecutive month that the unemployment rate was below 5%. The unemployment rate for all of 1999 was approximately 4.2%, down from 4.5% in 1998. Tight labor markets remain a theme of Federal Reserve concerns regarding inflation. Productivity enhancements and relatively constant levels of workers' hours are believed to be mitigating historically inflationary conditions.

Summary and Outlook

Economic growth, as measured by growth in GDP, accelerated to 5.8% in the fourth quarter of 1999, after registering a revised 5.7% annualized rate in the third quarter. Annual growth in GDP for 1999 was 4.0%. Stock markets finished the year at record levels. Both the Dow and S&P 500 experienced double-digit growth for the fifth straight year, while the NASDAQ posted an 85.6% gain in 1999. Bond prices generally declined throughout the year but showed particular weakness on rising yields late in the fourth quarter. Fourth-quarter inflation reflected a seasonally adjusted annualized rate of 2.2%, representing a decrease from the third-quarter rate of 4.2%. The rate of inflation for 1999 was 2.7%, higher than the 1.6% rate for 1998. After leaving interest rates unchanged at its October 5 meeting, the Federal Reserve Open Markets Committee raised interest rates by a quarter of a percentage point at its November 16 meeting. No change was made at the December 21 meeting. Economic growth is expected to moderate somewhat from recent levels, but should remain historically favorable with GDP growing at 3% to 4%. Inflation is expected to remain relatively mild at below 3%, but increasing fuel prices are posing a significant threat to future price stability.

EXERCISE 11: What two economic indicators are probably the most important in valuation?

a. Unemployment levels and Gross Domestic Product (GDP)
b. Dow Jones Industrial Average and Producer Price Index
c. GDP and inflation
d. Inflation and unemployment levels

National Economic Impact on Valuation

Analyzing the national economy is an important step in performing a valuation because it helps to identify any risk that the economy may have in relation to the Company. In this case, the economy appears to be performing well.

EXERCISE 12: In valuing a small geographically concentrated business, which of these types of economic data should be considered?

a. International, national, regional, local
b. National, regional, local
c. Regional, local
d. Local only

REGIONAL ECONOMIC DATA (AS OF DECEMBER 8, 1999)

The economy remained strong in October and early November, but was expanding more slowly than earlier in the year. Reports on consumer spending were mixed, with some noting strong sales growth for the first weekend of the 1999 holiday shopping season.

Construction activity generally was strong, despite softening on the residential side. Overall manufacturing output remained strong, but conditions were varied across industry segments. Lenders reported conditions similar to those noted in the last report, and reports reported no signs of Y2K-related surges in inventory borrowing or cash demand. The labor markets remained much tighter than the rest of the nation, and seasonal demand put additional strain on some sectors of the market. The fall harvest was complete, as was the planting of winter wheat. A survey of agricultural bankers indicated that slow farm loan repayments continued to be a problem.

Consumer Spending

Reports on consumer spending activity were mixed. Prior to the Thanksgiving weekend, sales were well below most merchants' expectations. However, several retailers reported double-digit sales gains from a year ago for the Thanksgiving weekend and most merchants expected a strong holiday sales season. Most retailers' reports cited unusually warm weather as contributing to lackluster pre-Thanksgiving sales results, especially for cold-weather apparel. By contrast, sales of appliances, electronics, and lawn and garden goods had continued to be strong.

Retailers reported that inventories for most goods were in line with their planned levels, but inventories of winter merchandise were high. They also noted that they had not changed their promotional activity from a year earlier. Auto dealers reported that lighter floor traffic and a slowdown in light vehicle sales continued through October and into mid-November. One large auto group noted that service activity was also down and that used-car prices weakened considerably.

Construction and Real Estate

Overall real estate and construction activity was robust but softer than earlier in the year. Demand for both new and existing homes continued to ease in October and early November, but most reports described the market as strong. Those realtors contacted indicated that sales in October and early November were down about 10% from very strong results a year earlier. Home builders' reports appeared to be more positive than realtors' reports, with most reports indicating new home sales were unchanged or down slightly. Conditions in the nonresidential sector remained strong and steady for the most part, according to most reports.

Development of light industrial space was steady to down slightly, as was the development of infrastructure projects. A report from one of the largest metro areas suggested that a few large office projects that have recently broken ground might be the last of the current downtown office expansion. Some contractors noted that many customers have changed strategies, preferring to hire the contractor viewed as most likely to complete the job on schedule rather than going with the low bidder.

Manufacturing

The manufacturing sector generally remained strong, although activity varied by industry segment. According to most automakers, orders for light vehicles remained strong nationwide. Inventories were generally in good shape, although they were reportedly lean for select models. Despite these conditions, the pricing environment remained soft, with an increase in incentive spending noted by some analysts. Producers of agricultural and heavy construction equipment reported further softening in output in recent weeks, and most planned to reduce inventories further next year, although not as aggressively as this year. Reports expected domestic demand would be relatively soft in the coming year while foreign demand was expected to pick up. Wallboard producers indicated that demand remained very strong and factories continued to run near capacity. With new capacity coming on stream, however, price increases were expected to moderate in the coming months. A large manufacturer of telecommunications equipment noted that orders continued to recover from weak sales early in the year, due in large part to strengthening demand in Asian markets.

Banking and Finance

Lending activity continued to be mixed in October and early November. Business lending remained robust, and most bankers suggested that growth was steady. A few reports indicated that overall asset quality on commercial loans might have deteriorated slightly, since intense competition for customers led some lenders to relax standards slightly. Some bankers appeared to be less optimistic about the near-term commercial lending outlook than they had been in recent months. Household loan demand softened further, according to most lenders, as new mortgage and refinancing activity continued to slow. Reports noted that asset quality on consumer loans improved as existing bank and store credit-card balances were paid down, delinquencies slowed, and personal bankruptcies decreased. A report from one large money center bank attributed this improvement to a lagged effect from strong refinancing activity earlier in the year, and as a result, did not expect the improvement to endure. None of the bankers contacted noted any unusual borrowing by businesses that would indicate an inventory buildup ahead of the year 2000 rollover, nor was there any noticeable increase in the demand for cash by consumers.

Labor Markets

Labor markets remained very tight in October and early November, and worker shortages appeared to intensify as the holiday hiring season began. Retailers and others who increase hiring for the holidays were finding it particularly difficult to staff positions this year. According to one report, many traditional seasonal workers (such as students, homemakers, etc.) were already employed elsewhere, either part- or full-time, as a result of overall strength in the economy. Some retailers reportedly have gone to extraordinary lengths to attract seasonal hires by offering, among other things, increased wages, steeper in-store discounts, and even tuition reimbursement for part-time workers.

Demand for workers in most other sectors remained strong as well. Temporary help firms in some metro areas reported increasing demand for manufacturing workers, while there were a few reports of slackening demand for financial service professionals, partly as a result of slowing mortgage applications. On balance, reports suggested that overall wage pressures had not intensified further in recent weeks. Staffing services reports indicated that wages were increasing fastest in the administrative/clerical occupations while a slowdown in wage growth was noted for information technology professionals. Reports from a large trucking firm noted the continued shortage of drivers is especially serious during current high seasonal demand for transporting goods. Most reports continued to argue that worker shortages were hampering the economic expansion.

Agriculture

The fall corn and soybean harvest was essentially complete in surrounding states. Storage space for corn and soybeans was reported to be tight in some areas, due to strong yields and a quick harvest pace that caused grain deliveries to bunch up at elevators. Winter wheat planting was finished and most of the crop had emerged, but its condition had deteriorated in some areas due to dry weather. A survey of agricultural bankers indicated that farmland values were steady to weak during the third quarter in several states, with rising values in only two states. Bankers also indicated that slow farm loan repayments continued to be a problem, and a majority believed there will be an increase in the incidence of financially stressed farmers selling assets during the fall and winter.

Regional Economic Impact on Valuation

The regional economy should also be analyzed in performing a valuation to help to determine specific risks associated with the particular region in which the Company operates. In this instance, the regional economy is performing very well in many areas.

LOCAL ECONOMY

Anycity, Anystate was founded in 1810. It has an estimated population of 670,000 citizens and is approximately 326 square miles in area. The economy is made up primarily of trade, services, and manufacturing. Anycity has the 12th strongest economy in the nation, according to a 1998 economic analysis. The analysis studied factors such as employment, per capita personal income and construction, and retail employment.

According to a 1998 study, Anycity, Anystate was one of the top ten metropolitan areas in the nation as a hot spot for starting and growing young companies. The survey measured the number of significant start-up firms created during the last ten years and the number of ten-year-old firms that grew substantially during the last four years. Also, in November 1997, a national magazine named Anycity one of the top ten "most improved cities" for business in the United States. Anystate was ranked seventh based on cost of living, educational opportunities, quality of life, and business issues. Construction activity also remained good.

Local Economic Impact on Valuation

The local economy is another important aspect to consider when performing a business valuation. The local economy represents the immediate environment in which the Company operates. The economy of Anycity, Anystate appears to be doing very well. Thus, in our opinion, there is little risk associated with the local economy that will affect the Company.

INDUSTRY OUTLOOK: WATER AND SEWER SYSTEMS

Water supply construction increased 5% in 1998, while sewerage construction was about the same as the level in 1997. Both of these construction categories did well in the mid-1990s, reflecting high levels of building construction as well as work on long-deferred projects. The strong construction market expected in 2000 will help both categories do well. In the longer term, waterworks probably will be one of the more rapidly growing categories of public construction. The aqueduct systems of most older cities are so old that extensive replacement work must be done each year. The current level of construction in the United States is much lower than that needed to replace waterworks every 50 years, which is the recommended practice. Most water utilities are in a good position to raise the needed capital, so a steady increase in replacement construction is likely through 2000.

The Safe Drinking Water Act requires numerous upgrades and replacements of water supply facilities. The Water Resources Act has expanded the role of the

Federal government in municipal water supply and appears to have facilitated increased Federal funding for water supply construction. After 1999, sewerage construction probably will continue to increase, although at a growth rate lower than that of the overall economy. Federal spending may not keep up with inflation, but the state and local share will increase steadily. A growing market factor is the need to repair, modernize, and replace the sewage treatment plants that were built during the boom of the 1970s. The sustained recovery in building construction also will support sewerage construction.

Impact on Valuation

The outlook for this industry is good. The Company is a subcontractor that does mainly water-line and sewer work. The water and sewer portion of the construction sector appears to be growing and is expected to grow in the next few years. The fact that there is a need of repairs and modernization of sewage treatment plants that were built a few decades ago also provides a positive outlook for the Company.

EXERCISE 13: Which industry outlook factors are generally the most important in supporting valuation assumptions?

a. Growth rates, profit margins, and risk
b. Regulatory and legal issues
c. Unemployment figures
d. Minority discounts and/or control premiums

HISTORICAL FINANCIAL ANALYSIS AND OVERVIEW OF THE COMPANY

Financial statement amounts labeled "Dec-98" represent the nine-month period, April 1, 1998 through December 31, 1998, due to change of year end.

EXERCISE 14: What is the most important use of historical financial data?

a. To determine how the company has performed
b. To assist in supporting anticipated performance
c. To highlight profitability
d. To determine average profits

EXERCISE 15: Analysts typically spread five years of financial statements because:

a. Revenue Ruling 59-60 requires five years.

> b. Uniform Standards of Professional Appraisal Practice requires five years.
> c. An economic cycle is often captured in five years.
> d. Most business plans are based on five years of projections.

Income Statements

REVENUES

Revenues are generally the first component to be reviewed by financial analysts. All other things equal, trends in revenues will translate into trends in profit margins, as well as the Company's ultimate fate. Increases in revenues, all things equal, should lead to higher profitability as the Company's fixed costs are spread over a wider revenue base, leading to lower fixed costs per dollar of revenue. Table 1.1 represents the actual revenues of the Company for each year and the growth trend associated with each year.

Table 1.1: Actual Revenues and Growth Trend						
	Mar-95	**Mar-96**	**Mar-97**	**Mar-98**	**Dec-98**	**Dec-99**
Revenues	$12,198,433	$11,345,938	$10,726,214	$11,558,858	$12,278,556	$14,819,373
% Change		-7.0%	-5.5%	7.8%	N/A	20.7%

As can be seen, the Company's revenues have increased toward the latter part of the analysis period. The revenues for the nine-month period ending December 1998 were higher than any of the previous 12-month periods. Over the period, 1995 to 1999, the compound growth rate in revenues was approximately 4%.

COST OF GOODS SOLD

To compare the Company to the industry, we used the 1999/2000 Benchmark Studies (fictitious). We believe that the appropriate industry classification for the Company is Standard Industrial Classification Code 1623: Construction: Water, Sewer, Pipeline, Communication and Power Line—General Contractors. According to the Benchmark Studies, the cost of goods sold averaged 78.2%. As presented in Table 1.2, the Company's cost of goods sold as a percentage of revenues was 78.8% in 1999, which is comparable to the industry average.

Table 1.2: Cost of Goods Sold and Percentage of Revenues						
	Mar-95	**Mar-96**	**Mar-97**	**Mar-98**	**Dec-98**	**Dec-99**
Cost of Goods Sold	$9,774,937	$9,301,970	$8,193,650	$8,804,580	$8,868,450	$11,676,380
% of Sales	80.1%	82.0%	76.4%	76.2%	72.2%	78.8%

OPERATING EXPENSES

According to the *Benchmark Studies*, operating expenses as a percentage of sales for companies in this industry were approximately 14.2% in 1999. As presented in Table 1.3, the Company's operating expense as a percentage of sales was approximately 8.1% in 1999, significantly lower than that of the industry average.

Table 1.3: Operating Expenses and Percentage of Revenues						
	Mar-95	**Mar-96**	**Mar-97**	**Mar-98**	**Dec-98**	**Dec-99**
Operating Expenses	$1,135,984	$818,233	$1,213,537	$1,563,721	$872,841	$1,202,237
% of Sales	9.3%	7.2%	11.3%	13.5%	7.1%	8.1%

Balance Sheets

ASSETS

Current assets usually consist of cash and cash equivalents, accounts receivable, inventory, and other current assets, which usually consist of prepaid expenses.

ASSET MIX

Over the period, the majority of the Company's assets has been in fixed assets and contract receivables. Table 1.4 illustrates the Company's asset mix as a percentage of total assets:

Table 1.4: Asset Mix Percentages							
	Mar-95	**Mar-96**	**Mar-97**	**Mar-98**	**Dec-98**	**Dec-99**	**Benchmark**
Cash and Equivalents	13.8%	9.0%	10.2%	10.5%	1.7%	4.6%	11.2%
Contract Receivables	19.6%	15.8%	12.6%	10.1%	39.3%	34.3%	39.9%
Inventories	0.2%	0.2%	0.3%	0.2%	0.1%	0.6%	1.0%
Other Current Assets	5.8%	8.9%	14.2%	22.3%	9.7%	5.9%	7.7%
Net Fixed Assets	54.4%	58.8%	59.6%	55.3%	47.9%	53.3%	33.5%
Other Assets	6.2%	7.1%	3.3%	1.6%	1.3%	1.3%	6.7%

As shown in Table 1.4, the Company's asset mix was stable for the most part. The contract receivables increased significantly in 1998 and 1999 due to the change in the reporting periods. The contract receivables tend to be higher at the December 31 year end than they were at the March 31 year end. The Company also has a much higher percentage of net fixed assets than the industry average. The Company maintained a lower cash balance than the industry in the past few years, but that again is mainly due to the change in the fiscal year ends.

LIABILITIES

The majority of the liabilities consisted of long-term debt, including the current portion. Table 1.5 illustrates the Company's liabilities mix as a percentage of total liabilities and stockholders' equity.

Table 1.5: Liability Mix Percentages							
	Mar-95	**Mar-96**	**Mar-97**	**Mar-98**	**Dec-98**	**Dec-99**	**Benchmark**
Short-Term Notes	2.2%	2.5%	2.4%	2.9%	8.7%	2.9%	3.4%
Current Portion of LTD	0.0%	0.0%	0.0%	0.0%	3.9%	6.8%	4.8%
Accounts Payable	3.2%	7.4%	3.1%	4.3%	6.3%	7.7%	15.2%
Other Current Liabilities	12.9%	6.2%	4.1%	15.9%	4.3%	5.9%	12.8%
Long-Term Debt	10.4%	12.6%	14.5%	13.4%	6.7%	4.1%	12.9%
Equity	71.3%	71.3%	75.9%	63.5%	70.0%	72.6%	50.9%

The liability section of the balance sheet was also stable. The largest liabilities were the accounts payable and the long-term debt. The equity as a percent is much higher than the industry average.

EQUITY

Stockholders' equity refers to the difference between the book value of a company's assets and its liabilities. The stockholders' equity increased each year over the period analyzed. During the entire period from March 1995 to December 1999, the stockholders' equity grew 109.8%.

Financial Ratio Analysis

Ratios for the nine-month period ending December 31, 1998, are not presented.

EXERCISE 16: The main drawbacks of publicly available benchmark financial ratios are:

   a. There are very few SIC codes.
   b. They calculate the ratios incorrectly.
   c. The companies that make up the data cannot be used to determine pricing ratios or capitalization rates.
   d. The information is from public companies.

The industry statistics used in the ratio analysis were taken from *Benchmark Studies*. The median statistics are for businesses whose primary Standard Industrial Classification Code 1623: Construction: Water, Sewer, Pipeline, Communication and Power Line—General Contractors.

   Ratios are divided into four groups, each representing an important aspect of the Company's financial position. The groups are liquidity, activity, leverage, and profitability.

LIQUIDITY RATIOS

Liquidity analysis assesses the risk level and ability of a company to meet its current obligations. It represents the availability of cash and the company's ability to eventually be converted into cash.

CURRENT RATIO

The current ratio compares current assets to current liabilities. It measures the margin of safety a company has for paying short-term debts in the event of a reduction in current assets. It also gives an idea of a company's ability to meet day-to-day payment obligations. Generally, a higher ratio is better.

Table 1.6: Current Ratios					
	Mar-95	**Mar-96**	**Mar-97**	**Mar-98**	**Dec-99**
Company	2.3	2.1	3.9	1.9	2.0
Industry	1.4	1.2	1.2	1.5	1.5

The Company's current ratio was consistantly above the industry average over the period, as shown in Table 1.6. The Company's ratio is higher than the industry due to lower current liabilities.

Quick Ratio

The quick ratio adds accounts receivables to cash and short-term investments and compares the sum to current liabilities. The resulting ratio measures a company's ability to cover its current liabilities without having to convert inventory to cash. Generally a higher ratio is better.

Table 1.7: Quick Ratios					
	Mar-95	**Mar-96**	**Mar-97**	**Mar-98**	**Dec-99**
Company	1.9	1.5	2.4	0.9	1.7
Industry	1.1	1.0	1.0	1.2	1.2

As shown in Table 1.7, the Company's ratios fluctuated over the period. The basic difference between the current and quick ratio is that the quick ratio includes only cash and receivables as the numerator. Thus, inventory is not included. As can be seen from the table, the industry averages contained a larger inventory base due to the lower ratio. The Company carried a minimal inventory of materials and supplies. In 1998, the Company's ratio was lower than the industry average due to a large increase in current liabilities in that year. Other than that year, the Company has been very liquid and could easily cover its current maturities.

Conclusion of Liquidity Ratios

The Company appears to have lower risk than that of the industry. The current ratio and the quick ratio are above the industry average for the most part. Thus, the

Company would have little difficulty covering its obligations when compared to other companies within the industry.

ACTIVITY RATIOS

Activity ratios, also known as "efficiency ratios," describe the relationship between the Company's level of operations and the assets needed to sustain the activity. The higher the ratio, the more efficient the Company's operations, as relatively fewer assets are required to maintain a given level of operations. Although these ratios do not measure profitability or liquidity directly, they are ultimately important factors affecting those performance indicators.

Collection Period Ratio

The collection period ratio, also known as the "days' sales in receivables," multiplies accounts receivable at year end by 365, then divides the result by net sales for the year. This ratio measures how much control a company has over its accounts receivable, and indicates how many days, on the average, it takes that company to convert accounts receivable to cash. Generally, the smaller the number of days, the better.

Table 1.8: Collection Period Ratios					
	Mar-95	**Mar-96**	**Mar-97**	**Mar-98**	**Dec-99**
Company	19	19	16	16	58
Industry	55	54	59	63	60

Compared to the industry, the Company was better at collecting receivables. For the years represented in Table 1.8, the Company converted its accounts receivable to cash more quickly than the other companies within the industry. The Company's collection period ratio was higher in 1999 due to exceptional circumstances concerning two accounts.

Fixed Assets Activity Ratio

The fixed assets activity ratio compares net sales to fixed assets. It indicates a company's ability to generate net sales from the use of its fixed assets. Largely depreciated fixed assets or a labor-intensive operation may cause a distortion of this ratio. Generally, a higher ratio is better.

Table 1.9: Fixed Assets Activity Ratios					
	Mar-95	**Mar-96**	**Mar-97**	**Mar-98**	**Dec-99**
Company	6.9	5.2	4.7	4.1	4.1
Industry	5.8	6.2	6.1	6.9	6.4

The Company appears worse than the industry average during the period, as demonstrated in Table 1.9. The Company appears to have not utilized its fixed assets in generating revenues as effectively as the industry. However, the Company owns all of its equipment and machinery as opposed to renting. Thus, the higher amount of fixed assets causes the ratio to be low as opposed to the industry figures. Most companies of this nature do not own all of their equipment. The industry averages most likely represent companies that both rent and own their respective equipment and machinery.

Asset Management Ratio

The asset management ratio compares net sales to total assets. It measures a company's ability to generate sales volume using its assets. It is useful in comparing companies within specific industry groups on their effective employment of assets. Generally, a higher ratio is better.

Table 1.10: Asset Management Ratios					
	Mar-95	**Mar-96**	**Mar-97**	**Mar-98**	**Dec-99**
Company	3.7	3.0	2.8	2.3	2.2
Industry	2.1	2.0	1.9	2.4	2.2

The Company's average decreased each year. The Company's trend (as shown in Table 1.10) was worse than the industry the most recent two years. The Company is not generating sales volume using its assets as effectively as in the past, but is comparable to other companies in the industry currently.

Conclusion of Activity Ratios

The Company seems to be doing better and worse than the industry in this category. The Company does collect its receivable quicker than other companies within the industry, for the most part. However, the Company is not as effective as other companies within the industry with fixed assets, but this may be affected by the large level of owned fixed assets.

LEVERAGE RATIOS

Leverage ratios measure the relative exposure of the creditors versus the shareholders of a business. Leveraged companies accrue excess returns to their shareholders as long as the rate of return on the investments financed by debt is greater than the cost of debt. However, financial leverage brings additional risks primarily in the form of fixed costs that would adversely affect profitability if revenues decline. Additionally, the priority of interest and debt can have a severe negative impact on a company when adversity strikes. The inability to meet these obligations may lead to default and possibly bankruptcy.

Net Fixed Assets to Equity

The net fixed assets to equity ratio divides net fixed assets by a company's equity. It measures a company's ability to support the acquisition of fixed assets by using the original investment plus retained earnings. Generally, a low ratio is better.

Table 1.11: Net Fixed Assets to Equity Ratios

	Mar-95	Mar-96	Mar-97	Mar-98	Dec-99
Company	0.8	0.8	0.8	0.9	0.7
Industry	0.7	0.8	0.7	0.8	0.6

Overall, the Company is close to the industry averages. The Company's ratio was pretty stable over the period, as shown in Table 1.11. Generally, the Company would have no problem supporting the acquisition of fixed assets with retained earnings.

Total Debt to Equity Ratio

The debt to equity ratio compares a company's total liabilities to its net worth. It expresses the degree of protection provided by the owners for the creditors. Generally, a lower ratio is better.

Table 1.12: Debt to Equity Ratios

	Mar-95	Mar-96	Mar-97	Mar-98	Dec-99
Company	0.4	0.4	0.3	0.6	0.4
Industry	1.3	1.2	1.0	1.1	1.0

The Company's ratio has been better than the industry averages for every year. A lower ratio indicates less debt in relation to equity. As presented in Table 1.12, the Company had less debt than the industry.

Conclusion of Leverage Ratios

The Company is leveraged and contains some debt and related interest expense, but its debt is still not as high as the industry averages. The Company should have little trouble supporting the purchase of fixed assets with retained earnings. The Company also has the capacity to take on some long-term debt if necessary.

PROFITABILITY RATIOS

Profitability ratios measure the ability of a company to generate returns for its stockholders.

Return on Equity

The return on equity ratio compares pretax income to equity. It measures a company's ability to generate a profit on the owner's investment. Generally, a higher ratio is better.

Table 1.13: Return on Equity Ratios

	Mar-95	Mar-96	Mar-97	Mar-98	Dec-99
Company	54.9%	47.3%	46.8%	41.4%	40.3%
Industry	30.5%	32.7%	31.9%	28.8%	31.2%

Although the Company's return on equity ratio has deteriorated during the period under analysis, it is still higher than the industry average, as presented in Table 1.13.

Return on Assets Ratio

The return on asset ratio is calculated by dividing pretax income by total assets. This ratio expresses the pretax return on total assets and measures the effectiveness of management in employing available resources. Generally, a higher ratio is better.

Table 1.14: Return on Asset Ratios					
	Mar-95	**Mar-96**	**Mar-97**	**Mar-98**	**Dec-99**
Company	39.7%	33.7%	35.5%	26.3%	29.3%
Industry	21.2%	26.2%	19.8%	23.2%	19.9%

Table 1.14 shows the Company's ratio was better than the industry average for each year in the analysis period.

Conclusion of Profitability Ratios

The Company is profitable and appears to be outperforming the industry, although there is a recent decrease in the margins.

EXERCISE 17: Indicate whether you believe that LEGGO is a better or worse performer based on the financial ratios previously presented.

_____

_____

_____

APPRAISAL OF FAIR MARKET VALUE

Valuation Approaches

Conventional appraisal theory provides several approaches for valuing closely held businesses. The asset approach looks to an enterprise's underlying assets in terms of either their net going concern or their liquidation value. The income approach looks at an enterprise's ongoing cash flows or earnings and apply appropriate capitalization or discounting techniques. Finally, the market approach derives value multiples from guideline company data or transactions.

EXERCISE 18: All three approaches to value must be applied in all valuations.

a. True
b. False

Asset Approach

ADJUSTED BOOK VALUE METHOD

The adjusted book value method consists of determining the fair market value of a company's assets and subtracting the fair market value of its liabilities to arrive at the fair market value of the equity. Both tangible and intangible assets are valued. Appraisals are used to value certain assets, and the remaining assets and liabilities are often included at book value, which is often assumed to approximate fair market value. This method does not provide a strong measure of value for goodwill or other intangible assets, which are more reasonably supported through the Company's income stream. In this case, the value under the adjusted book value method was less than the values calculated under the income and market approaches. Thus, the adjusted book value method was not utilized in the determination of a conclusion of value for the Company.

EXCESS CASH FLOW METHOD

The excess cash flow method, which is sometimes referred to as the excess earnings or formula method, is based on the excess cash flow or earnings available after a percentage return on the tangible assets used in a business have been subtracted. This residual amount of cash flow is capitalized at a percentage return for intangible assets of the business to derive the intangible asset value. This method is commonly used for very small businesses and in marital dissolution proceedings. The Internal Revenue Service's position on this method is that it should only be used when no better method exists.[7] It was not used in the valuation of LEGGO since more appropriate methods were available.

EXERCISE 19:   In what type of valuation setting is the excess cash flow method most often used?

    a. ESOPs (Employee stock ownership plans)
    b. Estate tax
    c. Dissenting rights
    d. Marital dissolution

EXERCISE 20:   On which Revenue Ruling is the excess cash flow method based?

    a. Revenue Ruling 59-60
    b. Revenue Ruling 83-120
    c. Revenue Ruling 68-609
    d. Revenue Ruling 77-287

---

[7] Revenue Ruling 68-609.

Income Approach

CAPITALIZED CASH FLOW METHOD (PREDEBT/INVESTED CAPITAL BASIS)

The capitalized cash flow method determines the value of a Company as the present value of all of the future cash flows that the business can generate to infinity. An appropriate cash flow is determined, then divided by a risk-adjusted capitalization rate, here the weighted average cost of capital. In this instance, control cash flows were used. This method was used to determine the Company's indicated value. The value is stated on a marketable, control interest basis.

EXERCISE 21: Which method(s) is(are) considered valid under the income approach?

  a. Guideline public company method
  b. Discounted cash flow method
  c. Capitalized cash flow method
  d. Excess cash flow method

EXERCISE 22: In which situation(s) would a capitalized cash flow method be more applicable?

  a. When a company's future performance is anticipated to change from its prior performance
  b. In litigation settings
  c. When a single historical or pro forma amount of cash flow is anticipated to be earned with a constant growth in the future
  d. When valuing very small businesses

EXERCISE 23: List the two main bases when using the capitalized cash flow (CCF) or discounted cash flow (DCF) methods of the income approach.

  1._____

  2._____

Determination of Appropriate Control Cash Flow

Under the capitalized cash flow method, we used a predebt/invested capital basis for our calculation. This is due, in part, to the fact that the interest being valued is on a control interest basis. This control interest can influence the amount of debt held by the Company. We began our analysis with the adjusted pretax earnings at the date of valuation and for the five years prior to the date of valuation. The adjustments that were made to arrive at adjusted pretax earnings include an adjustment to officers' compensation, a control adjustment. We then made adjustments for interest expense, nonrecurring items, and items that are not reflective of operations to the pretax earnings.

EXERCISE 24: Under the direct equity basis, what are the components of net cash flow?

_____

_____

_____

_____

EXERCISE 25: For the invested capital basis of the income approach, list the components of net cash flow.

_____

_____

_____

_____

EXERCISE 26: What is the difference between minority cash flows and control cash flows?

_____

_____

_____

_____

EXERCISE 27: Which adjustment(s) are made when valuing both minority and control cash flows?

    a. Nonrecurring items
    b. Nonoperating assets
    c. Excess compensation
    d. Perquisites
    e. Taxes

EXERCISE 28:   Assume the company does not have any control adjustments and the company is run to the benefit of all shareholders without any shareholders taking out cash flow over or above what they are entitled. Is this value control or minority?

_____

_____

_____

_____

The first adjustment was to add back the depreciation expense. This is a noncash expense and should be added back to arrive at an appropriate cash flow. The adjustment for the gains and losses on the sale of marketable securities was made because the marketable securities are considered an excess/nonoperating asset. All income and expenses related to excess/nonoperating assets are taken out of the income stream, because the total value of these assets is unrelated to the indicated value of operations. The reason for the adjustments to dividend income, income from the investment in a partnership, and unrealized gains on marketable securities is the same. These assets relate to excess/nonoperating assets and must be taken out of the income stream. The second adjustment was an adjustment to the interest income.

EXERCISE 29:   List some of the nonoperating/excess assets that are sometimes encountered in a business valuation.

_____

_____

_____

_____

EXERCISE 30:   In valuing a *controlling interest* in a corporation, most analysts agree that the nonoperating and/or excess assets of the business must be removed out of the operating business, then added back at fair market value.

   a. True
   b. False

EXERCISE 31:   In valuing a *minority interest* of a company, most analysts agree that the nonoperating and/or excess assets of the business must be removed out of the operating business, then added back at fair market value.

   a. True
   b. False

The resulting amount for each year (adjusted income before income tax) was then averaged. We believe a straight average is appropriate due to the cyclical nature of the Company. However, the Company changed year ends in 1998. Since we have nine months of data at December 31, 1998, an adjustment was made accordingly.

EXERCISE 32:   In the valuation of LEGGO, the analyst decided to use a straight average of the adjusted income before income taxes for five historical years. Besides a straight average, what other method(s) can be used to determine the appropriate cash flow to be capitalized into perpetuity?

   a. Weighted average
   b. Most recent fiscal year
   c. Most recent trailing 12 months
   d. Trend line analysis/next year's budget
   e. DCF average of next three years

EXERCISE 33:   Analysts will generally use a straight historical average where the earnings and cash flows are more volatile.

   a. True
   b. False

The next step was to deduct an estimated ongoing depreciation expense in order to calculate state and Federal taxes. In this instance, the ongoing depreciation expense was estimated to be $650,000 based on estimated future capital expenditures. After the ongoing depreciation was deducted, state and Federal taxes were calculated at a combined rate of 40% and deducted. The amount that resulted was adjusted income predebt and after-tax.

EXERCISE 34:   Which situation is most appropriate when adjusting cash flows for depreciation and capital expenditures?

   a. Capital expenditures should exceed depreciation.
   b. Depreciation should exceed capital expenditures.
   c. Depreciation and capital expenditures should be similar.
   d. The actual unadjusted amounts should be capitalized.

EXERCISE 35:   Assuming taxes are to be deducted, what two choices are there in making the tax adjustments?

   a. Tax each year historically, then determine the average.
   b. Taxes should never be deducted in the value of an S corporation.
   c. Make all adjustments in the historical period pretax, determine the average, then deduct for taxes.

Three further adjustments were then made to the predebt and after-tax income. The ongoing depreciation that was deducted to calculate taxes was added back because it is not a cash expense. The estimated future capital expenditures were then deducted. In this case, it was estimated that future capital expenditures would approximate $650,000 per year based on historical trends. The final adjustment was a working capital adjustment. The formula for this adjustment is based on industry data, as shown in Table 1.15. After making these final three adjustments, predebt and after-tax cash flow resulted. We believe that this cash flow is representative of future operations. The cash flow was then divided by a risk-adjusted capitalization rate using weighted average cost of capital, which is discussed below, to derive a value of the operations.

Table 1.15: Working Capital Adjustment Formula					
Current Year Revenue	X	Expected Growth Rate	=	Projected Revenue
Projected Revenue	–	Current Year Revenue	=	Change in Revenue
Change in Revenue	÷	Sales to Working Capital Ratio	=	Working Capital Adjustment

EXERCISE 36:   Which economic benefit stream(s) can be used for cash flow in a capitalized cash flow method?

    a. After-tax income
    b. Pretax income
    c. Net cash flow
    d. EBITDA (Earnings before interest, taxes, depreciation, and amortization)
    e. Revenues
    f. Debt-free net income
    g. Debt-free cash flow

DETERMINATION OF WEIGHTED AVERAGE COST OF CAPITAL

EXERCISE 37:   When using the direct equity basis instead of the invested capital basis, assumptions of capital structure can be avoided.
    a. True
    b. False

There are a number of steps involved in calculating the weighted average cost of capital (WACC). These steps involve calculating the cost of equity, the cost of debt, and the determination of an optimal capital structure for the Company using industry averages. The WACC formula is:

$$\text{WACC} = \text{We(Ke)} + \text{Wd (Kpt)}(1 - t)$$

Where

$$\text{We} = \text{Percentage of equity in the capital structure (at market value)}$$
$$\text{Ke} = \text{Cost of equity}$$
$$\text{Wd} = \text{Percentage of debt in the capital structure (at market value)}$$
$$\text{Kpt} = \text{Cost of debt, pretax}$$
$$t = \text{Tax rate}$$

EXERCISE 38: When using the invested capital basis to determine a control value, you should always use an optimal capital structure in the weighted average cost of capital.

    a. True
    b. False

Cost of Equity

EXERCISE 39: Name the two methods most often used to derive a cost of equity in the income approach.

1._____

2._____

EXERCISE 40: When using the capital asset pricing model (CAPM) to derive an equity cost of capital for a controlling interest, it is sometimes necessary to adjust beta for differences between the capital structure of the public companies and the capital structure of the subject company being valued. This is not necessary if the capital structure is assumed to be the same. Given the following information, and if the CAPM was used for LEGGO, calculate the unlevered and relevered beta.

a. Average beta of guideline public companies = 1.4

    Tax rate = 40%

    Market value capital structure = 35% debt, 65% equity

    The formula for unlevered beta is:

$$Bu = Bl / (1 + (1 - t)(Wd / We))$$

    Where

        Bu = Beta unlevered

        Bl = Beta levered

        t = Tax rate for the company

        Wd = Percentage of debt in the capital structure (at market value)

        We = Percentage of equity in the capital structure (at market value)

b. Assuming that LEGGO has a capital structure of 25% debt and 75% equity and that the CAPM can be used, what would be the beta?

    The formula to relever the beta is:

$$Bl = Bu (1 + (1 - t)(Wd / We))$$

EXERCISE 41: Should build-up method and CAPM rates of return be applied to income or cash flow?

_____

_____

_____

_____

EXERCISE 42: Which of these rates of return are derived using Ibbotson data?

   a. Minority rates of return
   b. Control rates of return
   c. Both
   d. Neutral

We used a build-up method to calculate the cost of equity. The first step was to begin with the risk-free rate of return, represented by the yield on long-term (20-year) constant maturity U.S. Treasury Coupon Bonds of 6.83%, as reported in the *Federal Reserve Bulletin* at December 31, 1999.

EXERCISE 43: Why are long-term 20-year U.S. Treasury coupon bonds most often used for the risk-free rate of return in both the build-up method and the CAPM?

_____

_____

_____

_____

The second and third steps are to add the common stock equity risk premium of 8.0% and the small stock risk premium of 4.35% (10th decile), both calculated in Ibbotson Associates *SBBI 1999 Yearbook*.

EXERCISE 44: The common stock equity risk premium was 8.0% as of the valuation date from the *SBBI 1999 Yearbook*. It is 7.8% from the *SBBI 2001 Yearbook*. What benchmark is this return based on?

   a. S&P 500
   b. New York Stock Exchange
   c. Dow Jones Industrial Average
   d. Russell 5000

EXERCISE 45:   In applying a small stock risk premium, what are the choices that analysts can make using the Ibbotson data?

    a. 10th decile annual beta
    b. 10th decile monthly beta
    c. 10th decile sum beta
    d. 10A monthly beta
    e. 10B monthly beta
    f. Micro-cap annual beta
    g. Micro-cap monthly beta
    h. Micro-cap sum beta
    i. All of the above

The final step is to add a company-specific premium that takes into account additional risks specific to the Company. These additional risks include:

- *Company's depth of management.* The Company appears to have sufficient depth of management.
- *The importance of key personnel to the Company.* The Company does have several key employees whose loss would have a negative impact on the Company.
- *The growth potential in the Company's market.* The water and sewer portion of the construction sector appears to be growing and is expected to grow in the next few years. (See earlier discussion on the industry outlook section.)
- *The stability of the Company's earnings and gross profits.* The Company has a consistent history of generating profits.
- *The Company's bidding success rates.* The Company has had good bidding success. In addition, the Company has maintained good profit margins. This indicates that the Company's bidding success is not due to underpricing contracts.
- *The financial structure of the Company.* The Company is financially sound.
- *The geographic location of the Company.* The Company is located in Anycity, Anystate. (See earlier discussion on the local economy.)
- *The Company's order backlogs.* The Company has a sufficient amount of contract backlogs.
- *The diversification of the Company's customer base.* The majority of the Company's revenues is generated from only a few customers. The Company could be negatively impacted should any of these customers be lost.

After considering the financial ratio analysis and these risk factors, plus the size of the company as compared to the Ibbotson companies, it is our opinion that a company-specific premium of 4% is appropriate for the Company.

EXERCISE 46:   A list of risk factors was previously presented for LEGGO to calculate the specific risk premium. Discuss the different methods for determining what the actual specific risk premium should be.

_____

_____

EXERCISE 47: Specific company risk premiums can be determined from Ibbotson data.

  a. True
  b. False

EXERCISE 48: Using the information in the text, calculate the cost of equity for LEGGO.

Rs	=	Risk-free rate of return	=	____
RPm	=	Risk premium common stock	=	____
RPs	=	Risk premium small stock	=	____
RPu	=	Company-specific risk premium	=	____
Ke	=	Cost of equity	=	____

The total of these four factors provides a net cost of equity, which is also called the equity rate, of 23% (rounded).

Cost of Debt

Next, we determined the cost of debt. To calculate this rate, we began by determining the Company's actual borrowing rate at the date of valuation. The borrowing rate of the Company at the date of valuation was at prime. We also added a risk premium of 1% to the prime rate. The prime rate at December 31, 1999 was 8.5%. Therefore, the Company's borrowing rate was 9.5%. To this rate, which is called the debt rate, a 40% tax rate is deducted. The result is the after-tax cost of debt of approximately 6% (rounded).

EXERCISE 49: Which of these factors causes the cost of debt to be tax-affected?

  a. Debt principal is tax deductible.
  b. Interest expense is tax deductible.
  c. It should not be tax-affected since equity is not tax-affected.
  d. Debt and interest are tax deductible.

Weighted Average Cost of Capital

Finally, we determined the WACC using the debt and equity rates that were already calculated. The equity discount rate is multiplied by an equity percentage and the debt discount rate is multiplied by a debt percentage as determined based on average capital structure for a company in this industry. In this instance, a 75% equity multiple and a 25% debt multiple were determined from industry averages. The percentages were then multiplied by the equity and debt discount rates calculated earlier and then summed to arrive at the WACC discount rate. This rate was calculated to be 18.75%.

EXERCISE 50: Using the information in the text, calculate the weighted average cost of capital for LEGGO.

EXERCISE 51: Which methods can be used to determine the weights in the weighted average cost of capital?

     a. Iterative process
     b. Guideline public companies
     c. Aggregated public industry data
     d. Risk Management Associates
     e. Troy
     f. Book values
     g. Anticipated capital structure

EXERCISE 52: Explain the iterative process for determining the weights in the weighted average cost of capital.

EXERCISE 53: Changing the amount of debt in the capital structure of the company has no effect on the return on equity.

     a. True
     b. False

EXERCISE 54: When valuing a controlling interest in a company, should you use the optimal capital structure based on public data or the capital structure anticipated to be employed by the owner of the company?

_____

_____

_____

_____

From this amount, a 3% growth factor is deducted to arrive at a net cash flow capitalization rate for the next year. The 3% growth factor is a long-term inflationary component used to adjust the capitalization rate. The rate derived after deducting the 3% was divided by 1 plus the growth rate to arrive at a net cash flow capitalization rate for the current year. In this instance, the rate amounts to 15% (rounded).

EXERCISE 55: Calculate the capitalization rate from the information in the text (apply to historical cash flow).

_____

_____

_____

_____

EXERCISE 56: Items used to support growth rates in the capitalized cash flow method of the income approach include:

    a. Inflation
    b. Nominal Gross Domestic Product
    c. Industry growth rate
    d. Actual historical company growth rate
    e. All of the above

Capitalized Cash Flow Method Conclusion of Value on a Marketable, Control Interest Basis

The indicated value of the Company's invested capital determined under this method was $6,673,093, which was stated on a marketable, control interest basis. The final step was to add nonoperating/excess assets and subtract any structured debt that the Company possessed at the date of valuation. In this instance, the Company possessed excess/nonoperating assets of $388,580. These assets included marketable securities, an investment in a partnership, other receivables, and life insurance premiums receivable. The Company also held structured debt of $918,121. Thus, after adding the nonoperating assets and subtracting the interest-bearing debt, a value of $6,143,552 is derived, as shown in Table 1.16.

Table 1.16: Income Approach—Capitalized Cash Flow Method	
	Calculated Values
Invested Capital	$6,673,093
Add: Nonoperating Assets	388,580
Less: Interest-Bearing Debt	(918,121)
Value on a Marketable, Control Interest Basis	$6,143,552

DISCOUNTED CASH FLOW METHOD

EXERCISE 57: When is it more appropriate to use a discounted cash flow method instead of a capitalized cash flow method?

_____

_____

_____

_____

The discounted cash flow method is a multiple period valuation model that converts a future series of economic income or cash flow into value by reducing it to present worth at a rate of return (discount rate) that reflects the risk inherent therein. The income might be pretax, after-tax, debt-free, free cash flow, or some other measure deemed appropriate and adjusted by the analyst. Future income or cash flow is determined through projections provided by the Company. However, no such projections were available or attainable. Furthermore, given the trends and growth propects of the company, the capitalized cash flow method was deemed more appropriate.

Market Approach

GUIDELINE COMPANY TRANSACTIONS METHOD

The guideline company transactions method values a company by finding acquisitions of similar companies in the marketplace and applying the multiples at which those companies sold to the subject company data to derive a value. In this instance, we researched various databases and found applicable transactions in two of them: Pratt's Stats and IBA (Institute of Business Appraisers). The transactions discovered within these databases are considered relevant.

EXERCISE 58: Which of these are general transaction databases used by analysts in valuing companies?

a. Pratt's Stats
b. RMA
c. Ibbotson Associates
d. Institute of Business Appraisers
e. Done Deals
f. Bizcomps
g. Mergerstat Review

EXERCISE 59: What is one of the most significant problems when using transaction data?

_____

_____

_____

_____

Pratt's Stats Database

Pratt's Stats database provides a list of transactions of companies in various industry sectors. In this instance, we researched the water, sewer, and pipeline construction sector and found nine sale transactions that took place from 1996 to the date of valuation. Using this database, we calculated values based on gross revenues and net income, as shown in Table 1.17.

Table 1.17: Pratt's Stats Database Values	
	Calculated Values
Sales Price to Gross Revenue	$6,915,495
Sales Price to Net Income	6,974,419
Average = Value on Nonmarketable, Control Interest Basis	$6,944,957

IBA Database

The IBA database provides a list of transactions of companies in various industry sectors. In this instance, we researched the water, sewer, and pipeline construction sector and found four transactions that took place from 1991 to the date of valuation. Using this database, we calculated values based on gross revenues and discretionary cash flows. To each value, however, we added and deducted some balance sheet items. The multiples derived from the IBA database apply only to the value of fixed assets and intangibles. Thus, to get to a total entity value, all current assets must be added and all liabilities must be deducted. The values using this database are presented in Table 1.18.

Table 1.18: IBA Database Values	
	Calculated Values
Sales Price to Gross Revenue	$4,630,801
Sales Price to Discretionary Cash Flows	3,267,016
Average	3,948,908
Add: Current Assets	3,090,597
Less: Total Liabilities	(1,864,359)
Value on Nonmarketable, Control Interest Basis	$5,175,146

Database Conclusion of Value on a Nonmarketable, Control Interest Basis

Table 1.19 presents the conclusions of value for each database after adding the non-operating assets that the Company possesses.

Table 1.19: Database Conclusions of Value	Pratt's Stats	IBA
Nonmarketable, Control Interest Value	$6,944,957	$5,175,146
Add: Non-Operating Assets	388,580	388,580
Total Indicated Value of LEGGO on a Nonmarketable, Control Interest Basis	$7,333,537	$5,563,726

EXERCISE 60: Is a controlling interest nonmarketable?

_____

_____

_____

_____

GUIDELINE PUBLIC COMPANY METHOD

A market approach using guideline public companies requires estimates of a capitalization rate (or multiple) derived from publicly traded guideline companies, and ongoing earnings (or a variation thereof, such as EBIT) for the subject entity.

Search for Guideline Public Companies

Guideline public companies provide a reasonable basis for comparison to the relevant investment characteristics of a company being valued. They are most often publicly traded companies in the same or similar business as the valuation subject.

However, if there is insufficient evidence in the same business, it may be necessary to consider companies with an underlying similarity of relevant investment characteristics such as markets, products, growth, cyclical variability, and other salient factors.

Our procedure for deriving group guideline companies involves:

- Identifying the industry in which the Company operates
- Identifying the Standard Industrial Classification Code for the industry in which the Company operates
- Using Internet search tools to search filings with the SEC for businesses that are similar to the subject company
- Screening the initial group of companies to eliminate those that have negative earnings, those with a negative long-term debt to equity ratio, and those whose stock price could not be obtained
- Reviewing in detail the financial and operational aspects of the remaining potential guideline companies, and eliminating those whose services differ from the subject company

Based on these criteria, our search identified two publicly traded companies that we believe are similar to the Company. The companies selected were:

1. *Kaneb Services, Inc.: headquartered in Richardson, Texas.* This company provides on-site services such as sealing under-pressure leaks for chemical plants, pipelines, and power companies.
2. *Infracorps, Inc.: headquartered in Richmond, Virginia.* This company specializes in the installation and renovation of water, wastewater, and gas utility pipelines. The company is now focusing on trenchless technology to repair subsurface pipelines.

EXERCISE 61:   Size is often a consideration in selecting guideline public companies. General criterion for using size as a selection parameter is:

   a. Two times
   b. Five times
   c. Ten times
   d. None of the above

EXERCISE 62:   In the valuation of LEGGO, only one company, Infracorps, was comparable by both industry and size. Given that fact, which option would probably result in the best presentation of the GPCM in the valuation of LEGGO?

   a. Only use Infracorps.
   b. Use both Infracorps and Kaneb.
   c. Reject the guideline public company method.
   d. Use both companies but only as a reasonableness test for the other approaches.

EXERCISE 63: Guideline public company methods are not applicable to smaller businesses such as LEGGO.

   a. True
   b. False

EXERCISE 64: Which selection criteria are generally used by analysts in choosing guideline public companies?

   a. Size
   b. Return on equity
   c. Profit margin
   d. Industry similarity
   e. Similar products and services
   f. Growth rates
   g. Investors' similarities

We have chosen to use four multiples to value the Company: earnings before interest and taxes (EBIT), revenues, assets, and equity. We believe that the asset and equity multiples are appropriate because construction companies tend to be asset intensive. We also believe that the EBIT and revenue multiples are appropriate because the Company has a strong income statement and is profitable. We have calculated both one-year and three-year multiples due to the cyclical nature of the industry. No adjustments have been made to the financial statements of the guideline companies as we believe none are necessary.

EXERCISE 65: Which of these are commonly used guideline public company valuation multiples?

   a. Price/earnings
   b. Invested capital/revenues
   c. Price/gross profits
   d. Invested capital/book value of equity
   e. Invested capital/EBITDA
   f. Invested capital/EBIT
   g. Price/assets
   h. Invested capital/debt-free net income
   i. Invested capital/debt-free cash flow

EXERCISE 66: When using the guideline public company method, at what point in time are the prices of the public companies' stock?

   a. 30-day average
   b. As of valuation date

c. Six-month average
d. Three-year average

EXERCISE 67: What type of value is the result of the application of the guideline public company method?

a. Control
b. Minority
c. Neutral

Guideline Public Company Method Conclusion of Value on a Marketable, Control Interest Basis

Applying multiples to the one- and three-year averages of the Company's EBIT, revenues, assets, and equity provides the values shown in Table 1.20. We have not applied any size premiums to the Company or fundamental discounts to the guideline company multiples in this case. We also put more weight on the income measures of value. As mentioned previously, we must add the nonoperating assets to the value to arrive at a total indicated value.

Table 1.20: Total Selected Values—Guideline Public Company Method		
	One-year Values	Three-year Values
Selected Value	$5,000,000	$6,000,000
Add: Nonoperating Assets	388,580	388,580
Value on Marketable, Control Interest Basis	$5,388,580	$6,388,580

EXERCISE 68: In selecting multiples from guideline public companies for application to a subject company such as LEGGO, what options do analysts typically have?

a. Mean average of the multiples
b. Median average of the multiples
c. Individual guideline company multiples
d. Average multiples with a fundamental discount
e. All of the above

EXERCISE 69: Which of these time periods can be used to derive valuation multiples from publicly traded companies?

a. Most recent four quarters
b. Most recent fiscal year end

c. Three-year average
d. Five-year average
e. One-year projected
f. Three-year future average

LACK OF MARKETABILITY DISCOUNT

EXERCISE 70: Discounts for lack of marketability can be applied to 100% controlling interests in a company such as LEGGO

a. True
b. False

EXERCISE 71: Which discounts for lack of marketability studies and/or data are typically relied on in determining discounts?

a. Mergerstat Review
b. Restricted stock studies
c. IPO studies
d. Court cases
e. Flotation costs
f. CAPM
g. Ibbotson Associates
h. Quantitative Marketability Discount Model (QMDM)

EXERCISE 72: Although we are valuing a 100% controlling interest in LEGGO, there are numerous other levels of ownership interests that can exist in a closely held company. Provide some examples of other levels of ownership.

_____

_____

_____

_____

_____

A marketability discount is intended, among other things, to account for the issues a controlling owner must face as he or she begins to liquidate his or her controlling interest in the company. There are a number of studies and cases over the years that have attempted to identify this discount.

> **EXERCISE 73:** A discount for lack of marketability should be applied to all of the valuation methods used in the valuation of LEGGO.
>
> a. True
> b. False

Selection of Applicable Discount for Lack of Marketability

To quantify the discount for lack of marketability applicable to the control, marketable ownership interest in the Company, we considered these factors to have an impact on the magnitude of the discount:

- Uncertain time horizon to complete the offering or sale
- Cost to prepare for and execute the offering or sale
- Risk concerning eventual sale price
- Noncash and deferred transaction proceeds
- Marketability implied in underlying valuation methodology

Based on our analysis of the factors we consider to affect the lack of marketability discount, it is our opinion that the appropriate discount for lack of marketability is 5% for a control interest as of December 31, 1999.

CORRELATION OF VALUES

To reach a final conclusion for the value of the stockholders' equity on a nonmarketable, control interest basis, the methods used were subjectively weighted according to their merits as indicators of value, as shown in Table 1.21. In this instance, we believe that the capitalized cash flow method provides the best indication of value because of the discernible trends of the company. This value is supported by the guideline company transactions method (GCTM) (Pratt's Stats and IBA Databases) and the guideline public company method (GPCM) (one-year and three-year). The guideline company transaction method was not chosen as the best indication of value due to the age of some of the transactions and the lack of detailed knowledge of the terms of the transactions. The guideline public company method was also not chosen as the best indication of value since there were only two companies, and one was larger and not as good a fit based on the industry description.

Table 1.21: Value Indications			
Method	Marketable Control Interest Basis	Discount for Lack of Marketability	Nonmarketable Control Interest Basis
Capitalized Cash Flow Method	$6,143,552	5%	$5,835,374
GCTM Pratt's Stats Database			7,333,537
GCTM IBA Database			5,563,726
GPCM — One-year	5,388,580	5%	5,119,151
GPCM — Three-year	6,388,580	5%	6,069,151

EXERCISE 74: Which method can be used to correlate and reconcile value?

a. Straight average of the indications of value
b. Numerical weights assigned to each of the value indications
c. Qualitative judgment in selection of value
d. All of the above

TOTAL CONCLUSION OF VALUE ON A NONMARKETABLE, CONTROL INTEREST BASIS

In our opinion, the fair market value of 100% of the common stock of LEGGO, on a nonmarketable, control interest basis, as of December 31, 1999, for management purposes and internal planning, is approximately (rounded):

FIVE MILLION EIGHT HUNDRED THOUSAND DOLLARS
$5,800,000

ADDENDUM 1: DISCOUNT CASE STUDY EXERCISES

Exercise A

Assume that we are determining the fair market value of a minority nonmarketable interest in a company for gift tax purposes. The minority marketable value derived by various methods is $100 per share. We are in a state where you need over 50% for full control. What is the relative discount for lack of marketability (DLOM) in these situations?

   a. Value of a 10% interest with one 90% owner

   _____

   _____

   _____

   b. Value of a 10% interest with nine other 10% owners

   _____

   _____

   _____

   c. Value of a 50% interest with one other 50% owner

   _____

   _____

   _____

   d. Value of a 33.33% interest with two other 33.33% owners

   _____

   _____

   _____

   e. Value of a 2% interest with two 49% owners

   _____

   _____

   _____

Exercise B

Again, assume we are determining the fair market value of a company for gift tax purposes. In this case study we are valuing a 100% controlling interest on a stand-alone basis in a closely held company. What is the discount for lack of marketability in these situations where the prediscount value is determined by using:

a. P/E ratios from control transactions information (i.e., Pratt's Stats)

_____

_____

_____

b. P/E ratios from guideline public companies

_____

_____

_____

c. Discounted cash flow (DCF) with a discount rate determined using Ibbotson information

_____

_____

_____

d. Capitalized cash flow method

_____

_____

_____

e. Asset approach

_____

_____

_____

CHAPTER 2

Valuation Case Study Exercises: Solutions and Explanations

EXERCISE 1: The purpose of the valuation of LEGGO is to assist management in internal planning. What other purposes are there?

ANSWER: Valuations are used for a variety of purposes including estate tax, income tax, gift tax, ESOPs, marital dissolution, buying companies, selling companies, shareholder oppression cases, dissenting rights cases, financial reporting, reorganization and bankruptcy, minority stockholder disputes, various types of litigation, and internal planning.

EXERCISE 2: Which of the following is the "as of" date for valuation?

a. Anytime within one year
b. "As of" a single point in time
c. "As of" a single point in time or six months later
d. Date that the report is signed

ANSWER: b. "As of" a single point in time

The valuation date is always as "of a" single point in time, typically a day. Valuation of a business is a dynamic, not a static, exercise. Values can change constantly such that a value today may be very different from the value a year from now or even just a few months from now. In the estate tax area, valuations are as of the date of death or six months later. However, this is only for estate tax. The date that the analyst signs the report usually does not coincide with the "as of" date. The signature date is most often after the valuation date.

EXERCISE 3: Valuation conclusions can be presented as:

a. A range of values
b. A single value
c. An estimate of value
d. All of the above

ANSWER: d. All of the above

Value conclusions can be presented in a variety of formats. Most often it is either a single value or a range of values. Values are always estimates, since subjective judgment is applied.

EXERCISE 4:   This valuation is being done on a nonmarketable, control interest basis. It is also on a control stand-alone basis. Name the four levels of value that are considered in a valuation.

ANSWER: 1. Control synergistic
              2. Control stand-alone
              3. Minority marketable
              4. Minority nonmarketable

Control synergistic value reflects the synergies and attributes in a deal between two companies. It is usually investment value. Control stand-alone value is the value of a company that reflects the management philosophies and strategy of the current owners and management team. Minority marketable value is the value of a single share of public company stock, an often-used starting point when valuing private companies. Minority nonmarketable value is the value of a minority interest in a private company that reflects the lack of control and lack of marketability of the interest.

This valuation is also prepared on a nonmarketable controlling interest basis. Some analysts believe that there is no such thing as a nonmarketable controlling interest. Their point is that 100% controlling interest is as marketable as any company of like kind that wants to be sold. Other analysts believe that a company can be nonmarketable controlling depending on the underlying valuation methodologies used. For example, when valuing a 100% controlling interest in a private company, the methodologies used typically rely on public company stock data that reflect the fact that the public company interest can be sold in a very short amount of time. If the public company data are applied to determine a controlling interest in a company, the same level of marketability and liquidity would be implied. You cannot sell an entire company in just a few days as you can with public stock. As such, some discount may be appropriate.

EXERCISE 5:   Which of these are standards of value?

   a. Fair market value, fair value financial reporting, investment value
   b. Fair value investment reporting, fair value state actions, intrinsic value
   c. Investment value, intrinsic value, equal value
   d. Fair market value, equal value, investment value

ANSWER: a. Fair market value, fair value financial reporting, investment
             value

There are five standards of value: fair market value, investment value, intrinsic value, fair value financial reporting, and fair value state actions.

EXERCISE 6: Valuation of S corporations is one of the most controversial issues in business valuations today. The main issue is whether to and how to tax effect S corporation income. What four options are there in valuing S corporations?

ANSWER: 1. Tax effect at the corporate rate
2. Tax effect at the personal rate
3. Do not tax effect at all
4. A combination or hybrid of the other options

Most analysts agree that S corporation should be tax effected when valuing a controlling interest. For example, there is no evidence that valuation multiples in deals for companies is any different if the company is a C corporation or an S corporation. The controversy is greater in the valuation of minority interests in S corporation. It is based on the fact and circumstances in each situation and is based in part on the distribution policy of the S corporation.

EXERCISE 7: We are valuing a 100% controlling interest in LEGGO. The percentage of ownership of individual shareholders is not an issue here. However, assume we are valuing the 85% of Tom Profit as opposed to the 100% in LEGGO. The value of an 85% interest in LEGGO would be based on 85% of the 100% control value in LEGGO.

   a. True
   b. False

ANSWER: b. False

An 85% interest in the company may not be equal to 85% of the 100% controlling interest value. The sum of the parts may not equal the whole. Although Tom still controls the corporation with his 85% interest, there is the possibility of a nuisance value attributable to the other three 5% interests. Tom does not have complete control and could be exposed at some time in the future to a dissenting rights action or shareholder oppression action. As such, 85% interest would probably be worth somewhat less than a proportional amount of the 100% controlling interest value in LEGGO.

EXERCISE 8: Revenue Ruling 59-60 is only applicable to estate, gift, and income tax valuations.

   a. True
   b. False

ANSWER: b. False

Technically, Revenue Ruling 59-60 should be followed when valuing interests for estate, gift, and income taxes. However, Revenue Ruling 59-60 is often relied on and quoted for other valuations as well. It has withstood the test of time.

EXERCISE 9: These are the only eight tenets of value in Revenue Ruling 59-60 that need to be considered.

    a. True
    b. False

ANSWER: b. False

Although there are eight main tenants of value contained in Revenue Ruling 59-60, there is a multitude of other important factors contained in the Revenue Ruling that must also be considered. Other factors include key person discounts, operating versus holding companies, acceptable approaches and methods, and types of historical information.

EXERCISE 10: What types of industries would most likely be affected by anticipated changes in interest rates?

ANSWER: Residential housing
                   Banking
                   Auto
                   Manufacturing

Although all industries are ultimately affected by changes in interest rates, these industries would be impacted more because changes in interest rates change both supply and demand as well as profit margins.

EXERCISE 11: What two economic indicators are probably the most important in valuation?

    a. Unemployment levels and Gross Domestic Product (GDP)
    b. Dow Jones Industrial Average and Producer Price Index
    c. GDP and inflation
    d. Inflation and unemployment levels

ANSWER: c. GDP and inflation

Although all economic indicators can be important, typically the two most important ones are historical and anticipated changes in GDP, which measures the real growth of the U.S. economy, and inflation, typically measured through changes in the Consumer Price Index. These two factors affect all industries and can be critical in choosing growth rates in both the discounted cash flow and capitalized cash flow methods of the income approach.

EXERCISE 12: In valuing a small geographically concentrated business, which of these types of economic data should be considered?

    a. International, national, regional, local
    b. National, regional, local

c. Regional, local

d. Local only

ANSWER: b. National, regional, local

Although a small geographically concentrated business would most likely be affected by local and regional data, the national outlook should also be analyzed in preparing the business valuation. It is true that there are often differences in both the local and regional economy versus the national economy. However, in many industries, what is happening at the national level will eventually trickle down to the regional and local levels. There are exceptions to this rule and each valuation can be different. It is highly unlikely that the international economic situation would impact a small local business.

EXERCISE 13: Which industry outlook factors are generally the most important in supporting valuation assumptions?

a. Growth rates, profit margins, and risk

b. Regulatory and legal issues

c. Unemployment figures

d. Minority discounts and/or control premiums

ANSWER: a. Growth rates, profit margins, and risk

When applicable and available, the industry data should tie to the assumptions used in the valuation for growth rates, profit margins, and risk factors. Regulatory and legal issues and unemployment figures are also important but only to the extent that they affect growth, profits, and risks. Discounts and premiums are separate issues.

EXERCISE 14: What is the most important use of historical financial data?

a. To determine how the company has performed

b. To assist in supporting anticipated performance

c. To highlight profitability

d. To determine average profits

ANSWER: b. To assist in supporting anticipated performance

All of the items listed above are important components of a historic review of financial data. However, when applicable, the main purpose of the historical review is to support anticipated performance and the assumptions in the valuation models. The analysis of the historical operating performance of a company also indicates how well the management team is performing overall and can lead to information concerning trends.

Alternatively, history may not repeat itself and/or history may not be indicative of future performance. For example, the company may not have performed well in the past due to such factors as loss of a key person or litigation. The absence of those items going forward would indicate better performance. The analysis of the historic information should also be made in light of the local, regional, and national economy, as well as the industry outlook. All these items can be used to support assumptions in the valuation models.

EXERCISE 15:   Analysts typically spread five years of financial statements because:

  a. Revenue Ruling 59-60 requires five years.
  b. Uniform Standards of Professional Appraisal Practice requires five years.
  c. An economic cycle is often captured in five years.
  d. Most business plans are based on five years of projections.

ANSWER: c. An economic cycle is often captured in five years.

There is no magic to looking at five years of data. In some industries only the most recent year is relevant or just a few years. In other industries five to ten years may be more appropriate. The underlying theme is that it captures enough financial information to indicate trends, the performance of the company and an economic cycle. Although Revenue Ruling 59-60 suggests that five years of data be reviewed, it is not required. USPAP does not have any requirements concerning the number of years of financial information. Although it may be true that many projections include five years of data, this has no real relevance in terms of a historical review of information.

EXERCISE 16:   The main drawbacks of publicly available benchmark financial ratios are:

  a. There are very few SIC codes.
  b. They calculate the ratios incorrectly.
  c. The companies that make up the data cannot be used to determine pricing ratios or capitalization rates.
  d. The information is from public companies.

ANSWER: c. The companies that make up the data cannot be used to determine pricing ratios or capitalization rates.

Most of the national databases do have fairly extensive amounts of information by SIC code and the ratios typically are calculated properly. Most of the information is from closely held companies.

   The main drawback of the data is that none of it is tied to pricing ratios or valuation multiples such as price to earnings or invested capital to EBITDA. There is also no tie to any type of discount or capitalization rate. Therefore, some analysts believe that these types of comparisons are less meaningful. Alternatively, when using the guideline public company method of the market approach, ratios can be tied to valuation multiples. You can take a look at how the subject company compares to the various ratios of the public companies, then make adjustments to the public company multiples to reflect those differences. This cannot be done when using public benchmark data that again have no references or ties to valuation multiplies or capitalization rates. However, they can help in a general risk assessment.

It is also important to recognize that many of the ratios are calculated differently and that consistency is important when comparing the subject company being valued to the ratios in the benchmark data.

EXERCISE 17: Indicate whether you believe that LEGGO is a better or worse performer based on the financial ratios previously presented.

ANSWER: Although each ratio is important, some are more useful than others. For example, profit margins and leverage ratios are typically more important than other ratios. In general, it appears that LEGGO is more liquid. In terms of activity ratios, it appears that they are under-performing based on fixed assets, but this may be due to owning more of their fixed assets as opposed to leasing them. In terms of leverage, it appears that the Company uses less debt than its industry counterparts and could add additional debt if it chooses. The Company's return on equity ratio and return on assets ratio are much higher, indicating that it may be generating higher profit margins than the industry. Overall, it appears that LEGGO is outperforming its peers based on the benchmark data presented.

EXERCISE 18: All three approaches to value must be applied in all valuations.

   a. True
   b. False

ANSWER: b. False

Although it is true that all three approaches to value should be considered in each valuation, they need not all be applied in every valuation. Most analysts do not use the full asset approach (tangible and intangible assets) in valuing an operating company because increases in the accuracy of the appraisal, if any, are not worth the time and expense of having all the assets valued. The value of all the aggregated assets, including intangible assets, is considered in the value derived from the income and market approaches. The asset approach is often the primary approach in valuing investment or holding companies.

EXERCISE 19: In what type of valuation setting is the excess cash flow method most often used?

a. ESOPs (Employee stock ownership plans)
b. Estate tax
c. Dissenting rights
d. Marital dissolution

ANSWER: d. Marital dissolution

Although the excess cash flow method can be used in any valuation, it is most often seen in marital dissolutions. Analysts may use this method because the court in a jurisdiction is familiar with it. In some situations, exclusion of the excess cash flow method could be perceived as an omission.

EXERCISE 20: On which Revenue Ruling is the excess cash flow method based?

a. Revenue Ruling 59-60
b. Revenue Ruling 83-120
c. Revenue Ruling 68-609
d. Revenue Ruling 77-287

ANSWER: c. Revenue Ruling 68-609

The excess cash flow method, sometimes referred to as the formula method or the excess earnings method, was first discussed in ARM 34, which was used to determine goodwill in breweries due to prohibition. This eventually led to Revenue Ruling 68-609. Revenue Ruling 59-60 contains the basic tenants and procedures for valuing closely held businesses. Revenue Ruling 83-120 deals with valuation of preferred stock. Revenue Ruling 77-287 deals with the valuation of restricted securities.

EXERCISE 21: Which method(s) is(are) considered valid under the income approach?

a. Guideline public company method
b. Discounted cash flow method
c. Capitalized cash flow method
d. Excess cash flow method

ANSWER: b. Discounted cash flow method, and
c. Capitalized cash flow method

Discounted cash flow and capitalized cash flow are the two main methods under the income approach. There are variations of these two methods. The guideline public company method is a market approach, and the excess cash flow method is a hybrid of the income and asset approaches.

EXERCISE 22:   In which situation(s) would a capitalized cash flow method be most applicable?

    a. When a company's future performance is anticipated to change from its prior performance
    b. In litigation settings
    c. When a single historical or pro forma amount of cash flow is anticipated to be earned with a constant growth in the future
    d. When valuing very small businesses

ANSWER: c. When a single historical or pro forma amount of cash flow is anticipated to be earned with a constant growth in the future, and
                d. When valuing very small businesses

Capitalized cash flow methods are most often used when future performance is anticipated to be at a steady rate based on either a historical figure, such as an average or recent year, or a pro forma single figure. Discounted cash flow is most often used when future performance is anticipated to be different from the past. Both discounted cash flow and capitalized cash flow methods are used in litigation, although some analysts believe that the capitalized cash flow method is more supportable because it is easier to explain. Capitalized cash flow methods are most often seen in valuations of small businesses, since that is how they are often bought and sold.

EXERCISE 23:   List the two main bases when using the capitalized cash flow (CCF) or discounted cash flow (DCF) methods of the income approach.

ANSWER: 1. Direct equity
              2. Invested capital

There is much debate in the valuation community about whether to use direct equity methods of valuation in which interest expense and debt principal are included, or to use invested capital methods in which interest expense and debt principal are excluded. Theoretically, the use of both models should give you a similar result. Both methods can be used in most valuations. However, in certain circumstances, one method may be better than the other. For example, the invested capital method may be used in control valuations where the capital structure of the company is anticipated to change. Alternatively, in a minority valuation, some analysts believe that the direct equity method is more appropriate, since the minority shareholder cannot change the capital structure of the company. It is often a matter of preference.

EXERCISE 24:   Under the direct equity basis, what are the components of net cash flow?

ANSWER:		Net income after tax
	Plus	Depreciation and noncash charges
	Minus	Capital expenditure requirements
	Plus/minus	Working capital requirements
	Plus	New debt principal paid in
	Minus	Debt principal paid out

EXERCISE 25: For the invested capital basis of the income approach, list the components of net cash flow.

ANSWER:		Net income after tax
	Plus	Interest expense times 1 minus the tax rate
	Plus	Depreciation and noncash charges
	Minus	Capital expenditure requirements
	Plus/minus	Working capital requirements (debt-free)

EXERCISE 26: What is the difference between minority cash flows and control cash flows?

ANSWER: The difference between control cash flows and minority cash flows is normalization adjustments. Normalization adjustments for control include excess compensation and perquisites. When such amounts are added back, it is considered a control value. When such amounts are left in as expenses, it is considered a minority value, since the minority shareholder cannot change the policies of the control owner.

EXERCISE 27: Which adjustment(s) are made when valuing both minority and control cash flows?

a. Nonrecurring items
b. Nonoperating assets
c. Excess compensation
d. Perquisites
e. Taxes

ANSWER: a. Nonrecurring items,
             b. Nonoperating assets, and
             e. Taxes

The goal of normalizing cash flows is to determine what a normalized amount would be into perpetuity. Nonrecurring items are typically removed from the cash flows. Most analysts will also adjust the P&L for the effect of removing nonoperating assets from the balance sheet. For example, there may be an adjustment for interest and dividend income associated with excess marketable securities, as is the situation here with LEGGO. Excess compensation and perquisites are only adjusted in control cash flows. When using after tax rates of return, taxes are typically an expense in minority and control cash flows.

EXERCISE 28: Assume the company does not have any control adjustments and the company is run to the benefit of all shareholders without any shareholders taking out cash flow over or above what they are entitled. Is this value control or minority?

ANSWER: The value would clearly be control stand-alone, since the capitalized cash flow is the cash flow of the entire company reflecting the benefits to all shareholders. Since the current owner of the company is operating to the benefit of all shareholders, it becomes a minority value as well. However, it is minority value only to the extent that the current owners continue their policies. Policies can change and/or new owners can come in, which increases the risk such that a discount for a lack of control or minority interest may still be appropriate. A possible adjustment for lack of control may be appropriate to reflect the risk of potential future changes in either the owner or the policies or both.

EXERCISE 29: List some of the nonoperating/excess assets that are sometimes encountered in a business valuation.

ANSWER: Marketable securities
Cash
Inventory
Working capital
Land
Buildings
Condominiums
Boats

EXERCISE 30: In valuing a *controlling interest* in a corporation, most analysts agree that the nonoperating and/or excess assets of the business must be removed out of the operating business, then added back at fair market value.

a. True
b. False

ANSWER: a. True

The rate of return requirements for excess assets and/or nonoperating assets are often less than the cost of capital of the company. As such, including the income and expenses of the nonoperating/excess assets in the P&L, and capitalizing such amounts at a higher rate of return, will undervalue the company. There are also situations where there are nonoperating assets that generate no income. The capitalization of cash flow without adjustment would result in a zero value for those assets. This is why these types of assets are typically removed from the balance sheet with appropriate P&L adjustments, then added back to the operating value of the business.

EXERCISE 31: In valuing a *minority interest* of a company, most analysts agree that the nonoperating and/or excess assets of the business must be removed out of the operating business, then added back at fair market value.

a. True
b. False

ANSWER: a. True

Although this is true for most analysts, there are still differences of opinions. Some analysts believe that the same methodology should be employed as in valuing a controlling interest, that is, value the nonoperating or excess assets separately and make the related P&L adjustments. They would then take a discount for lack of control and a discount for lack of marketability from the nonoperating asset value before they added it to the company's discounted operating value. Other analysts believe that a minority stockholder has no access to these types of assets and the P&L should be as it is, reflecting the way the company operates. The assets are not separately valued and added back. Again, this can create a situation where the value of nonoperating/excess assets may be zero.

EXERCISE 32: In the valuation of LEGGO, the analyst decided to use a straight average of the adjusted income before income taxes for five historical years. Besides a straight average, what other method(s) can be used to determine the appropriate cash flow to be capitalized into perpetuity?

a. Weighted average
b. Most recent fiscal year
c. Most recent trailing 12 months
d. Trend line analysis/next year's budget
e. DCF average of next three years

ANSWER: a. Weighted average,
b. Most recent fiscal year,
c. Most recent trailing 12 months, and
d. Trend line analysis/next year budget

The first four items can be considered in valuing and determining how cash flow should be capitalized. An example of a weighted average is (3,2,1), which would be used for a three-year average, with the most recent year given the weight of 3, the second year 2, and the most distant year 1. Some analysts will use (5,4,3,2,1) for five years of data. The weighted average is typically used when the analyst believes there may be an increasing trend but wants to reflect the possibility that there could be some underperforming years. Fiscal year end and trailing 12 months are typically used when there is anticipation that the most recent information is indicative of the future. Some analysts will use an estimate of next year's budget if they believe it is more indicative of the potential performance of the company. DCF is typically used when historical information is not anticipated to continue. DCF and capitalized cash flow methods do not average future years, only historical years.

EXERCISE 33: Analysts will generally use a straight historical average where the earnings and cash flows are more volatile.

    a. True
    b. False

ANSWER: a. True

This is the situation with LEGGO. Although there is some trend upward for LEGGO, the construction industry is fairly cyclical such that a straight historical average is more appropriate here. The other methods are often more appropriate where there is more of a trend in the historical results.

EXERCISE 34: Which situation is most appropriate when adjusting cash flows for depreciation and capital expenditures?

    a. Capital expenditures should exceed depreciation.
    b. Depreciation should exceed capital expenditures.
    c. Depreciation and capital expenditures should be similar.
    d. The actual unadjusted amounts should be capitalized.

ANSWER: c. Depreciation and capital expenditures should be similar.

A common mistake made in business valuation is to capitalize cash flow into perpetuity where the depreciation greatly exceeds the future capital expenditure requirements. This is obviously an impossible situation, since future capital expenditures have to be made in order to generate future depreciation. Many analysts will normalize depreciation and capital expenditures by making them equal or similar. This equalization process is a simplifying assumption, since capital expenditures would slightly exceed depreciation due to the inflationary pressure in a stable business. However, this usually (but not always) has a nominal effect on value. There are situations in which depreciation can exceed capital expenditures within a definite period of time. This occurs when there is a previous purchase of a long-life asset such as a building, or where goodwill or other intangible assets are amortized over a longer period of time. In those situations, it would be appropriate to have depreciation exceed capital expenditures.

EXERCISE 35: Assuming taxes are to be deducted, what two choices are there in making the tax adjustments?

    a. Tax each year historically, then determine the average.
    b. Taxes should never be deducted in the value of an S corporation.
    c. Make all adjustments in the historical period pretax, determine the average, then deduct for taxes.

ANSWER: a. Tax each year historically, then determine the average, and
           c. Make all adjustments in the historical period pretax, determine the average, then deduct for taxes.

Some analysts will go back and compute taxes in each of the years used in the average income as opposed to making all the adjustments pretax, calculating the average, then adjusting for taxes. When the tax rates are the same, this will not have an impact. However, in C corporations, where taxes may differ for each year due to certain types of planning, an average of five years after-tax income may be different than the average of five years pretax, which is aggregated with one tax amount applied to it. There may be years when the taxes would be less than the marginal rate. As such, some analysts believe that an average tax-affected rate is more appropriate. Other analysts believe that the company will eventually end up paying close to the marginal rate into perpetuity, and that would be the more appropriate rate.

EXERCISE 36: Which economic benefit stream(s) can be used for cash flow in a capitalized cash flow method?

    a. After-tax income
    b. Pretax income
    c. Net cash flow
    d. EBITDA (Earnings before interest, taxes, depreciation, and amortization)
    e. Revenues
    f. Debt-free net income
    g. Debt-free cash flow

ANSWER: a. After-tax income
           b. Pretax income
           c. Net cash flow
           f. Debt-free net income
           g. Debt-free cash flow

Cash flow is often used in many business valuations. However, there are circumstances, particularly with small businesses, when income is capitalized both on an after-tax and a pretax basis. Debt-free net income is used in the invested capital basis and is after-tax income with interest expense added back. Debt-free cash flow is debt-free net income with depreciation added back. Although theoretically EBITDA could be a capitalizeable amount, it is more often used in the market approach than the income approach. Revenues are seldom capitalized in the income approach, although they can be capitalized through the market approach.

There is some debate in the valuation industry concerning the use of either cash flow or income when performing the income approach. However, this is frequently a moot point because analysts often equalize depreciation and capital expenditures. The only other real adjustment would be incremental working capital. Not all businesses require incremental working capital, particularly cash businesses or businesses whose receivables are turned quickly. As such, and particularly in small businesses, cash flow and income may be equal or similar. However, there are many businesses that require working capital to fund growth. In those situations, working capital should be considered as a cash outflow. Cash flow in a growing business would typically be less than income in those businesses with working capital needs. Debt would also have to be normalized in terms of debt principal in and debt principal out. However, again, if they are normalized, they net out to net income.

EXERCISE 37: When using the direct equity basis instead of the invested capital basis, assumptions of capital structure can be avoided.

   a. True
   b. False

ANSWER: b. False

One of the reasons often given for using the direct equity basis is that the analyst can avoid making assumptions of capital structure, that is, what percent debt and what percent equity a company will use. However, in a direct equity basis there needs to be assumptions of debt principal in and debt principal out, and they need to be normalized. Anytime you normalize the amount of debt that is used in a company, you are explicitly assuming a capital structure. As such, debt is a consideration in using the direct equity basis.

EXERCISE 38: When using the invested capital basis to determine a control value, you should use always an optimal capital structure in the weighted average cost of capital.

   a. True
   b. False

ANSWER: b. False

Although many analysts will use an optimal capital structure, often determined based on a review of public company capital structures, it is not always the basis to use for control value. If the management of a company decides to operate with a different capital structure than what may be considered optimal, it would still be a control value on a stand-alone basis reflecting the current policies of management.

EXERCISE 39:   Name the two methods most often used to derive a cost of equity in the income approach.

ANSWER: 1. Capital asset pricing model (CAPM)
             2. Build-up method

There is controversy in the valuation industry about whether the CAPM should be used to value small businesses. Some analysts believe that CAPM should not be used to value even large businesses. The only difference between the CAPM and the build-up method is the use of beta. It is often difficult to find betas for small publicly traded companies that could be applicable to small private companies. There are many different sources of betas and many different ways to calculate betas. Betas can also differ for the same public company at the same point in time.

Betas are sometimes available that could be used in a CAPM for small companies. There are industries where there are large numbers of public small companies where betas may be available. However, if there are no reasonably similar companies whose betas could be used as a proxy for the small closely held company, then the build-up method may be the best method to use. However, if the betas are reasonable and can be used, then the CAPM may be considered as well. Each of these situations is fact and circumstance specific and could differ depending on the type of company, the industry of the subject company, and the size of the company.

EXERCISE 40:   When using the CAPM to derive an equity cost of capital for a controlling interest, it is sometimes necessary to adjust beta for differences between the capital structure of the public companies and the capital structure of the subject company being valued. This is not necessary if the capital structure is assumed to be the same. Given the following information, and if the CAPM was used for LEGGO, calculate the unlevered and relevered beta.

a. Average beta of guideline public companies = 1.4
    Tax rate = 40%
    Market value capital structure = 35% debt, 65% equity

    The formula for unlevered beta is:
    $$Bu \;=\; Bl \,/\, (1 + (1 - t)\,(Wd \,/\, We))$$

Where

$$
\begin{aligned}
Bu &= \text{Beta unlevered} \\
Bl &= \text{Beta levered} \\
t &= \text{Tax rate for the company} \\
Wd &= \text{Percentage of debt in the capital structure (at market value)} \\
We &= \text{Percentage of equity in the capital structure (at market value)}
\end{aligned}
$$

b. Assuming that LEGGO has a capital structure of 25% debt and 75% equity and that the CAPM can be used, what would be the beta?

The formula to relever the beta is:
$$Bl = Bu \,(1 + (1 - t)\,(Wd / We))$$

ANSWER: a.
$$
\begin{aligned}
Bu &= 1.4 / (1 + (1 - .40)(.35 / .65)) \\
&= 1.4 / 1 + .6 \,(.54) \\
&= 1.4 / 1.32 \\
&= 1.06
\end{aligned}
$$

b.
$$
\begin{aligned}
Bl &= 1.06 \,(1 + (1 - .40)(.25 / .75)) \\
Bl &= 1.06 \,(1 + (.6) \,(.33)) \\
Bl &= 1.06 \,(1.20) \\
Bl &= 1.27
\end{aligned}
$$

EXERCISE 41: Should build-up method and capital asset pricing model (CAPM) rates of return be applied to income or cash flow?

ANSWER: The current general consensus is that these are cash flow rates of return. They are also rates of return after corporate tax but before personal investor tax. The rates of return are based on dividends and capital appreciation. Dividends are paid after tax by public corporations, and capital appreciation is also after-tax due to retained earnings used to grow the business. However, these returns are pretax to an individual investor. Ibbotson agrees that traditional rates of return derived using their data, whether CAPM or build-up method, should be applied to after-tax cash flows.

EXERCISE 42: Which of these rates of return are derived using Ibbotson data?

a. Minority rates of return
b. Control rates of return
c. Both
d. Neutral

ANSWER: d. Neutral

There is some controversy concerning whether the rates of return derived using Ibbotson data are minority rates of return or control rates of return. However, Ibbotson is very clear in stating that it believes they are not minority returns even though the data are based on returns of shares of stock that are on a minority basis. Ibbotson believes the returns are neutral. Most analysts today believe that control or minority features are in the cash flows to be capitalized versus the discount or capitalization rate. A controlling shareholder in a public company would not necessarily be able to maximize or increase the returns over and above what the minority shareholders are experiencing. The management and board of directors of publicly traded companies must maximize returns for all shareholders regardless of how the company is held, supporting the concept of a neutral return.

EXERCISE 43: Why are long-term 20-year U.S. Treasury coupon bonds most often used for the risk-free rate of return in both the build-up method and the CAPM?

ANSWER: Most analysts use a 20-year risk-free rate of return from a U.S. Treasury bond because this is the basis from which Ibbotson derives its risk premiums. There is no such thing as an original issue 20-year bond. Analysts and Ibbotson use 30-year Treasury bonds that have 20 years remaining.

EXERCISE 44: The common stock equity risk premium was 8.0% as of the valuation date from the *SBBI 1999 Yearbook*. It is 7.8% from the *SBBI 2001 Yearbook*. What benchmark is this return based on?

    a. S&P 500
    b. New York Stock Exchange
    c. Dow Jones Industrial Average
    d. Russell 5000

ANSWER: The risk premium used in this report is from the S&P 500. This is the most commonly used benchmark for determining equity premiums for the marketplace.

EXERCISE 45: In applying a small stock risk premium, what are the choices that analysts can make using the Ibbotson data?

    a. 10th decile annual beta
    b. 10th decile monthly beta
    c. 10th decile sum beta
    d. 10A monthly beta

    e. 10B monthly beta
    f. Micro-cap annual beta
    g. Micro-cap monthly beta
    h. Micro-cap sum beta
    i. All of the above

ANSWER: i. All of the above

In the valuation of LEGGO, the analysts decided to use the 10th decile monthly beta. All of these small stock premiums are the premiums in excess of CAPM that Ibbotson uses to derive small stock risk premium. Some analysts will use the 10th decile whereas others will use the micro-cap strata, which is the 9th and 10th deciles. There are also differences of opinion as to which small stock premiums should be used based on the type of beta. It could be monthly betas, annual betas, or sum betas. Monthly and annual betas are based on the timing of the calculation. Sum betas are sometimes referred to as lagged betas and reflect the fact that small stock market reactions may lag the market by a certain amount of time. Some analysts use a micro-cap small stock risk premium because the average includes more companies. In 1999, the micro-cap risk premium was 2.6% versus the 4.35% used for the 10th decile. In the *2001 Yearbook* the micro-cap risk premium was also 2.6%. In the *2001 Yearbook*, Ibbotson has segmented its information into deciles 10A and 10B. The 10B decile risk premium was 8.42%. Although the 10B decile risk premium is based on smaller companies, it is also based on a lower number of companies that make up the average. There is currently no clear requirement for selecting small stock risk premiums, and the controversy continues about whether to use the 10th decile, micro-cap, or 10B strata, as well as the type of beta on which the information is based.

EXERCISE 46: A list of risk factors was previously presented for LEGGO to calculate the specific risk premium. Discuss the different methods for determining what the actual specific risk premium should be.

ANSWER: In this valuation the analyst made a subjective selection of an aggregate 4% risk premium. This was based on the analyst's judgment concerning the additional risk of the previously described items. This is a common method of selecting specific risk premiums. Other methods that can be used are some type of numerical system placed on the categories (i.e., -3, -2, -1, 0, 1, 2, 3). However, this sometimes implies accuracy that may not exist and may be difficult to defend in a litigation setting. Other analysts use a plus and minus system to determine the potential amount of specific risk.

EXERCISE 47: Specific company risk premiums can be determined from Ibbotson data.

    a. True
    b. False

ANSWER: b. False

Specific company risk premium data are not included in the Ibbotson *SBBI yearbooks*. In fact, there are no empirical studies indicating specific risk premiums. This is a subjective area for the analyst.

EXERCISE 48:   Using the information in the text, calculate the cost of equity for LEGGO.

Rs	=	Risk-free rate of return	=	____
RPm	=	Risk premium common stock	=	____
RPs	=	Risk premium small stock	=	____
RPu	=	Company-specific risk premium	=	____
Ke	=	Cost of equity	=	____

ANSWER: 6.83% + 8.0% + 4.35% + 4.0% = 23% (rounded)

EXERCISE 49:   Which of these factors causes the cost of debt to be tax-affected?

a. Debt principal is tax deductible.
b. Interest expense is tax deductible.
c. It should not be tax-affected since equity is not tax-affected.
d. Debt and interest are tax deductible.

ANSWER: b. Interest expense is tax deductible

Principal is never tax deductible for a corporation (ESOP exception). Since interest expense is a cost of debt and is tax deductible, there is an adjustment for taxes. Equity returns derived by using Ibbotson data are already on an after-tax basis, so no adjustments need to be made to equity returns.

EXERCISE 50:   Using the information in the text, calculate the weighted average cost of capital for LEGGO.

ANSWER: 75% (23%) + 25% (6%) = 18.75%

EXERCISE 51:   Which methods can be used to determine the weights in the weighted average cost of capital?

a. Iterative process
b. Guideline public companies

c. Aggregated public industry data
d. Risk Management Associates
e. Troy
f. Book values
g. Anticipated capital structure

ANSWER: a. Iterative
b. Guideline public companies
c. Aggregated public industry data
g. Anticipated capital structure

Both guideline public company information and aggregated public industry data are often viewed as optimal capital structures with the idea that public companies use an optimal amount of debt to lower their weighted average cost of capital. Iterative processes can be used for both minority and controlling interests but are more typically used in minority valuations. Clients will often have an anticipated capital structure that can also be employed. Risk Management Associates, Troy, and book value information are all based on book values, not fair market values. The weights to be used in the weighted average cost of capital are fair market value weights, not book value weights.

EXERCISE 52:   Explain the iterative process for determining the weights in the weighted average cost of capital.

ANSWER: The analyst will choose the capital structure to value the company, then determine the percent of debt based on that value using the actual debt of the company. If it is different, then you redo the capital structure until it iterates to the proper capital structure that is in existence. This is easily accomplished by the use of spreadsheets.

EXERCISE 53:   Changing the amount of debt in the capital structure of the company has no effect on the return on equity.

a. True
b. False

ANSWER: b. False

As you change the capital structure of the company through an iterative process, the increases in debt may increase the rates of return on equity as well. The more debt the company takes on, the higher the return on equity. This can be reflected directly through the use of CAPM by levering and unlevering betas based on the different debt levels. If the build-up method is used, the adjustment is more subjective.

EXERCISE 54:   When valuing a controlling interest in a company, should you use the optimal capital structure based on public data or the capital structure anticipated to be employed by the owner of the company?

ANSWER: This answer depends on the type of valuation being performed. The valuation could be from the perspective of a sale to an owner that could employ a different capital structure. The company may be valued on a stand-alone basis, and the owners may want to know what it is worth to them with the existing capital structure. In the valuation of LEGGO, the Company was valued using industry capital weights.

EXERCISE 55:   Calculate the capitalization rate from the information in the text (apply to historical cash flow).

ANSWER: $(18.75\% - 3\%)/1.03$ = 15.29%

                                        = 15% rounded

EXERCISE 56:   Items used to support growth rates in the capitalized cash flow method of the income approach include:

    a. Inflation
    b. Nominal Gross Domestic Product
    c. Industry growth rate
    d. Actual historical company growth rate
    e. All of the above

ANSWER: e. All of the above

The selection of the growth rate can have a tremendous impact on the value conclusion. Value is very sensitive to growth. Many analysts use the inflation rate as the perpetual growth rate in the capitalized capital cash flow method, which is used here for LEGGO. Others use the average nominal (real and inflation) growth of the GDP of the United States which has been 6% when measured from 1926 to the present. Still other analysts use what they believe to be the anticipated or long-term industry growth rate. Economic and industry information can be helpful in supporting the growth rate. A company's historical growth is also a consideration.

EXERCISE 57:   When is it more appropriate to use a discounted cash flow method instead of a capitalized cash flow method?

ANSWER: If a company anticipates growing at a steady rate in the future, it is unnecessary to prepare a discounted cash flow method. A capitalized cash flow method, as used here in the valuation of LEGGO, is sufficient. Discounted cash flow methods are typically used when short-term growth is anticipated to be different from long-term growth and/or the company's cash flow has not reached a stabilized or normalized period that can be capitalized into perpetuity.

EXERCISE 58: Which of these are general transaction databases used by analysts in valuing companies?

- a. Pratt's Stats
- b. RMA
- c. Ibbotson Associates
- d. Institute of Business Appraisers
- e. Done Deals
- f. Bizcomps
- g. Mergerstat Review

ANSWER: a. Pratt's Stats
d. Institute of Business Appraisers
e. Done Deals
f. Bizcomps
g. Mergerstat Review

Ibbotson does not provide any transaction information. RMA provides book value ratios of companies.

EXERCISE 59: What is one of the most significant problems when using transaction data?

ANSWER: One of the common mistakes made in the application of transaction multiples is to aggregate the transactions from the different databases. This will result in an inaccurate valuation, since each of the databases collects and presents its data in a different format. Some of the databases use invested capital multiples, some use equity multiples, some include working capital, some include debt, some include inventory, and so on. When using these databases, it is recommended that information from each database be used and applied separately to the subject company's earnings parameters as it was done here in LEGGO. This will avoid any possible inaccuracies.

EXERCISE 60: Is a controlling interest nonmarketable?

ANSWER: Some analysts believe that the term *nonmarketable* as it applies to a controlling interest is inappropriate. However, the price of the transaction should reflect some reasonable amount of time to sell the company such that marketability issues are included in the value. The marketability, or lack thereof, is already reflected in the transaction price.

EXERCISE 61: Size is often a consideration in selecting guideline public companies. General criterion for using size as a selection parameter is:

    a. Two times
    b. Five times
    c. Ten times
    d. None of the above

ANSWER: d. None of the above

There is really no general criterion for selecting guideline public companies based on size. A rule of thumb used by some analysts is no greater than ten times revenue. However, this is not always applicable. The reason analysts adjust for size is not so much because the guideline public companies are larger but because size typically indicates that the company is more diversified both in product lines and geography. Furthermore, larger companies tend to have more management depth.

EXERCISE 62: In the valuation of LEGGO, only one company, Infracorps, was comparable by both industry and size. Given that fact, which option would probably result in the best presentation of the GPCM in the valuation of LEGGO?

    a. Only use Infracorps.
    b. Use both Infracorps and Kaneb.
    c. Reject the guideline public company method.
    d. Use both companies but only as a reasonableness test for the other approaches.

ANSWER: d. Use both companies but only as a reasonableness test for the other approaches.

Kaneb's revenue is 30 times as large as LEGGO, whereas Infracorps' revenue is twice as large. Some analysts would eliminate Kaneb because it is so much larger than LEGGO. Furthermore, it does not operate in the same industry. Infracorps seems to be a better fit in terms of size as well as the types of construction services it provides. Some analysts would have eliminated Kaneb and only relied on Infracorps. That would result in reliance on one guideline public company, a presentation that may be more difficult to defend. Other analysts would completely reject the guideline public company method as it applies to LEGGO. Given the lack of good guideline companies, the analyst here decided to use the guideline public company method only as a reasonableness test for the income approach.

EXERCISE 63: Guideline public company methods are not applicable to smaller businesses such as LEGGO.

   a. True
   b. False

ANSWER: b. False

Some analysts do believe that guideline public companies are not applicable to small businesses. However, some of these analysts may be surprised by the number of potential publicly traded companies that are similar in size in certain industries. At the very least, in valuing a small company, a cursory review of public companies should be undertaken to determine if there are any similar companies.

EXERCISE 64: Which selection criteria are generally used by analysts in choosing guideline public companies?

   a. Size
   b. Return on equity
   c. Profit margin
   d. Industry similarity
   e. Similar products and services
   f. Growth rates
   g. Investors' similarities

ANSWER: a. Size
         d. Industry similarity
         e. Similar products and services

Analysts typically screen initially by industry similarity including similar products and services. They screen by size. Once an initial selection of companies is made, they will often look at profit margins, return on equity, and growth rates. However, these are typically not looked at in the initial screening. Some analysts will also look at similarity in terms of investor preferences. They believe that the selection process for guideline public companies can be expanded outside the particular industry in which the company operates. They will look for similar investment characteristics such as growth, return on equity, profit margin, and so forth. Their belief is that a prudent investor would invest in companies that have similar characteristics regardless of industry. Generally, the courts have been reluctant to accept companies outside the subject company's industry that are not at least somewhat similar by product, market, and so on.

EXERCISE 65: Which of these are commonly used guideline company valuation multiples?

a. Price/earnings
b. Invested capital/revenues
c. Price/gross profits
d. Invested capital/book value of equity
e. Invested capital/EBITDA
f. Invested capital/EBIT
g. Price/assets
h. Invested capital/debt-free net income
i. Invested capital/debt-free cash flow

ANSWER: a. Price/earnings
           b. Invested capital/revenues
           e. Invested capital/EBITDA
           f. Invested capital/EBIT
           h. Invested capital/debt-free net income
           i. Invested capital/debt-free cash flow

There are a variety of multiples that can be used to value a company. In the valuation of LEGGO, the analysts used invested capital to EBIT, invested capital to revenue, invested capital to assets, and price to equity. This is a subjective area, and the analyst should consider all potential multiples and decide which ones may be the best fit. It is preferable for the numerator and denominator to be similar. For example, if price of equity is in the numerator, then the earnings parameters should be the earnings available to equity in the denominator. If the numerator is invested capital, then the denominator should be the earnings parameters available for invested capital. Price/gross profit, invested capital/book value of equity, and price to assets would not be the best multiples to use here.

EXERCISE 66:   When using the guideline public company method, at what point in time are the prices of the public companies' stock?

a. 30-day average
b. As of valuation date
c. Six-month average
d. Three-year average

ANSWER: b. As of valuation date

There has been some recent controversy due to the current volatility of the stock market. Since stock prices in P/E multiples can change so rapidly, some analysts believe that some type of average stock price or P/E multiple should be used as opposed to a P/E multiple based on a particular point in time. However, traditional valuation theory holds that the value should be at a single point in time, typically as of a single day. They believe that whatever the day the valuation is, that is the day the stock price should be used. In addition, some analysts use the current price divided by a projected income or cash flow figure. They believe that this is a better fit of the price of the stock to the anticipated performance of the company.

EXERCISE 67: What type of value is the result of the application of the guideline public company method?

    a. Control
    b. Minority
    c. Neutral

ANSWER: c. Neutral

This is a controversial area. Those that believe it is a minority value argue that the underlying stocks are minority such that the application of a valuation multiple would result in a minority value. Others argue that the valuation multiples are nothing more than inverted capitalization rates derived from the public market. As such, the underlying theory about minority/control being in the cash flows for the income approach should also apply to the market approach. If that is true, then the application of valuation multiples would be neutral and control/minority would, like the income approach, be an adjustment to the earnings parameter to which the valuation multiples are applied.

EXERCISE 68: In selecting multiples from guideline public companies for application to a subject company such as LEGGO, what options do analysts typically have?

    a. Mean average of the multiples
    b. Median average of the multiples
    c. Individual guideline company multiples
    d. Average multiples with a fundamental discount
    e. All of the above

ANSWER: e. All of the above

Some analysts use an average of multiples to derive a value. Some use a mean average that is the sum of the indications divided by the number of indications. Others believe that the median average is a better fit because it excludes outliers since it is the midpoint. Still other analysts believe that you should look at each guideline company separately, decide which ones are more comparable, and rely on those multiples rather than an average of the multiples. Some analysts will use averages, then take a fundamental discount from the average to reflect the subject company's differences. This fundamental discount is often used to adjust for size.

EXERCISE 69: Which of these time periods can be used to derive valuation multiples from publicly traded companies?

    a. Most recent four quarters
    b. Most recent fiscal year-end
    c. Three-year average
    d. Five-year average
    e. One-year projected
    f. Three-year future average

ANSWER: a. Most recent four quarters
                   b. Most recent fiscal year-end
                   c. Three-year average
                   d. Five-year average
                   e. One-year projected

Analysts must decide whether the multiples derived from publicly traded companies should be the most recent multiples, typically based on an annual fiscal year-end or four-quarter trailing figure or a multiple of some average earnings such as a three-year or five-year average. If it is believed that an average multiple would be more indicative of future performance of a company, then that may be more appropriate. Many analysts use both—the most recent period as well as a historical period—and weight them according to what they think would be most indicative of the future value and performance of the company. Some analysts also use a multiple based on a one-year projected annual earnings parameter typically forecasted by investing banking houses that follow the company.

EXERCISE 70: Discounts for lack of marketability can be applied to 100% controlling interests in a company such as LEGGO.

    a. True
    b. False

ANSWER: a. True

There is continuing controversy about whether discounts for lack of marketability should be applied to controlling interests, particularly 100% controlling interests as we have in LEGGO. Some analysts believe that a 100% interest is marketable and no discount would apply. Other analysts believe that it depends on the underlying methodology used to derive the prediscount value. For example, when using valuation multiples or rates of return derived from public company data, the rates of return, or multiples reflect the fact that the public stock can be sold in a very short amount of time, typically within three days. You cannot sell a company within three days. These analysts believe that the underlying method assumes such marketability, which does not exist in a controlling interest in a private company. Thus, some level of discount may be appropriate. There are no known studies to determine discounts for lack of marketability of a 100% controlling interest in a business. Many analysts rely on discount for lack of marketability studies for minority interests and subjectively reduce the discount to reflect the 100% control.

EXERCISE 71:   Which discounts for lack of marketability studies and/or data are typically relied on in determining discounts?

    a. Mergerstat Review
    b. Restricted stock studies
    c. IPO studies
    d. Court cases
    e. Flotation costs
    f. CAPM
    g. Ibbotson Associates
    h. Quantitative Marketability Discount Model (QMDM)

ANSWER: b. Restricted stock studies
                c. IPO studies
                e. Flotation costs
                h. QMDM

Analysts typically rely on restricted stock studies, which compare restricted or letter stocks to their publicly traded counterparts, and to IPO studies, which look at the value of companies within a few months of when they went public. Flotation costs are sometimes looked at when valuing much larger companies. However, they assume that the company is an IPO candidate. QMDM is the Quantitative Marketability Discount Model, which looks at holding periods for investments for minority interests in closely held companies. It is a present value technique that has limited acceptance at the current time. *Mergerstat Review* reports control premiums; CAPM is the model for deriving discount rates; and Ibbotson contains data for calculating risk premiums. Court cases will indicate discounts for lack of marketability, but they are very fact and circumstance specific and should seldom be relied on in determining discounts. Knowledge of court cases can be important, but they should not be used as the primary method for discounts.

EXERCISE 72:   Although we are valuing a 100% controlling interest in LEGGO, there are numerous other levels of ownership interests that can exist in a closely held company. Provide some examples of other levels of ownership.

ANSWER: 100% ownership
                Less than 100% ownership but greater than majority
                Majority interest
                Operating control
                Two 50% interest

Largest minority block of stock
Minority with swing vote
Minority can elect board member
Pure minority (no control rights)

Each of these may have a different discount for lack of control and/or lack of marketability.

EXERCISE 73: A discount for lack of marketability should be applied to all of the valuation methods used in the valuation of LEGGO.

  a. True
  b. False

ANSWER: b. False

As previously mentioned, the Capitalized Cash Flow Method and the Guideline Public Company Method are based on securities that can be sold within three days. This does not exist for LEGGO. As such, a small discount for lack of marketability, subjectively derived and based on judgment, may be appropriate. In the application of the transaction databases, the transaction prices already reflect any potential discount for lack of marketability. No discount is applied.

EXERCISE 74: Which method can be used to correlate and reconcile value?

  a. Straight average of the indications of value
  b. Numerical weights assigned to each of the value indications
  c. Qualitative judgment in selection of value
  d. All of the above

ANSWER: d. All of the above

In correlating and reconciling values, many analysts simply average all of the indications of value. This implies that each method has equal weight, validity, and accuracy. This is seldom the case in a business valuation including the situation here with LEGGO. Other analysts will assign weights to each of the methods, such as 0.5 to the income approach, 0.2 to the guideline public company approach, 0.1 to transactions, and so on. However, this may again imply accuracy that does not exist. Also, if you are only putting a 10% weight on a method, you may be indicating that the method may not be very accurate. In the valuation of LEGGO, the analyst looked at each one of the methodologies and decided that the income approach was the most relevant. The analyst believes that the other methods support that value.

ADDENDUM 1: DISCOUNT CASE STUDY EXERCISES

EXERCISE A: Assume that we are determining the fair market value of a minority nonmarketable interest in a company for gift tax purposes. The minority marketable value derived by various methods is $100 per share. We are in a state where you need over 50% for full control. What is the relative discount for lack of marketability (DLOM) in these situations?

    a. Value of a 10% interest with one 90% owner
    b. Value of a 10% interest with nine other 10% owners
    c. Value of a 50% interest with one other 50% owner
    d. Value of a 33.33% interest with two other 33.33% owners
    e. Value of a 2% interest with two 49% owners

ANSWER: a. This is a typical minority ownership with very few rights. The 90% owner has full control, and, absent any shareholder oppression or dissenting rights issues, can pretty much do what they want concerning the direction of the company, including selling the company and distributions. The 10% owner is almost completely at the mercy of the 90% owner.

    b. This is a much better situation than "a," since no one has control. A 10% owner would need to team up with five other owners to control the company. As such, they have more potential for influence than the situation in "a."

    c. In owning a 50% interest with one other 50% owner, each owner possesses veto power. Although they cannot do anything without agreement of the other owner, they can veto anything the other owner does. This is a better situation than in "a" or "b." There would still be a discount for lack of control and marketability, but not as great as in "a" and "b."

    d. In this situation there is more ability to influence the company since a one-third owner would only have to team up with another one-third owner. There is some risk that two one-third owners could collaborate on the direction of the company.

    e. This is the classic situation of swing value. Each one of the owners may be willing to couple with the 2% owner to direct the company. However, there are many situations where there are two major owners of a company with a small minority share where the two major owners collaborate. This may not necessarily be to the benefit of the small minority owner. The value of a 2% interest may go up when the two 49% owners are in a dispute.

EXERCISE B: Again, assume we are determining the fair market value of a company for gift tax purposes. In this case study we are valuing a 100% controlling interest on a stand-alone basis in a closely held company. What is the discount for lack of marketability in these situations where the prediscount value is determined by using:

a. P/E ratios from control transactions information (i.e., Pratt's Stats)
b. P/E ratios from guideline public companies
c. Discounted cash flow (DCF) with a discount rate determined using Ibbotson information
d. Capitalized cash flow method
e. Asset approach

ANSWER: a. Many analysts believe that the application of control transaction information results in a value that already reflects the marketability of the company. This is because most control transactions are of private companies.

b. Many analysts believe that when using P/E ratios from public companies, the marketability and liquidity of the public company stocks are inherent in the multiples when applied to a private company. That level of liquidity does not exist, even for a 100% interest. In those situations, many analysts will take a discount for lack of marketability based on the DLOM studies for minority interests, which are then subjectively reduced.

c. This is similar to "b." Since the discount rate is determined using Ibbotson information based on publicly traded company rates of return, they too, reflect much greater marketability and liquidity than exists in a 100% controlling interest in a private company. Some subjectively determined level of discount may be appropriate.

d. Same situation for capitalized cash flow as for DCF when using Ibbotson information.

e. When valuing a company through an asset approach, the marketability of the asset is included in the individual values of those assets. A discount for lack of marketability may be appropriate, since selling an entire company may be more difficult than selling individual assets. Some analysts will apply some level of discount, again usually based on DLOM studies based on minority interests reduced for the 100% controlling interest being valued.

CHAPTER 3

ValTips

INTRODUCTION

In the companion book, *Financial Valuations: Applications and Models* (FV), there are numerous ValTips throughout the chapters of the text that are used to highlight important concepts, application issues, and pitfalls to avoid. We have re-created these ValTips in this chapter with certain modifications to make them presentable on a stand-alone basis. These ValTips are organized and identified by the chapter/section in FV.

CHAPTER 1:   INTRODUCTION TO FINANCIAL VALUATION

1. Relying on the wrong standard of value can result in a very different value, and, in a dispute setting, the possible dismissal of the value altogether.
2. Although many states use the term *fair market value* in their marital dissolution cases, the definition of fair market value may vary from state to state and will not necessarily be the same definition as in the tax area.
3. Some companies are worth more dead than alive. It is important for the analyst, particularly when valuing an entire company, to determine if the going concern value exceeds the liquidation value. For a minority interest, there are situations where the going concern value is less than liquidation value. However, the minority shareholder cannot force a liquidation if the controlling shareholder desires to continue the business as a going concern.
4. Price and cost can equal value but do not necessarily have to equal value. Furthermore, value is future-looking. Although historical information can be used to set a value, it is the expectation of future economic benefits that is the primary value driver. Investors buy tomorrow's cash flow, not yesterday's or even today's.

CHAPTER 2:   RESEARCH AND ITS PRESENTATION

1. Because of the complexity of the data assembling process, most analysts use checklists that detail the types of information they are seeking. Chapter 5 of this workbook contains many useful checklists. The use of these tools can help ensure that the valuation analyst covers the necessary bases in gathering information.

2. One of the biggest mistakes the valuation analyst can make in valuation research is to start looking for information without a plan.

3. 10-Ks of public companies often have detailed analyses of the industry.

4. If you are looking for a one-stop source for business and financial data, consider one of the major information services. These services, which include such names as Dialog, Lexis-Nexis, Factiva, OneSource, Alacra, Proquest, and Bloomberg, offer the most extensive collections of periodicals, legal information, and financial data available.

5. The analyst will need to consider the key external factors that affect value, such as interest rates, inflation, technological changes, dependence on natural resources, and legislation.

6. The *Beige Book* contains information on current economic conditions in each district, gathered through reports from interviews with key business professionals, economists, and market experts.

7. *Industry Insider™ Trade Association Research* (available online through Investext), is currently the only online collection of trade association research. It includes industry-specific information such as statistics, economic indicators, analysis, trends, forecasts, and surveys.

8. The EDGAR database contains information on thousands of public companies.

9. A common mistake made by inexperienced valuation analysts is to wait until the last minute to do the industry and economic analysis, then drop it into the text without any discussion of how it relates to the valuation conclusion.

CHAPTER 3: FINANCIAL STATEMENT AND COMPANY RISK ANALYSIS

1. The analyst must take special care to set expectations in both the engagement letter and the valuation report regarding the degree of responsibility assumed regarding generally accepted accounting principles (GAAP) departures. The analyst should also be prepared to adjust the historical financial statements for any obvious and meaningful departures from GAAP that are discovered in the course of review.

2. The valuation report should provide substantive commentary regarding methods and ratios chosen and results of the comparative analysis.

3. Analysts should not mix year-end data with beginning and ending year average data when preparing comparisons of the subject company to industry benchmark data and ratios.

4. In order to use benchmark industry ratios appropriately, the analyst will want to be familiar with their scope and limitations, as well as differences among them regarding data presentation and computation methods.

CHAPTER 4: INCOME APPROACH

1. Failure to develop the appropriate normalizing adjustments—that is, nonrecurring and extraordinary items—may result in a significant overstatement or understatement of value.

2. By making certain adjustments to the future economic benefit—that is, the numerator in any income approach method—the analyst can develop a control or noncontrol value.

3. Normalization adjustments affect the pretax income of the entity being valued. Consequently, the control adjustments will result in a corresponding modification in the income tax of the entity, if applicable.

4. Adjustments to the income and cash flow of a company are the primary determinants of whether the capitalized value is minority or control.

5. When there are controlling interest influences in the benefit stream or operations of the entity and a minority interest is being valued, it may be preferable to provide a minority value directly by not making adjustments. This will avoid the problems related to determining and defending the application of a more general level of minority discount.

6. Financial statements prepared based on GAAP are considered the desirable standard for both accounting and valuation. Statements prepared on a tax basis or cash basis often may need adjustment. Other departures from GAAP may be analyzed and considered for adjustment as well.

7. As with the control-oriented adjustments, extraordinary, nonrecurring, or unusual item adjustments affect the profit or loss accounts of a company on a pretax basis. Therefore, certain income tax–related adjustments may be necessary. These types of adjustments are made in both minority and control valuations.

8. Valuing nonoperating assets may involve the expertise of someone who specializes in the valuation of these particular assets, such as a real estate appraiser. Engagement letters should clearly set out these responsibilities and the related appraisal expenses.

9. Synergistic value is investment value, which may not be fair market value.

10. In many small companies, income and cash flow are the same or similar.

11. Regardless of the method employed, there is no substitute for dialogue with management to provide critical insight into future projections.

12. Theoretically, the length of the explicit period in the discounted cash flow (DCF) is determined by identifying the year when all the following years will change at a constant rate. Practically, however, performance and financial position after three to five years is often difficult to estimate for many companies.

13. There are circumstances where the past is not indicative of the future. In these situations, care must be exercised in analyzing projected performance. There has to be adequate support for the assumptions on which the projections are based.

14. The valuation analyst uses normalized historical data, management insights, and trend analysis to analyze formal projections for the explicit period of the DCF. These projections may take into account balance sheet and income statement items that affect the defined benefit stream and may involve not only projected income statements but also projected balance sheets and statements of cash flow to increase income statement projection accuracy.

15. The more certain the future streams of cash flow are in a DCF, the more valuable the asset or entity is.

16. The terminal value of a DCF is critically important, since it often represents a substantial portion of the total value of an entity.

17. The value driver method for terminal year calculations can result in a lower terminal value than the Gordon growth model. This is sometimes due to inaccurate assumptions in the Gordon growth model.

18. Property (i.e., real estate) also may be segregated from operating tangible assets at the outset and added back later. Rent expense is properly substituted for real estate–related expenses if the decision is to separately value the operating real estate.

19. If the control excess cash flow method is used and a minority value is the interest that is being valued, a discount for lack of control must be determined and applied.

20. Assets that are normally considered operating assets may in reality be nonoperating. For example, excess cash and cash equivalents are actually nonoperating assets and can be isolated from the operating assets during normalization.

21. The company's lending rate may be higher if personal guarantees are required from the company's owners, officers, and so forth.

22. Whatever rate of return is used for goodwill in the excess cash flow method, the aggregate return on all assets should approximate the weighted average cost of invested capital for the entity.

CHAPTER 5:   COST OF CAPITAL/RATES OF RETURN

1. Identifying the value drivers of an enterprise and developing action steps to limit or reduce controllable (i.e., internally oriented versus external) risks can be of great benefit to many closely held businesses.

2. The value of a company can be expressed as the present value of all of the future economic benefits that are expected to be generated by the company.

3. Values are reflections of the future, not the past or even the present.

4. In valuing a company, analysts need to estimate sustainable growth into perpetuity, not just short-term growth.

5. Since 1926, the U.S. economy has been able to sustain a nominal growth rate of approximately 6% over time. This is a combination of the real growth rate and inflation.

6. Overall, the deciding factor in determining how to reflect growth in the rates of return will be informed professional judgment.

7. For publicly held companies, systematic risk is captured by a measurement referred to as the *beta* of the enterprise.

8. It is common to assume a privately held company's beta as 1.0 and develop separate risk factors to include in its overall rate of return calculations, or to use a beta for an industry group or from guideline public companies.

9. The estimation of unsystematic risks is one of the more difficult aspects of calculating rates of return.

10. Every business enterprise will have its own unique attributes and risks, which can be incorporated into the rate of return.

11. There is no direct source for returns on 20-year Treasury bonds. Analysts can consult the *Wall Street Journal* to find the quoted market yields on 30-year bonds with approximately 20 years of maturity left. Another source for this data is the St. Louis branch of the Federal Reserve Bank, which maintains an extensive inventory of historical yield rates on all types of government securities, including a continuing proxy for the 20-year constant maturity Treasury bond. This can be found online at *www.stls.frb.org/fred/data/irates/gs20*.

12. Lists of small company risk factors can be used to analyze the attributes of a specific subject company and to select the level of adjustment for size and unsystem-

atic risk. It is important, however, to avoid a double counting, since adjustments for size can often implicitly include adjustments for other operating attributes.

13. While the amount of industry risk premia data available from Ibbotson Associates is expected to grow over time, many analysts in the valuation community are not yet comfortable with the direct application of industry risk premia adjustments. However, analysts can consider this new empirical evidence where the subject falls within one of the Ibbotson-defined industries and there is a need to assess industry risk, that may not be captured in the build-up method.

14. Caution should be used whenever a methodology assigns specific numerical adjustments to various categories of specific company risks in the build-up or CAPM rate. Due to the subjective nature of the numerical assignments for each category, one can easily get trapped upon cross-examination in testimony as to whether it might be considered reasonable for each of the factors to be, say, half a percent higher or lower, thereby causing a significant change in the resulting capitalization or discount rate being developed.

15. The format and content of an analytical framework for analyzing unsystematic risk will vary considerably depending on the nature of the assignment and the depth of analysis required. However, the articulation of the analyst's thought process by use of diagnostic tools can be a means of competitive differentiation, whether the tools are included in the final report or only in engagement work papers.

16. The betas published by different sources can display different results due to differing time periods, methodologies, and adjustments. Therefore, care should be exercised.

17. A good source of information for determining industry capital structures can be found in the Ibbotson Associates *Cost of Capital* publications. If the guideline public company method is being used, the public companies can be a source of capital structure components.

18. Since traditionally derived discount and capitalization rates are cash flow rates, not earnings rates, an upward subjective adjustment would have to be made to convert the rate for application to earnings.

19. It is important to recognize the increasingly "noisy" nature of public company reported valuation multiples including P/E. As indicated in the August 21, 2001, *Wall Street Journal*,[1] many public companies have moved away from using GAAP earnings for the E of the P/E. They may instead utilize other earnings measures, such as operating earnings before extraordinary items, core earnings, and even pro forma earnings. Each of these revised definitions of earnings allows reporting entities to exclude certain one-time, exceptional, special, or noncash expenses, and, in turn, the net income of the enterprise is higher. According to the *Wall Street Journal* article, more than 300 of the 500 entities making up the S&P 500 now exclude some ordinary expenses as defined by GAAP from the operating earnings numbers provided to investors and analysts.

20. Arbitrage pricing theory (APT) is not widely used in business valuation assignments for cost of capital determinations due to the unavailability of usable data for the components of the model.

---

[1] Jonathan Weil, "What's the P/E Ratio? Well, Depends on What Is Meant by Earnings," *Wall Street Journal*, August 21, 2001.

21. There has been much debate over the merits of the Black-Green model. Many analysts have determined that the method is not empirically grounded and can be misleading, especially with regard to the suggested ranges of rate adjustments for each category. However, the detailed list of questions for the various factors can be very useful as an analytical tool and for work paper support.

22. The value from the excess cash flow method should approximate that derived from the capitalized cash flow method.

CHAPTER 6: MARKET APPROACH

1. The prices paid for businesses and business interests reflect investor expectations. Consequently, any valuation methods that use stock or sale prices of businesses, such as the market approach, must necessarily be prospective in nature.

2. The values derived from both the market and income approaches implicitly include all assets, both tangible and intangible.

3. Implicit in the prices of publicly traded companies and transactions is some assumption about growth. Generally, the higher the expected growth, the higher the value, all else being equal.

4. There are two distinct pools from which guideline company information can be drawn: (1) actual transactions and (2) publicly traded companies. Understanding the value implications of using these different types of data is crucial in properly applying the market approach.

5. For many very small businesses, the guideline company transaction method may be the only method within the market approach that makes sense.

6. Because detailed information is often not available for transactions, it is difficult to know the structure of the transactions or the motivation of the buyer or seller.

7. Detailed financial statements of acquired companies are usually not available for transactions. Therefore, it is impossible to make certain adjustments to the data underlying the pricing ratios, assuming such adjustments are necessary.

8. When using electronic sources of public company data, the analyst may have to consult the individual companies' filings for the underlying detail. This is not to suggest that adjustments do not have to be made to either of the values to make them truly comparable; rather, the point is that the values in these electronic databases are usually good starting points.

9. There is the perception that public companies are much too large to be used as comps in many situations. While this may be true for the smallest of subject companies, such as mom-and-pop operations, small professional practices, or sole proprietors, there is usually enough size variation among public companies that they should be considered for most other valuations.

10. In a recent study of all publicly held companies, 16% had sales of $10 million or less for the last 12 months.

11. In a recent study, the median asset size of all public companies is also surprisingly small at $161 million, with 13% of all public companies having assets of $10 million or less. The largest U.S. company is, not surprisingly, Citigroup, Inc., with almost $1 trillion in total assets.

12. In a recent study, one-quarter of all public companies have market capitalizations of $11 million or less.

13. In a recent study, almost one-half of all publicly traded companies lost money for the last 12 months on a net income (after-tax) basis. Only about 18% of all U.S. companies had net income profit margins of more than 10%.

14. Examining detailed business descriptions of the possible guideline companies is an essential step in the guideline public company analysis. Some data vendors provide good descriptions of a company's business(es); however, they are never more detailed than the data found in a company's 10-K filing.

15. One challenge involved with showing a list of potential guideline public companies to management is that they will often not view any of the companies as comparable, since they believe their company is truly unique. It is unlikely that the market niche into which the subject company fits really appreciates some of the nuances that make the subject truly unique. Unless these nuances result in prospects for the subject that are substantially different from those of the potential guideline companies, these companies can usually be used.

16. Perhaps the most important of comparative indicators is size. Size can be expressed in terms of sales, total assets, or market capitalization. Numerous studies have indicated that smaller companies have lower pricing multiples than larger companies. The main reason is that smaller companies typically have more business and financial risk than large companies.[2]

17. Expected growth is much more important in the determination of value than historical growth.

18. Another issue is whether trading of a guideline company's stock is sufficiently large to give meaningful and realistic values for that company. While companies with low trading volumes may be very similar to the subject in terms of business and financial characteristics, if their stocks' prices are questionable, there is no point in using the valuation ratios that are based on these prices.

19. The analysts may have to choose between (a) a very small group of companies whose business descriptions are very similar to that of the subject and (b) a larger group of companies with some of the companys' descriptions not as good a match with the subject.

20. The debt number used in the market approach should be its market value; however, on a practical basis, most analysts simply use the book value of the debt as a proxy for market value.

21. Using percentiles of valuation multiples rather than simple averages or composites has the advantage of providing a range of values and protecting the information from the effects of outliers.

22. It should be noted that when using transactions, there is much less data available. In particular, usually there is no data on which to compute growth rates or long-term margins. This lack of information might limit the confidence in the results obtained from this method.

---

[2] More risk means investors will require a higher rate of return on their investment; and the way to get this is by lowering the price.

23. Excess working capital can be determined by comparing the working capital ratio of the subject with those of the guideline companies, or by using industry norms.

24. Making certain adjustments can change the character of the resulting value— many times from a minority to a controlling value.

25. The quality and quantity of publicly traded company information will affect the confidence in the results from the market approach.

26. Whether to use the Market Value of Equity or Market Value of Invested Capital will be a function of the purpose of the valuation, the capital structures of the subject and guideline companies, and the analyst's preference.

27. The term *capital structure* refers to the relationship between the market values of debt and equity—never the book value of equity.

28. In theory, the best denominator to use in a valuation multiple would be one based on expectations—that is, using next year's expected revenues or income. It is an appropriate match with the numerator, since the value of equity or invested capital is a prospective concept, containing the market's best assessment of the prospects for the future.

29. Overall, EBITDA and EBIT multiples tend to be frequent indications across many industries.

30. Although rules of thumb should seldom be used as the sole way of valuing a business, they do provide some good industry knowledge, and investor insight.

31. Negative valuation multiples, which usually arise from losses, are not meaningful and should be ignored.

32. The final determination of which particular pricing multiple(s) to use must be based on an understanding of how the subject compares to the guideline companies in terms of the important factors (i.e., growth, size, longevity, profitability, etc.).

33. The application of market multiples from different databases results in varying types of value (e.g., with or without inventory or working capital).

34. Sometimes large differences between values derived from the income approach and the market approach can be explained by differences in growth assumptions.

CHAPTER 7: ASSET APPROACH

1. *Book value*, which pertains to cost basis accounting financial statements, is not fair market value.

2. The asset approach is sometimes used in the valuation of very small businesses or professional practices where there is little or no goodwill.

3. Although the asset approach can be used in almost any valuation, it is seldom used in the valuation of operating companies. The time and costs involved in valuing individual tangible and intangible assets typically is not justified, because there is little if any increase in the accuracy of the valuation. The value of all tangible and intangible assets is captured, in aggregate, in the proper application of the income and market approaches. In many valuations there is no real need to break out the amount of value associated with individual assets, including goodwill.

4. If the net asset/cost approach is used in valuing a minority interest of a closely held company, the value indication derived will usually have to be adjusted from control to minority and from a marketable to a nonmarketable basis.

5. The notes of the financial statements often contain useful information concerning contingent liabilities.

CHAPTER 8:   VALUATION DISCOUNTS AND PREMIUMS

1. Two of the fundamental tools used by valuation professionals are discounts, which reduce the value of interests in closely held businesses, and premiums. which increase the value of those interests.

2. Premiums and discounts may be classified as entity-level or shareholder-level depending on whether the driver for the premium or discount affects the entity as a whole (such as an environmental discount), or whether the driver reflects the characteristics of the shareholder's ownership by adjusting value either positively or negatively.

3. Control premiums quantify the value of controlling the destiny of the company. Acquisition or strategic premiums quantify the quality of a particular investment as viewed by a specific investor.

4. It should be noted that lack of control and liquidity are not necessarily separate and distinct entities. A majority shareholder may be able to affect liquidity in ways that a minority shareholder cannot. Pursuing a sale, a merger, or an initial public offering are examples of such situations. Thus, the two discounts should be considered in conjunction with each other.

5. From the point of view of the minority shareholder, the majority shareholder's ability to control gives the majority shareholder the ability to reduce or eliminate the return on the minority shareholder's investment.

6. In most states, majority control is not absolute.

7. The determination or the quantification of the amount of the minority discount or the discount for lack of control is difficult due to the lack of empirical evidence in this area.

8. The Mergerstat data includes synergistic and acquisition premiums along with the control premium. Segregation of these premiums is difficult.

9. The use of minority cash flows in the income approach produces a minority interest value. Minority cash flows are those cash flows without any adjustments for controlling shareholders actions such as excess compensation, rent payments, or perquisites.

10. Whether you start with control cash flows or minority cash flows, it is important to consistently apply this methodology throughout the minority value engagement.

11. Marketability is the term that expresses the relative ease and promptness with which a security or commodity may be sold when desired.

12. While some experts support a discount, there remains no generally accepted empirical evidence to support a discount for the lack of marketability for a controlling interest.

13. There are a number of studies and a wealth of empirical evidence for a lack of marketability discount for minority interests. These studies are usually based on two types of analyses. The first type of study is based on the difference between the initial public offering (IPO) price of a company and transactions in the same company's stock prior to the IPO. These are referred to as IPO studies or Private Placement Studies. The second measures the difference between the private price of a restricted security and the publicly traded stock price of the same company. These are referred to as Restricted Stock Studies.

14. The IRS, in Revenue Ruling 77-287, dealt with the issue of valuing restricted stocks. It was issued ". . . to provide information and guidance to taxpayers,

Internal Revenue Service personnel, and others concerned with the valuation, for Federal tax purposes, of securities that cannot be immediately resold because they are restricted from resale pursuant to Federal securities laws."

15. In addition to the discounts for lack of control and marketability, there are several other potential discounts. Some analysts consider these discounts in the calculation of a discount or capitalization factor while others separately quantify and apply the discounts.

16. Restrictions under certain agreements limit the ability to sell or transfer ownership interests.

17. In valuing a closely hold company, an adjustment for information access and reliability may be in order.

18. An ongoing disagreement between the IRS and many tax practitioners revolves around the treatment of the costs related to liquidating the assets in the estate. Certain costs such as brokers' fees, state and local transfer taxes, and holding period interest would be incurred to realize the property's fair market value.

19. At the very least, trapped capital gains discount should be considered if liquidation is imminent and the entity holds assets with unrealized appreciation.

20. A key person or thin management entity-level discount would be appropriate in the valuation of a closely held company where an owner or employee is responsible for generating a significant portion of the business's sales or profits. This key person may be a revenue generator, possess technical knowledge, or have close relationships with suppliers, customers, banks, and so forth.

21. Blockage discounts are based on the theory that a large block of publicly traded stock cannot ordinarily be sold as readily as a few shares of stock.

22. In the valuation of a closely held real estate investment holding company, a discount for potential market absorption should be considered.

23. When a smaller closely held company is being compared to a larger publicly traded company, an adjustment for size may be appropriate.

24. Small companies often have a limited access to capital, limited ability to weather a market downturn, limited resources to develop and market new products, and so forth. Smaller companies can also have a higher cost of capital than larger companies.

25. The blind application of discounts, without a thorough understanding of the subject company as compared to the underlying data used for the discounts, can lead to misleading valuation results.

CHAPTER 9:   REPORT WRITING

1. A full written report should provide all detail necessary to permit another qualified analyst to use the same information to replicate the work done and reach an informed valuation conclusion.

2. Although many analysts often comply with the Uniform Standards of Professional Appraisal Practice (USPAP) as a general rule, most of the analysts' report writings are not conducted under the circumstances specified by USPAP and are not required to be USPAP reports.

3. There are two primary types of valuation reports produced by analysts: "complete" and "other."

4. In certain engagements, such as litigation, the analyst might not be granted access to the facilities. In that event, the introduction section should explain this, and what was done to obtain the knowledge normally gained during a site visit.

5. Analysts usually do not audit or perform reviews or any other assurance procedures on the historical financial information provided by company management. They often accept the information as accurate and state this in the assumptions.

6. Some analysts include the assumptions and limiting conditions in the engagement letter as well as the report.

CHAPTER 10:   BUSINESS VALUATION STANDARDS

1. The Internal Revenue Service has not officially adopted USPAP.

2. Terminology used in USPAP standards is not uniform across the professions doing appraising work. For example, USPAP Standard 3 discusses the review of other appraisers' work. To certified public accountants (CPAs) doing business valuation, the term *review* carries a meaning that is unique to the accounting profession and represents a level of service related to financial statements.

3. The pertinent sections of USPAP for the business appraiser include the preamble, the ethics rule, the competency rule, the departure rule, the jurisdictional exception, and the supplemental standards. Standard 9 covers development of a business appraisal and Standard 10 covers reporting.

4. For CPAs, the word *certify* has special meaning concerning attestation of financial information. Some CPAs will add a sentence in their reports that they are not certifying any financial information but are adhering to the appraisal certification requirements of USPAP.

CHAPTER 11:   ESTATE, GIFT, AND INCOME TAX VALUATIONS

1. Use of the alternative date (6 months after the date of death) in an estate tax valuation may help to minimize estate taxes. For example, if the decedent was the key person in a closely held business, then the business's financial performance may decline during the period subsequent to death. The actual financial results will serve to support the proposition that the business was dependent on the decedent.

2. It is often the case that events that would otherwise affect a subject company's value occur subsequent to the valuation date. Such events should generally not be considered for purposes of estate and gift tax valuations. The key to determining what events should be considered is what facts were known or reasonably knowable as of the valuation date.

3. Many analysts make the mistake of focusing on a subject company's past historical performance as the primary determinant of value. It is the expectation of the company's future performance as of the valuation date that determines value. The past performance is only relative to the extent that it is indicative of the company's future performance.

4. Value is dependent on investors' expectations of a company's *future* earnings capacity. If an unprofitable operation can be discontinued without adversely affecting the company's other lines of business, then the future earnings capacity (and hence the value) of the remaining lines of business may be materially greater than if the values of all operating lines were aggregated—that is, the sum of *some* of the parts may be greater than the whole.

5. This definition of dividend-paying capacity is equivalent to equity net cash flows—that is, *those cash flows available to pay out to equity holders (in the form of dividends) after funding operations of the business.*[3]

6. Revenue Ruling 59-60 does not specifically address the use of the market approach/guideline company transaction method in valuing closely held companies, as these data have only had widespread availability in recent years. However, the guidelines relating to comparability of the business lines and consideration of other relevant factors presented in Revenue Ruling 59-60 for the application of the guideline public company method may be applicable to the guideline company transaction method as well.

7. Revenue Ruling 59-60 supports the use of an asset approach for valuing investment or holding companies. Therefore, use of an asset approach when valuing family limited partnerships and limited liability companies with similar characteristics is considered reasonable in view of Revenue Ruling 59-60.

8. Inexperienced analysts often make the mistake of arbitrarily averaging each of the various valuation approaches/methodologies used in valuing a closely held company. For example, if three approaches are used, each approach may be assigned an equal one-third weighting. As noted in Revenue Ruling 59-60, such an approach would serve no purpose. Rather, each valuation is subject to particular facts and circumstances, which must be considered in selecting the most appropriate approach(es) and level of reliance when determining the final estimate of value.

CHAPTER 12:   VALUATION OF FAMILY LIMITED PARTNERSHIPS (FLPs)

1. Once a valuation analyst has a solid understanding of the bundle of rights, they are better prepared to determine how to capture the impact on value in the subject's benefit stream, rate of return, discount applied to enterprise value, or a combination of these. This will involve gaining a picture of not only the rights that exist but more importantly those rights that do not.

2. Term restriction is important from a valuation perspective because it defines the inability of the limited partners to receive a return on their investment prior to the completion of the partnership term.

3. A majority vote provision provides for rights for limited partners in certain circumstances that may enable them to affect some of the operations of the part-

---

[3] *International Glossary of Business Valuation Terms* (The C.L.A.R.E.N.C.E. Glossary Project comprised of the following professional organizations: American Institute of Certified Public Accountants, American Society of Appraisers, Canadian Institute of Chartered Business Valuators, National Association of Certified Valuation Analysts, and The Institute of Business Appraisers, 2001).

nership. As such, the impact of this type of provision will be partially dependent on the size of the limited partnership interest being valued.

4. If transfer provisions in the agreement are anything other than fair market value between family members, the agreement may be disregarded under the Internal Revenue Code, Chapter 14, Section 2703.

5. Most partnership agreements will have a clearly stated restriction on transferability of partnership interests. This is primarily to protect all partners from finding themselves legally bound to the partnership with individuals not of their choice. From a valuation perspective, such restrictions on transferability may have a material impact on the selection of the degree of discounts for lack of control and lack of marketability. However, if other provisions modify the transferability restrictions, they may provide a mitigating effect on the depth of the discounts.

6. Certain provisions provide a substantial level of authority to the general partner with input by the limited partners. However, many partnership agreements provide for a power of attorney clause whereby the limited partners specifically provide the authority for the general partner to act on their behalf. In addition, a restriction on transferability provides some level of protection to the limited partners regarding possible changes in partnership management. These restrictions as well as the general partner(s)' legally binding fiduciary responsibility toward the limited partners may allow for some level of discount for lack of control when valuing a general partner interest.

7. Just like the provision for the general partner capital accounts, there are provisions that make it clear that all contributions are to be credited to the partners' account in order to avoid "gift on formation" issues.

8. One of the benefits to a limited partnership structure is the protection afforded the limited partners from the debts and obligations of the partnership or of other partners.

9. Certain FLP provisions serve as the foundation for selecting appropriate discounts for lack of control and lack of marketability because:

   - A limited partner by definition does not have any right to manage or control the partnership, thus eliminating his or her ability to determine the amount and timing of any distributions or asset liquidations of the partnership. This effectively eliminates some of the sources of return on the partner's investment.
   - The inability to readily transfer the interest or withdraw from the partnership eliminates the other avenue for a limited partner to receive a return on his or her investment.

10. In order to avoid the negative impact that Section 2704(a) can have on the estate tax value of a limited partnership interest, it is better if the limited partner does *not* own a general interest in the partnership at death. Alternatively, the limited partner can gift all of his or her limited interest before he or she dies.

11. If fair market value is the appropriate standard of value, factors influencing the pricing of partnership interests in secondary transactions may be considered.

12. Assets within a particular category may produce different impacts on value. For instance, if an FLP is holding undeveloped land instead of an income-producing property, its value will be influenced by the inability of the undeveloped land to generate a return to partners other than through ongoing appreciation and possible liquidation of the asset.

13. The closed-end funds to be used should match as closely as possible the specific portfolio structure of the FLP. For instance, if the FLP is holding only technology stock and some blue chips, the selected closed-end funds should have a similar asset mix so that the market perception of risk will be appropriately reflected for the type of portfolio being held by the FLP.

14. As a point of reference, publicly traded open-end mutual funds issue and redeem shares directly to and from the fund itself. Consequently, if the demand for an open-end fund increases, the fund issues more shares. An open-end mutual fund normally prices unit purchases and redemptions at the transaction cost-adjusted net asset value. Therefore, these types of funds will continually dilute and grow with purchases and shrink with sales. Typically, they do not experience the price fluctuations that closed-end funds do.

15. An analysis of closed-end funds with similar investment characteristics to the subject FLP can provide an indication of the adjustment to net asset value that the market would require.

16. Since closed-end funds are publicly traded, the difference between the trading price and net asset value has nothing to do with marketability. In addition, be aware that some funds are thinly traded and, as a result, are not good indicators of market dynamics.

17. The derived discount from net asset value (NAV) can be viewed in two ways. The first is as a discount:

$$\text{NAV} \times (1-D) = \text{Value} \quad \text{where D} = \text{Discount}$$
$$\text{NAV} - \$1,000,000 \times (1 - .20) = \$800,000$$

or it can be viewed as a market multiple:

$$\text{NAV} \times \text{Multiple} = \text{Value}$$
$$\$1,000,000 \times .80 = \$800,000$$

CHAPTER 14: SHAREHOLDER DISPUTES

1. State statutes and judicial precedent control this area of valuation. Although analysts should not be acting as attorneys, it is important that they become generally familiar with the statutes and case law in the jurisdiction where the lawsuit has been filed.

2. Shareholder dispute cases arise under two different state statutes, dissenting shareholder actions, and minority oppression (dissolution) actions.

3. In both dissenting and oppressed shareholder disputes, the statutes are clear—the standard of value is fair value.

4. Not only is the standard of value important in determining the methodology that will be performed and the discounts and premiums that will or will not be applied, but the courts have also shown that they do not equate fair value and fair market value.

5. When preparing a fair value analysis, the valuation analyst must look at the state statute to establish the valuation date.

6. The courts look to the valuation analyst to provide a well-reasoned, objective valuation to aid the court in its findings. This requires the analyst to maintain his or her objectivity and independence.

7. Currently, the three approaches to value: market, income, and asset, are all acceptable in the shareholder dispute arena, although it is important to generally understand the appropriate court cases in the particular jurisdiction. Methodologists (or preferred methods) vary from one jurisdiction to the other.
8. Various courts interpret methodologies differently and will refer to commonly known methods by other names.

CHAPTER 15: VALUATION ISSUES IN ESOPs

1. Both private and publicly held corporations can establish employee stock ownership plans (ESOPs) to encourage their employees to think and act like owners.
2. Closely held companies and some thinly traded publicly held companies must be valued by an independent valuation analyst.
3. The ultimate responsibility for a financial valuation of a closely held company ESOP resides squarely with the plan trustee.
4. Every ESOP valuation must fulfill the regulations of both the Internal Revenue Service (IRS) and the Department of Labor (DOL).
5. The capital to conduct such transactions is generally borrowed by the ESOP from or through the sponsoring company, although the company can also simply contribute new shares of stock to an ESOP, or contribute cash to buy existing shares.
6. Expounding on the DOL "adequate consideration" requirement, the ESOP cannot pay more than fair market value for its shares.
7. Plan provisions written at the time of the inception of the ESOP are very important and have an effect on when distributions will occur.
8. The greater the employee turnover, the higher the expected level of repurchase obligation. The higher the growth of stock value of the sponsoring company, the more the per-share distributions must be. The impact on the dollar amount of the repurchase obligation can be substantial.
9. The effort to understand and plan strategies for dealing with repurchases is needed early in the life of an ESOP company.
10. By making loans through the ESOP, the company receives a number of tax benefits.
11. There is no limit on the term of an ESOP loan other than what lenders will accept. ESOP loans typically amortize over five to seven years.
12. The company measures compensation expense on the basis of the fair value (an accounting term not to be confused with fair market value) of the shares to be released, which can cause some dramatic fluctuations in recorded compensation expense.
13. ESOP valuations are usually those of a noncontrolling interest, unless compelling requisite relevant factors and empirical evidence are available to support a control value.
14. When valuing a minority block of stock of a closely held corporation, there is no range of discounts that will universally be applicable in any given circumstance.
15. A put right is the legal right, not the requirement, of a participant, under certain circumstances of plan termination, to convert their sponsoring company stock held in their individual accounts to cash under a detailed time-specific formula.

16. It is difficult to forecast repurchase obligations much further than a few years and to estimate the present value of future repurchase obligations.

17. In order to comply with the requirements of the DOL, the analyst's conclusion of fair market value must be reflected in a written document.

18. The valuation is generally made on an annual basis and may be used in several scenarios over which the analyst has little or no control.

CHAPTER 16:   VALUATION IN THE DIVORCE SETTING

1. The analyst must know the specific definition of value that is to be used in determining a value in a divorce setting. Failure to do so could result in the valuation being excluded if challenged.

2. The various definitions and components of goodwill have often caused confusion. Therefore, it is important to fully understand its meaning in the context being used.

3. Since state laws are so diverse, the analyst must constantly be alert to not only the espoused standard of value in a particular jurisdiction, but also the variations imposed by judicial decisions.

4. Personal goodwill is that goodwill that attaches to the persona and the personal efforts of the individual. It is generally considered to be difficult to transfer, if at all. Entity goodwill is the goodwill that attaches to the business enterprise.

5. If analysts present their case well and support the allocations with sound logic, the court will be more likely to accept their value conclusions as a reasonable approximation of the personal versus entity goodwill.

6. In the case of a law or accounting practice, location of the client might not be as important, except in smaller communities.

7. The analyst should consider the number of employees, the job titles and job descriptions, the pay scale, and the length of service in a goodwill review.

8. In determining the fair market value of a professional practice, the issue of control of clients, patients, customers, and so forth, relates to the transferable value of the practice. Thus, the issue of nonowner professionals and their impact on value should be considered in addition to the consideration of the owner's of personal entity goodwill.

9. The arguments set forth be proponents of a personal goodwill element for commercial businesses sound similar to a key person discount.

10. Generally, divorce decrees specify amounts of marital assets (identified in dollars) allocated to each spouse. The amounts are specific (as indicated) instead of a range of amounts. Therefore, the analyst in a divorce situation will normally be asked to determine a specific amount of value instead of a range of value.

11. Although noncompliance to standards does not necessarily invalidate the valuation report for the court (that decision is up to the judge), the cross-examining attorney can nevertheless use noncompliance as a tool for impeachment.

CHAPTER 17:   VALUATION ISSUES IN SMALL BUSINESSES

1. Small businesses tend to have lower-quality financial statements. Outside accountants are less likely to have prepared the financial statements. Their statements tend to be tax oriented rather than oriented to stockholder disclosure as in larger companies.

2. Adjustments from cash basis accounting to accrual basis accounting are common among the smallest companies. Other adjustments to place the statements more in compliance with GAAP are also more likely to be needed in small companies.

3. The characteristics of small businesses tend to result in overall higher risk than is found in larger businesses. Among small businesses, these characteristics tend to be extreme, and risk tends to increase as size decreases.

4. It may be necessary to make certain adjustments to improve comparability of the subject company to industry norms, publicly traded companies, or companies involved in market transactions considered in the valuation process.

5. When valuing a control interest in a small business, it is appropriate to adjust discretionary items. When valuing a minority interest, it is not always appropriate to adjust for discretionary items because the owner of a minority interest is not in a position to change these items.

6. Business brokers can provide insight into the qualitative factors being considered in a particular market.

7. Earnings in the latest 12 months and average earnings in recent years tend to be given the most weight in establishing prices for small businesses. Capitalization of earnings/cash flow is often an appropriate method for these small businesses.

8. Many valuation analysts assume that the guideline public company method is never applicable to small businesses. For the mom-and-pop very small business, this may be a safe assumption. For the small businesses at the other end of the spectrum, this assumption is not safe. There are a large number of publicly traded companies with market capitalization less than $50 million, putting them within reasonable range for some small businesses.

9. The valuation analyst must exercise caution using transaction databases because they define variables in different ways.

10. Revenue and discretionary earnings are two of the most common multiples used in the guideline company transaction method.

11. Value indications derived from the guideline company transaction method are on a control basis.

12. Although rules of thumb may provide insight on the value of a business, it is usually better to use them for reasonableness tests of the value conclusion.

13. The excess cash flow/earnings method is widely used for small businesses, but analysts frequently misuse it.

CHAPTER 18: VALUATION ISSUES IN PROFESSIONAL PRACTICES

1. Many professional practices obtain most of their patients or clients through referrals based on the reputation of specific professionals.

2. An important issue in valuing professional practices is distinguishing between the goodwill that is solely attributable to the professional (and difficult to transfer) and the goodwill that is attributable to the practice.

3. Although professional practices are valued for the same reasons as other types of businesses, litigation (including disputes among principals and marital dissolutions) and transactions (including the sale of a practice, an associate buying in, and buy-sell formulas) account for a large portion of the valuation work.

4. Goodwill may be the primary intangible asset found in professional practices. But the definition of goodwill differs in different scenarios.

5. When a professional practice is being valued for transaction or litigation purposes (depending on state law and judicial precedent), it may be important to identify professional and practice goodwill separately and to discuss the likelihood that a portion of the professional goodwill can be transferred in a transaction.

6. Analysts should have a clear understanding of state law as it pertains to marital dissolution in divorce valuations.

7. It is important to be sure the professional's earnings and/or the practice's economic income have been calculated in the same manner as the comparative compensation data in a divorce valuation.

8. In a small professional practice, value may be greater if a successor for the key professional is in place. Bringing in an associate and introducing the associate to clients or patients may facilitate the transfer of some professional goodwill and may increase the price received by the exiting professional.

9. When valuing professional practices, it is important to analyze and make appropriate adjustments to the financial statements. The widespread use of cash basis accounting may require a number of adjustments.

10. If the practice owns material amounts of nonoperating assets such as art collections and antiques in excess of what is customary in the decor of comparable offices, it may be necessary to value these assets separately from practice operations.

11. If the economic benefits stream being discounted or capitalized is pretax earnings or pretax earnings plus owners' compensation and benefits, the discount rate or the capitalization rate should be higher than if the benefits stream is after-tax net cash flow.

12. Guideline company transactions are often used as a reasonableness test of values obtained by other methods.

13. The usefulness of past transactions in the subject company is often limited by the way the transactions are structured. A substantial portion of the transferred practice value may be included through salary differentials, and it may be difficult to distinguish that portion of the salary differential attributable to the buyout of a practitioner. Prior transactions also sometimes reflect a punishment to the exiting practitioner for early withdrawal of capital and the practitioner's professional services.

14. Although rules of thumb may provide insight on the value of a professional practice, it is usually only appropriate to use them for reasonableness tests of the value conclusion.

CHAPTER 19: VALUATION OF HEALTHCARE SERVICE BUSINESSES

1. In the mergers and acquisition marketplace, the demand for business valuation services has shifted away from transactions involving physician practices toward other types of deals.

2. Reimbursement is a critical assumption in the financial projections of healthcare organizations. Many analysts make the inaccurate assumption that reimbursement will continue to increase at the national inflation rates. Analysts

must first understand the payor mix of the business being valued, including how specific payors reimburse for services and the prospect for future changes in that reimbursement.

3. The volatility of reimbursement for individual procedures can be very high. It is important to consider all prospective reimbursement changes when performing the valuation analysis.

4. Individual physicians exert a significant amount of control over the direction of patient referrals to healthcare service providers.

5. Valuation analysts should understand that the level of scrutiny may be very high when providing opinions of fair market value that could be subject to the Federal anti-kickback laws. A very large number of transactions are subject to the anti-kickback regulations.

6. It is important to identify applicable situations and seek advice from healthcare attorneys on the Federal fraud and abuse implications of valuations performed in the healthcare services industry.

7. Appropriately factoring the regulatory environment into the valuation is important when valuing healthcare businesses.

8. It may be necessary to consult a qualified tax lawyer in order to understand how to appropriately consider the tax laws when valuing a business that involves a tax-exempt enterprise.

9. If a valuation is being performed as a result of regulatory requirements, the valuation must apply the fair market value standard of value.

10. It is important to understand what is included in the revenue stream of the subject entity, since professional versus technical revenue generation involves different valuation dynamics.

11. A negative reimbursement trend for certain healthcare services is not uncommon. It may be erroneous to assume that reimbursement will increase at inflationary rates without having performed some level of reimbursement analysis.

12. One of the erroneous assumptions commonly made in healthcare valuations is that variable expenses are always solely a function of revenue.

13. The net result of volatile reimbursement levels for some healthcare entities is declining margins, making it important for the valuation analyst to carefully track variable costs.

14. Historically, public healthcare companies have been acquisitive and have had high valuation multiples. As a result, the multiples generated by public companies are usually not comparable to those of private businesses.

15. Many analysts try to force the use of guideline transaction multiples. This can increase the risk of a flawed valuation. Unfortunately, it is rare when the information is at the level of detail necessary to perform a stand-alone guideline transaction analysis.

16. Many minority interests in healthcare businesses do not exhibit the characteristics that affect the magnitude of discounts in other closely held businesses.

17. The analyst should read the operating and/or partnership agreement in order to determine the level of minority or marketability discounts, if any.

18. The regulatory and legal issues may pertain to the valuation of entities in many industry niches.

19. A common oversimplification is utilizing limited market transaction data without thoroughly understanding the transactions, potentially leading to faulty conclusions.

20. When valuing a dialysis center, it is important to understand the center's relationship with the nephrologist. It is critical in assessing risk.

Case Study #1: Valuation of a Surgery Center

1. It is important to understand the underlying components in the case mix, since the reimbursement rates for each specialty are not homogeneous.
2. The analysis will want to ascertain the likelihood that the top 10 surgeons will continue to perform cases at a center, which affects the specialty growth rates used in the projections.
3. Some analysts obtain a sampling of the surgery center's explanation of benefits (EOBs) from the most recent surgical cases to understand the dynamics of the payor mix. An adequate sampling of 25 to 30 EOBs with the associated gross and net charges for that procedure will provide an understanding of the main procedures performed under each specialty as well as help assess the reasonableness of the facility's overall charge rates.
4. Nonoperational expenses such as automobiles for personal use should be removed from the operating expense profile.

Case Study #2: Valuation of a Hospital

1. *Assets, limited as to use* and *investments* are considered excess assets and therefore may be added back to the resulting DCF value to arrive at the total value. Assets, limited as to use refers to those assets that are earmarked for specific activities (e.g., related future capital expenditures, etc.). Investments refer to cash/marketable securities.
2. Simply adding inpatient days plus outpatient cases would be erroneous, since patients who are treated on an outpatient basis in the hospital are not measured in terms of days. As a result, the hospital applies an outpatient conversion factor to convert the outpatient cases into outpatient days. This is necessary in order to arrive at adjusted patient days, the term for measuring a hospital's occupancy rate and capacity.

CHAPTER 20:   VALUATIONS OF INTANGIBLE ASSETS

1. This growth of intangible assets relative to tangible assets has been a major force propelling our U.S. economy.
2. Intangible assets receiving legal protection are called intellectual property, which is generally categorized as: patents, copyrights, trade names (-marks, -dress), trade secrets, and know-how.
3. There are approximately three dozen Statements which require consideration of fair value.[4]

---

[4] Michael Mard, *Task Force Report to Business Valuation Subcommittee* (2000).

4. Since return requirements increase as risk increases and since intangible assets are more risky for a company than are tangible assets, it is reasonable to conclude that the returns expected on intangible assets typically will be at or above the average rate of return (discount rate) for the company as a whole.

5. A principal difference between the two definitions of value is that fair value for the business enterprise considers synergies and attributes of the specific buyer and specific seller, while fair market value endeavors to be a more objective standard, contemplating a hypothetical willing buyer and a hypothetical willing seller.

6. Goodwill is the excess of the cost of an acquired entity over the net amounts assigned to assets acquired less liabilities assumed.[5]

7. Under SFAS No. 142, amortization of goodwill is not allowed. Instead, goodwill is tested annually for impairment.

8. A present value technique is often the best available technique with which to estimate the fair value of a group of assets (such as a reporting unit).

9. The second step of the goodwill impairment test is triggered if the carrying value of the reporting unit, including goodwill, exceeds the fair value of the reporting unit.

10. The subject of IPR&D has been comprehensively addressed in the AICPA Best Practices Guide, Assets Acquired in a Purchase Business Combination to be used in Research and Development Activities: A Focus on Software, Electronic Devices and Pharmaceutical Industries (IPR&D Practice Aid).

11. IPR&D can be generally defined as a research and development project that has not yet been completed. Acquired IPR&D is an intangible asset to be used in R&D activities.

12. To be recognized as assets, IPR&D projects must have substance, that is, sufficient cost and effort associated with the project to enable its fair value to be estimated with reasonable reliability.[6] Further, the IPR&D must be incomplete in that there are remaining technological, engineering, or regulatory risks.[7]

13. Including tax effects in the valuation process is common in the income and cost approaches, but not typical in the market approach, since any tax benefit is already factored into the quoted market price.

14. Transfer pricing takes place within non-arm's length transactions, generally between subsidiary and parent. Because of perceived abuses in establishing tax deductible charges between related entities, the IRS has been quite vigilant in reviewing such arrangements.

15. A company's tangible and intangible rates of return can be presented as in the figure below (example only).

---

[5] Financial Accounting Standards Board, Statement of Financial Accounting Standards No. 142, Goodwill and Other Intangible Assets, Appendix F (June 2001).

[6] Randy J. Larson et al., *Assets Acquired in a Business Combination to Be Used in Research and Development Activities: A Focus on Software, Electronic Devices, and Pharmaceutical Industries* (New York: AICPA, 2001), at 3.3.42.

[7] Ibid., at 3.3.55.

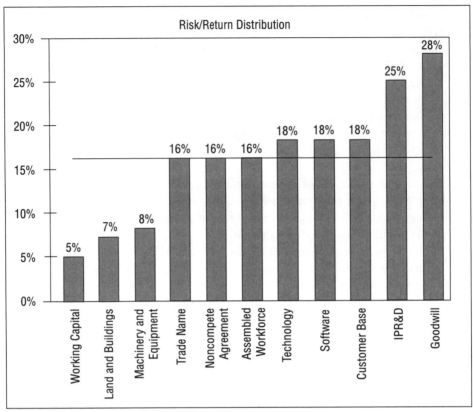

Where
a. The midline of the distribution represents the company's discount rate;
b. Items below the midline represent returns on tangible assets (such as working capital: 5%, and land and buildings: 7%;
c. Items above the midline represent returns on intangible assets (such as IPR&D: 25%, and customer base: 18%); and
d. The highest rate of return represents the riskiest asset, goodwill.

16. The risk premium assessed to a new product launch should decrease as a project successfully proceeds through its continuum of development since the uncertainty related to each subsequent stage diminishes.

17. Under GAAP, an acquiring company must record the fair value of the assets acquired in a business combination. SFAS No. 141 mandates such purchase accounting for all acquisitions.[8]

18. The appropriate rate of return in valuing the enterprise is the weighted average cost of capital, the weighted average of the return on equity capital, and the return on debt capital. The weights represent percentages of debt to total capital and equity to total capital. The rate of return on debt capital is adjusted to reflect the fact that interest payments are tax deductible to the corporation.

---

[8] Financial Accounting Standards Board, Statement of Financial Accounting Standards No. 141, *Business Combinations* (June 2001), at 13.

19. The formula for the amortization benefit of an amortizable intangible asset is:

    $$AB = PVCF \times (n / (n - ((PV(Dr,n, -1) \times (1 + Dr) {}^\wedge 0.5) \times T)) -1)$$

    Where

AB	=	Amortization benefit
PVCF	=	Present value of cash flows from the asset
n	=	15 year amortization period
Dr	=	Discount rate
$PV(Dr,n,-1) \times (1 + Dr)^\wedge 0.5$	=	Present value of an annuity of \$1 over 15 years, at the discount rate
T	=	Tax rate

20. Valuation of a customer base using the costs approach requires the identification of the selling costs associated with the generation of new customers. For example, management indicated that the split in selling costs was roughly equivalent to the revenue split between new and existing customers. Thus, the valuation is based on that split. Depending on the nature of the business, this split between new and existing customers may vary greatly. Thus, the valuation analyst will need to appropriately identify the costs associated with generating the new customers. This is probably most easily done based on an allocation of the sales team's time such as 40 percent spent on finding new customers, 60 percent to handle existing ones. Or, there may be certain sales or marketing people or departments that are devoted entirely to servicing existing accounts, while others spend all of their time finding new ones. In such cases, the costs can be broken out on a departmental or individual level. For many smaller businesses, top executives also spend a large amount of time in the generation of new customers, so these costs must also be considered in the analysis.

21. Use of the cost approach also assumes that the customers and selling effort required to obtain them are all relatively equivalent. If the company has a few customers that make up the majority of its business, then the cost approach may not be as appropriate to determine the value of the customer base.

22. It should be noted that the income approach is often recommended for valuing a customer base. For many consumer products and "old economy" businesses, the customer relationship may have much higher value than the technology associated with the products being sold, since these products are often a commodity or near commodity that may be easily substituted with products from another vendor. The customer relationship may allow the sale of multiple products and services through the same sales channels. An income approach may be more appropriate in these cases.

23. SFAS No. 141 specifically prohibits the recognition of assembled workforce as an intangible asset apart from goodwill.[9]

24. Trade names and trademarks must be considered individually to determine their remaining useful life. Trade names and trademarks that are associated with a company name or logo (e.g., McDonald's) typically have indefinite lives. Many product trade names and trademarks also will have an indefinite life if no reasonable estimate can be made of the end of the product life (e.g., Coca

[9] Financial Accounting Standards Board, Statement of Financial Accounting Standards No. 141, *Business Combinations*, (June 2001), at 39.

Cola). However, the analyst must be careful to find out whether there is a planned phase-out of a product or ascertain whether it can be estimated with reasonable certainty that a name will lose value or be abandoned over time. In such a case, a finite life is suggested and, therefore, an amortization period is warranted. Remember, for tax purposes generally all intangibles are amortizable over a 15-year life.

25. In the valuation of a successful business enterprise, there are often intangible assets that cannot be separately identified. These intangible assets are generally referred to as goodwill. The term *goodwill* however is sometimes used to describe the aggregate of all of the intangible assets of a business. In a more restricted sense, goodwill is the sum total of only the imponderable qualities that attract future new customers to the business.

26. By its nature, goodwill is the riskiest asset of the group and therefore should require a higher return than the overall business return.

CHAPTER 21:   MARKETING, MANAGING, AND MAKING MONEY IN A VALUATION SERVICES GROUP

1. Some practices whose revenues are primarily based on fixed fees make the mistake of failing to maintain or to evaluate time records and other information about efficiency and profitability that would indicate problem areas needing corrective action.

2. It is desirable that chargeable hours for engagements, on average, result in billings equal to 90% or more of the recorded hours.

3. On average, professionals in the practice should be charging billable hours to engagements for more than 70% of the standard hours available for them to work.

4. In spite of the higher rates offered by litigation services, many practitioners find that being an expert witness is disruptive to the processes needed to direct a practice that must deliver valuation reports on a regular basis.

5. Since a business valuation engagement is a consulting project, proactive planning and control is key to maximization of the efficiency, quality, and profitability of the work process and product.

6. Resource flexibility in staffing is a rich area for practice leaders to explore as they seek to smooth the peaks and valleys of the work flow.

7. Unless the practice has a bias toward quality and client value, there is less chance for good economics, at least for any sustained period of time.

8. Litigation service engagements especially need an organized and disciplined approach because so often the engagement objectives identified at the start are augmented and revised over the life of the project.

9. A practice may not want to accept engagements for individuals (as opposed to companies) as clients without substantial retainers being received.

10. In most situations, if you are good enough to be engaged, you are good enough to be partially paid in advance through retainers.

11. A work plan and budget provide a valuable tool to supervise and control the engagement team and are conducive to obtaining efficiency on the job.
12. Sometimes the best approach to take with an engagement that is going badly economically is to put the practice's best people on the job to finish.
13. An old adage, "People do what you inspect, not what you expect," applies here, since few team members will know or admit to the leader on a timely basis that they are off-track about the direction in which their work is headed.
14. A good rule of thumb for frequency of inspection by a practice leader or engagement manager is that the work of juniors/novices should be reviewed every two hours. The work of all other professionals should be inspected on a time interval of three hours for each year of their experience. This is highly effected by the type and complexity of the engagement.
15. Preparing a work plan and budget for known tasks and obtaining approval are beneficial to the client and attorney understanding the likely fee levels required.
16. Nothing should be assumed with the client and the client's attorney without frequent clear communication.

CHAPTER 22: BUSINESS (COMMERCIAL) DAMAGES

1. Although financial experts are usually not attorneys and are not expected by their professional standards to know the law, attorneys frequently choose experts who have some knowledge of the law that applies to a particular litigation matter.
2. Establishing reasonable certainty involves rigorous analysis, of which the identification and testing of key assumptions may be an important part. Some of these key assumptions are based on client representations.
3. Financial experts are sometimes requested by the attorney to opine on causation. The experts should evaluate whether they have the qualifications and foundation to render such an opinion.
4. Although *Daubert* involved a scientific expert, the court set forth four criteria by which a trial judge could evaluate the reliability of all expert testimony.[10]
   a. Whether a theory or technique can be (and has been) tested;
   b. Whether the theory or technique has been subjected to peer review and publication;
   c. The known or potential rate of error and the existence and maintenance of standards controlling the technique's operation; and
   d. Explicit identification of a relevant scientific community and an express determination of a particular degree of acceptance within that community.
5. In litigation, the financial expert can expect to be challenged regarding qualifications, the proper application of valuation theory, and the appropriateness of the underlying assumptions and facts.
6. One of the most challenging aspects of a lost profits calculation is determining how far into the future to project ongoing lost profits. The period of recovery

---

[10] William Daubert, et ux, etc., et al., Petitioners v. Merrell Dow Pharmaceuticals, Inc. (113 S. Ct. 2786, 125 C. Ed., 2d 469 [1993]).

largely depends on the facts and circumstances of the case, as well as the tests for reasonable certainty and proximate cause.

7. In many jurisdictions, the law mandates the treatment for interest, often by prescribing a statutory interest rate, generally based on simple rather than compound interest calculations.

8. The purpose of compensatory damages is to make the plaintiff whole—that is, the plaintiff should receive no more or no less than is necessary to make it whole.

9. In certain damage calculations, analysts will discount future *pretax* earnings by the appropriate *after-tax* discount rate, which may be different than in a business valuation.

CHAPTER 23: OTHER VALUATION SERVICES AREAS

A. Valuation Issues in Mergers and Acquisitions

1. In many instances, as a starting point in pricing a transaction, a buyer will analyze the value of a transaction using assumptions that are the same or similar to those that would be used under fair market value. This provides the buyer with a baseline valuation, which is a valuation of the target without any effects of the transaction itself.

2. The most common standard of value for a merger or acquisition is investment value.

3. Fair value is a standard of value in accounting pronouncements. For financial reporting purposes, the fair value of an asset is defined as "the amount at which the asset could be bought or sold in a current transaction between willing parties, that is, other than in a forced or liquidation sale."[11]

4. Synergies can be either operational or financial.

5. Selling previously acquired assets and companies can also lead to company synergies by allowing management to concentrate on what drives value in a company.

6. Many analysts fail to consider incremental costs when performing a pricing analysis or valuation of a potential target.

7. Analysts include value created from revenue enhancements, cost reductions, and creation of other efficiencies. However, valuation analysts should be aware of hidden costs in a transaction, such as postmerger integration issues and competitors' reactions when performing a valuation that includes the synergy of a transaction.

8. Under the new Statements (SFAS Nos. 141 and 142), goodwill will continue to be recognized as an asset in business combinations. However, the new Statements prohibit the amortization of goodwill. Instead they provide for an impairment test at the reporting unit level on at least an annual basis.

B. Valuations for Public Companies and/or Financial Reporting

1. The increasing importance of intangible assets and intellectual property to public companies' financial positions and strategic profiles also increases the need for valuation services.

---

[11] Financial Accounting Standards Board, Statement of Financial Accounting Standards No. 141, *Business Combinations,* Appendix F (June, 2001).

2. Unlike most other valuation assignments, the need for public company valuation services is often dictated by GAAP.

3. The standard of value most often used in financial reporting valuations is fair value.

4. When engaged to provide an opinion regarding the fair value of a particular public company's assets or liabilities, it is important to confirm with the company's auditor the exact definition of fair value to be utilized and to clearly identify which items are to be valued.

5. While a public corporation's traded stock has a readily determinable value and the company may have publicly traded options, there are distinct differences between employee stock options and publicly traded stock options that influence their value. Also, corporations may grant employee stock options on shares that are not publicly traded, including shares in subsidiaries and shares with voting rights different from the publicly traded stock.

6. In certain businesses, the lines are blurred between the intangible assets of the business and income-producing real estate. Some examples include: hotels, motels, hospitals, and skilled nursing centers, among others. By performing a purchase price allocation, the intangible assets can be separated from the real property and can then be amortized over a much shorter life.

7. The client will not typically be versed in the differences between these standards of value, so early communication and active listening are the keys to a successful engagement.

C. Valuation Issues in Buy-Sell Agreements

1. Every closely held business owner should have a Buy-Sell Agreement with their business partners/shareholders.

2. A Buy-Sell Agreement can set the ground rules for any matter the owners want to include. For this reason, there is no "one size fits all" when it comes to shareholder agreements. An owner who signs a "cookie-cutter" Buy-Sell Agreement is practically assured of disagreement and misunderstanding down the road.

3. Most disputes that arise as a result of a triggering event do so because the agreement is either unclear or misunderstood by the parties involved. Unfortunately, this is also the worst time to try to resolve such a dispute; it is better to be in the position of making these decisions when the parties are amicable.

4. The battles that accompany triggering events often occur at a time when the company needs most to be projecting assurances to their employees and customers. This can disrupt operations and ultimately serve to reduce the very value the owners are at odds over.

5. Rarely do formulas result in "easy" solutions when the time comes to put them into practice.

6. If a Buy-Sell Agreement entered into after October 8, 1990 contains a clause that would value the stock at less than fair market value, it will be disregarded for tax purposes.

7. Shareholders who have signed agreements that value the company's stock at something less than fair market value may find themselves in the unfortunate position of having transferred the stock for the price set by the agreement only to find that the IRS values it at something greater. This may result in an unexpected tax liability.

D. Valuation Issues in Pass-Through Entities

1. The valuation analyst should read the partnership agreement for the specific legal rights and responsibilities assigned to individual partners, and, if necessary, also consult with the entity's legal counsel.
2. When a company converts from a C corporation to an S corporation, a business valuation is often needed, particularly if a sale of company assets is expected within 10 years of S election. The valuation serves as a baseline for calculating built-in gains.
3. The issue of whether to deduct corporate-level taxes in a pass-through entity is a matter that is heavily disputed among valuation analysts and among the ranks of IRS valuation analysts. In fact, the IRS has often rejected any deduction for corporate taxes in direct violation of its own valuation guide, which clearly states that corporate-level taxes should be deducted.
4. In the determination of the cash flows of a business under a fair market value standard, considerable case law exists to support the concept of considering the entire pool of hypothetical buyers.
5. The IRS frequently takes the position, as in the recent tax court case, *Gross*,[12] that corporate-level taxes are not to be deducted in valuations of S corporations. However, in many cases, the strict guidance set forth in *Gross* should not apply.
6. For companies that distribute only part of their profits, ultimately the reality of settlements with the IRS is that it attempts to meet the taxpayer somewhere in the middle. However, valuation analysts should be looking to the economic reality of the interest being valued.
7. If the pool of buyers for pass-through entity stock is limited by S election restrictions, the discount could be higher. On the other hand, some S corporations distribute virtually all of their earnings, which puts more cash in the pockets of investors and leads to greater return on investment. This factor would lower the discount for lack of marketability. There are also situations where there are profits but no distribution. This would support a higher discount.
8. Some valuation analysts tax-affect S corporation earnings, then apply a traditionally derived after-tax discount. Other analysts use pretax earnings or cash flow, then apply a pretax discount rate. It is important to note that both of these methods result in an after-tax value, since the pretax rates are derived from data specific to tax-paying entities.

E. Valuing Debt

1. The value of a convertible bond is closely tied to the value of the underlying common stock as long as the per share price multiplied by the conversion ratio (i.e., the number of the shares represented by the convertible option) is greater than or equal to the par value of the bond.
2. Since a bond with a long period until maturity is riskier than a bond that will mature in the near future, the bond with the longer term to maturity usually has a higher discount rate than the bond with the shorter term to maturity.

---

[12] Estate of *Gross v. Commissioner*, 78 T.C.M. (CCH) 201 (1999), T.C. Memo 1999-254.

3. Since there are significant public trading markets for debt securities, it is easy to determine the present value of a publicly traded debt security.

4. The best method to estimate the yield to maturity of a debt security of a closely held company is a guideline company analysis.

F. Valuation Issues in Preferred Stock

1. Preferred stock is a "hybrid" security with features similar to both common stock and bonds. Like common stock, it represents equity ownership and much like a bond (debt holder) it can receive fixed income distributions and receives preferential treatment.

2. The dividend rate is the predetermined rate an issuer promises to pay the preferred shareholder.

3. A company that has issued preferred stock with cumulative dividend terms has an obligation to make all accumulated dividend payments to the preferred stockholders before declaring and paying a dividend on common stock.

4. Shares of preferred stock with noncumulative features do not carry a guarantee of dividend payments and, as a result, carry more risk.

5. Convertible preferred stock gives the investor the option to exchange the security for common stock.

6. Revenue Ruling 83-120 is intended to amplify Revenue Ruling 59-60 and set out other considerations regarding the valuation of preferred and common stock for gift tax and recapitalization of private companies.

7. The fair market value of a share of preferred stock is equal to the present value of the future cash payments, discounted back to the present using a discount rate that embodies the risk associated with the investment.

G. Restricted Stock Valuation

1. *Restricted stock* is stock of a publicly traded corporation that is restricted from public trading for a specified period of time. Restricted stock is often identical to its publicly traded counterpart except that it is not freely tradeable.

2. The seminal IRS revenue ruling in this area, Revenue Ruling 77-287, provides guidance for the valuation of restricted stock.

3. The Longstaff analysis[13] indicates that the greater the volatility of the stock, the greater the discount, and that the marketability discount is not a linear function of time because the greatest risks, and therefore the largest increases in the percentage discount, occur early in the restriction period.

H. Valuation of Early-Stage Technology Companies

1. To avoid excess compensation expense, companies often attempt to set the grant price of options equal to the underlying common stock's fair market value at the time of issuance.

---

[13] Frances A. Longstaff, "How Much Can Marketability Affect Security Values?" *Journal of Finance,* Vol. 1, No. 5 (December 1995), pp. 1767–1774.

2. A technology company's most important assets (intangibles) may not be recorded on the balance sheet.

3. The valuation professional may need to focus on when the company will attain sustainable profit margins and work backward to the valuation date.

4. As with more traditional companies, the largest impediment to properly using the guideline company transaction method in the technology arena is lack of information. Information on what bundle of assets and liabilities were acquired, what the true price and terms were, and whether strategic consideration was present is difficult to obtain.

5. Actual company transactions are the preferred market approach method if the analyst is fortunate enough to have a contemporaneous transaction in the subject company's securities.

6. Simultaneous gifts made by the same donor in the same security can have different fair market values.

7. Due to the potential for abnormally high growth in operations, revenue, and cash flows, the income approach discounted cash flow (DCF) method is usually the method used when valuing early-stage technology companies.

8. One of the first decisions the valuation analyst will face in implementing the income approach is whether to accept management projections as representing the most likely potential outcome or whether multiple scenarios should be projected and probability of occurrence assigned to each. In theory, the latter approach is best, but, due to practical considerations, projection risk is addressed most often in the discount rate and not through multiple-outcome scenarios.

9. Another threshold decision is whether forecast losses (particularly in the early years of the forecast with low or no revenue) should be discounted at a rate different from profits.

10. If venture capital rates of returns are referenced in selecting an appropriate discount rate, the valuation analyst may need to adjust the lack of marketability discount applied later because many venture capital discount rates are predicated on investments in nonmarketable securities.

I. Valuation Issues Related to Stock Options

1. Employee stock options (ESOs) are particularly attractive given the ability to defer the recognition of these grants as compensation and the fact that cash is not normally involved. Vesting rights are often embedded in these ESOs to promote employee retention by rewarding longevity.

2. Employee stock options are classified as either incentive stock options or non-qualified stock options.

3. Options that can be exercised during and up to the expiration date are known as American options, whereas options that can be exercised only upon the expiration date are known as European options.

4. If not exercised before the expiration date, the option simply expires with no additional value.

5. As a result of dilution, the value of a warrant may vary somewhat from the value of a call option with identical terms.

6. Even without being "in the money," an option may have value. This value is created by the possibility that the option could be exercised profitably in the future. There are three factors that determine time value: the volatility of the stock underlying the option, the risk-free rate of interest, and the length of time before the option expires.

7. A key limitation of the Black-Scholes model is that it was developed to price European call options in the absence of dividends.

8. Warrants are often sold in connection with other financial instruments as a "sweetener" to enhance the attractiveness of the placement of the financial instrument it is bundled with or to get favorable terms on another financial instrument.

9. The causes driving the need for a valuation are fairly universal: litigation/divorce, management planning, tax oriented (gift or estate), transaction oriented, or financial reporting.

10. If the underlying stock is lightly traded or not publicly traded, then volatility can be estimated using a representative sampling of guideline companies or an industry benchmark.

11. If an intervening event is identified in the analysis, it may be appropriate to exclude it from the volatility.

12. The final consideration is the marketability of the option itself. There are no studies available regarding the lack of marketability of closely held stock options.

J. Real Option Valuations

1. Traditional discounted cash flow models may not determine the value of flexible managerial decision making.

2. Real options is a managerial decision-making tool that utilizes financial option pricing models such as the Black-Scholes and applies them to "real" rather than just specific financial decisions.

3. Several other analytical techniques are available that may better suit an individual problem. These models include financial models, dynamic programming, and Monte Carlo simulation.

K. Maximizing Shareholder Value

1. One well known value creation program used by many companies is Economic Value Added (EVA) promoted by Stern Stewart. The concept behind EVA is that shareholder value is created by maximizing "economic profit" or the returns to the shareholders after taking a "charge" for capital investment of the company.

2. Economic profit in its most simple form is free cash flow generated by a company less its return on investment by the shareholders in the company. Economic profits take into consideration the opportunity cost of the investment.

3. For EVA purposes, developing a measure of a company's total cost of capital will involve using the actual capital structure of the company rather than an optimal capital structure, since the goal of measuring shareholder value is analyzing the actual cash flow returns to the shareholders less the actual opportunity cost of equity capital.

4. The best organizations at creating shareholder value incentivize their management to think like the owners of the business.

5. Management must have the authority to make decisions that create value, including the authority to make capital budgeting discussions, capital investment decisions, cost of capital decisions, as well as the authority to increase returns on capital.

6. There are four general ways to increase shareholder value:
   a. Create more cash flow without using more capital
   b. Use less capital
   c. Invest in higher return projects
   d. Lower the cost of capital

7. Valuation analysts are uniquely qualified to assist management with the design and implementation of value creation strategies. Analysts can expand traditional valuation methodologies to incorporate the concept of economic profits to analyze, model, and measure how value is created. Analysts can be indispensable to not only measure what the value is today, but how to increase value tomorrow.

CHAPTER 4

Income Approach Valuation Process Flowchart

INTRODUCTION

The income approach is usually the most often used approach in valuing operating companies. It is the most direct approach in that it is based on the actual earnings and cash flow parameters of a company, which are then directly correlated to a discount or capitalization rate that reflects the risk in achieving those earnings and cash flows. This is not to say it does not contain numerous subjective assumptions. It does. However, the data used to prepare this method continue to evolve and allow for more accurate valuations.

The purpose of the Income Approach Valuation Process Flowchart is to allow valuation analysts to follow a more structured process to determine how to apply the income approach properly. It also provides less experienced analysts with a roadmap to follow in selecting and supporting the various methods and assumptions used in the income approach. This guide also will provide all analysts with good documentation of the reasons the approach was applied in the manner ultimately determined.

The Income Approach Valuation Process Flowchart is presented in the form of an outline to allow your easy adoption to a checklist for compliance. It also follows a series of questions to answer and concepts to consider when preparing the income approach. The cost of capital topic is not part of this guide.

INCOME APPROACH VALUATION PROCESS FLOWCHART

Business Name: _____

Date of Valuation: _____

Disclaimer Excluding Any Warranties: This Income Approach Valuation Process Flowchart is designed to provide guidance to analysts, auditors, and management, but is not to be used as a substitute for professional judgment. This guide does not include nor address all the considerations and assumptions in a valuation. These procedures must be altered to fit each assignment; the various factors listed in this flowchart may not be necessary for every valuation. The practitioner takes sole responsibility for implementation of this guide. The implied warranties of merchantability and fitness of purpose and all other warranties, whether express or implied, are excluded from this transaction and shall not apply to this guide.

I.   Input five years of financial statements or tax returns.

    A. If five years do not exist, number of years input _____

    B. Reason for inputting less than five years _____

II.   Is a minority or control valuation being performed?

    _____ Minority   _____ Control

    A. Make all appropriate normalization adjustments including nonrecurring, nonoperating, and extraordinary items.

    B. If control value, list and explain all adjustments.

        1. Excess compensation

        2. Other perquisites

        3. Capital structure

        4. Other

III. Analyze historical trends and compare to industry information, economic information, and projected/anticipated performance.

    A. Revenue growth rates

        1. Investigate reasons for each year's growth.

        2. Explain all fluctuations.

            a. Generally upward

            b. Generally downward

            c. Erratic (up and down)

        3. Is historical growth in line with projected/anticipated performance? If not, explain the differences.

        4. Is historical growth and projected performance in line with industry and general economic growth rates? Explain.

    B. Gross margin

        1. Investigate reasons for each year's gross margins.

        2. Explain all fluctuations.

            a. Generally upward

            b. Generally downward

            c. Erratic (up and down)

        3. Is historical gross margin in line with projected/anticipated performance? If not, explain the differences.

        4. Is historical gross margin and projected performance in line with industry and general gross margins? Explain.

C. Selling, General and Administrative (S, G & A) expenses as a percent of revenue

1. Investigate reasons for each year's expenses.

2. Explain all fluctuations.

   a. Generally upward

   b. Generally downward

   c. Erratic (up and down)

3. Are historical S, G & A expenses in line with projected/anticipated performance? If not, explain the differences.

4. Are historical S, G & A expenses and projected performance in line with industry and general S, G & A expenses? Explain.

D. Operating income margin

1. Investigate reasons for each year's operating income margin.

2. Explain all fluctuations.

   a. Generally upward

   b. Generally downward

   c. Erratic (up and down)

3. Are historical operating income margins in line with projected/anticipated performance? If not, explain the differences.

4. Are historical operating income margins and projected performance in line with industry and general operating income margins? Explain.

E. Pretax income margin

1. Investigate reasons for each year's pretax income margin.

2. Explain all fluctuations.

   a. Generally upward

   b. Generally downward

   c. Erratic (up and down)

3. Are historical pretax income margins in line with projected/anticipated performance? If not, explain the differences.

4. Are historical pretax income margins and projected performance in line with industry and general pretax income margins? Explain.

F. Taxes

1. Are taxes anticipated to change? _____ Yes _____ No

2. Include both Federal and State taxes.

3. If net operating losses exist, explain how they were handled.

G. Net income growth rates

1. Investigate reasons for each year's net income growth.

2. Explain all fluctuations.

a. Generally upward

b. Generally downward

c. Erratic (up and down)

3. Are historical net income growth rates in line with projected/antici-pated performance? If not, explain the differences.

4. Are historical net income growth rates and projected performance in line with industry and general net income growth rates? Explain.

H. Working capital

1. If using a debt-free discounted cash flow (DCF) method, make sure you are using debt-free working capital, which excludes short-term interest-bearing debt including notes and the current portion of long-term debt.

2. Investigate reasons for each year's working capital.

3. Explain all fluctuations.

a. Generally upward

b. Generally downward

c. Erratic (up and down)

4. Are historical working capital requirements in line with projected/anticipated performance? If not, explain the differences.

5. Are historical working capital requirements and projected performance in line with industry and general working capital requirements? Explain.

I. Depreciation

1. Investigate reasons for each year's depreciation.

2. Explain all fluctuations.

a. Generally upward

b. Generally downward

c. Erratic (up and down)

3. Is historical depreciation in line with projected/anticipated perform-ance? If not, explain the differences.

4. Is historical depreciation and projected performance in line with indus-try and general depreciation? Explain.

J. Capital expenditures

1. Investigate reasons for each year's capital expenditures.

2. Explain all fluctuations.

    a. Generally upward

    b. Generally downward

    c. Erratic (up and down)

3. Are historical capital expenditures in line with projected/anticipated performance? If not, explain the differences.

4. Are historical capital expenditures and projected performance in line with industry and general capital expenditures? Explain.

IV. Are there any nonoperating or excess assets? Explain why they are nonoperating or excess assets.

    A. Identify all such assets, value separately, and make sure both income statement and balance sheet are adjusted both *historically* and *projected*. Remove the effect of nonoperating assets from the operating cash flows. Consider whether to discount nonoperating assets when valuing a minority interest.

        1. Cars, boats, condos, houses

        2. Real estate

        3. Idle machinery and equipment

        4. Working capital

        5. Cash

        6. Receivables

        7. Inventory

        8. Other

V. Are earnings and cash flow anticipated to continue consistent with past trends?

    A. Yes

        1. Consider using a capitalized cash flow (CCF) method instead of a DCF.

        2. If using a CCF method, choose the period(s) and explain your choice.

            a. Five-year straight average

            b. Three-year straight average

            c. Five-year weighted average

            d. Three-year weighted average

            e. Most recent 12 months trailing

            f. Most recent four quarters trailing

    g. Most recent fiscal year-end

    h. One-year forward

    i. Trend analysis

    j. Other _____

B. No

  1. If the future performance of the company is expected to change, consider using a DCF method. This usually means either growth rates or profit margins are anticipated to change, or a normalized level of cash flow has not been achieved currently. It may also mean that the business itself may be changing. Sometimes it may be appropriate or informative to use both methods of the income approach.

  2. Has client prepared projections of future cash flows?
    _____ Yes _____ No

  3. If no, who prepared projections? _____

  4. Do projections include:

    a. Revenue

    b. Gross profits

    c. Depreciation

      (1) Book (remember to consider deferred taxes)

      (2) Tax (deferred taxes are not considered)

    d. S, G & A

    e. Operating income

    f. Other income/expenses

      (1) Interest expense

      (2) Interest income

      (3) Nonoperating income or expenses, such as real estate, securities

    g. Pretax income

    h. Net income after tax

    i. Capital expenditure needs

    j. Incremental working capital needs (Must be debt-free working capital if using a debt-free or invested capital model. This means that all interest-bearing short-term debt is removed from the working capital calculation. This usually includes the current maturity of long-term debt.)

    k. Debt principal to be repaid

    l. New debt principal in (Must be normalized in CCF and terminal year of DCF)

    m. Deferred taxes if using book depreciation

    n. Decide whether to use a debt-free or debt-inclusive model and explain your decision. _____ Debt-free _____ Debt-inclusive

    o. Terminal-year value (What is your future anticipated perpetuity growth rate?)

VI. Is future growth rate greater than historical nominal Gross Domestic Product (GDP) growth of 6%? Explain. _____ Yes _____ No _____ Same

    A. Is future growth rate greater than forecasted nominal GDP growth?

        1. What is forecasted nominal GDP growth? _____

        2. Explain.

    B. Test growth rates in revenue versus earnings versus cash flow. If different, explain why.

    C. Is there a large difference between the terminal-year growth rate and the growth rate in the last year of the discrete period? _____ Yes _____ No

        1. Explain.

        2. Do not mix revenue growth rates with cash flow growth rates. They are often the same, but it is growth in normalized cash flow that is correct.

    D. If using the Gordon growth model (GGM), apply the value in the terminal year as a multiple of EBITDA or EBIT. _____ EBITDA _____ EBIT

        1. Is this consistent with the multiples used in the market approach?

            a. EBITDA

            b. EBIT

        2. Explain. It is sometimes justified to test this against the market multiples adjusted downward to reflect the risk of projecting a multiple in future years.

    E. Is the working capital assumption into perpetuity driven by the perpetuity growth rate? Explain. _____ Yes _____ No

VII. Do capital expenditures and depreciation equal each other in the terminal year?

    A. If yes, no further adjustment is necessary.

    B. If no, normalize them to be equal, or

        1. If there is a depreciation overhang, value it separately and add it to the value.

        2. If there is a capital expenditure overhang, value it separately and deduct it from the value.

VIII. Are projections and resultant value minority or control?
     _____ Minority _____ Control

  A. Explain. If all discrete expenses have been added back—excess compensation, perquisites, capital structure—the value is on a control stand-alone value. If such expenses have not been added back, then the resultant value is on a minority stand-alone basis because the cash flows reflect the diminished cash flows and value. If the company has no discrete expenses to add back, then the value is the same for both minority and control. In this situation, some practitioners will take a smaller minority discount when valuing a minority interest to reflect the fact that, although the controlling stockholder is not taking cash out today, they could change that policy in the future, so there is added risk that diminishes value. Be careful using minority discounts derived from control premium studies (*Mergerstat Review* and Houlihan, Lokey, Howard and Zukin [HLHZ]) to discount for stand-alone minority value, since those studies reflect mostly synergized premiums paid by strategic buyers of public companies.

  B. Is the resultant value a marketable value? _____ Yes _____ No

    1. Explain. If using Ibbotson Associates data, the value is a marketable value and assumes a cash sale in less than three days. As such, a further discount for marketability may be warranted for both a minority and control value. Some practitioners will discount minority interest at a greater amount than a controlling one. However, even a controlling interest cannot usually be sold in three days.

  C. Optional: Check terminal-year value using the Value Driver Formula (VDF)[1]

    1. VDF assumes that the company will always earn a return on new invested capital equal to its cost of capital and thus no increase in value. This is true regardless of the growth rate, since both returns on capital and the actual costs of new capital will grow at the same rate under this formula. VDF is sometimes used to check the individual components of the GGM for reasonableness.

    2. VDF = DFNI / WACC (DFNI is Debt-free Net Income)

    3. To check the components of GGM, we consider the value driver model:

      a. Continuing Value = FCF / (WACC − g) =
   [NOPLAT (1 − g / r)] / (WACC − g)

        (1) FCF = Free cash flow, or (DFNI + Depr. − CAPEX − ΔW / C)

        (2) NOPLAT = Net operating profits less adjusted taxes (this is the same as DFNI)

---

[1] Copeland et al., *Valuation, Measuring and Managing the Value of Companies*, 2nd ed. (John Wiley & Sons, Inc., 1996), pp. 288–290.

      (3) g = Growth rate in NOPLAT

      (4) r = Rate of return on new capital invested

  b. Using algebra, we deduce: FCF = NOPLAT $(1 - g / r)$, or FCF = DFNI $(1 - g / r)$

  c. Restating the formula:

      (1) DFNI + Depr. − CAPEX − ΔW / C = DFNI $(1 - g / r)$

      (2) As we know the individual components of the formula, we can test our conclusion of value by solving for g or r, such that:

         (a) g = r [1 − ((DFNI + Depr. − CAPEX − ΔW / C) / DFNI)], and

         (b) r = g / [1 − ((DFNI + Depr. − CAPEX − ΔW / C) / DFNI)]

      (3) If the calculated r is much greater or less than the discount rate used in your conclusion of value, maybe you need to reconsider your Depr., CAPEX, or ΔW / C growth, or even your discount rate.

4. What is VDF value?

  a. Is it higher or lower than GGM value?

      (1) If VDF is higher, then the company is destroying value by growing since the costs of capital must then be exceeding the return on capital.

      (2) If the VDF is lower, then the company is earning a return on capital higher than its cost of capital into perpetuity.

5. Conclusion: Correlate with other values derived from other valuation approaches/methods.

CHAPTER 5

Checklists

The information requests, checklists, and questionnaires (Guides) contained in this chapter are provided to assist analysts, auditors, and company management in compiling information that will aid the valuation process. Further tailoring of these sample Guides will be necessary after review of the specific circumstances of each valuation. Modifications may be influenced by business, legal, and regulatory environments. Hence in tailoring the recommended Guides to each assignment, the analyst, auditor, or management should apply his or her professional judgment in correlation with knowledge of the environment of the business.

The Guides in this chapter have been grouped by function:

General

- Business Valuation or Real Estate Appraisal
- Key Information Requirements

Valuation Information Request (VIR)

- General
- Accounting Practice
- Bank/Holding Company
- Eminent Domain
- ESOP
- Gas and Oil Rights
- High Tech Business
- Law Practice
- Partnership
- Professional Practice
- Services
- Medical Practice

Management Interview

- Management Interview—Operations
- Management Interview—Financial Review
- Accounting Practice
- Insurance Agency
- Law Practice
- Medical Practice

Intangible Assets

- Copyright VIR
- Customer Relationships VIR
- In-process Research and Development VIR
- Know-How VIR
- Patent VIR
- Software VIR
- Proprietary Processes/Products Technology VIR
- Trademark/Trade Name VIR
- Procedures for the Valuation of Intangible Assets
- Checklist for Business Valuations—Royalty Factors
- Patent Valuation Management Interview

Revenue Rulings

- 59-60
- 77-287
- 93-12

Review Checklists

- General
- Eminent Domain
- Contemporaneous
- USPAP Compliance
- Appraisal Review
- Nonanalyst's Guide to Reviewing Business Valuation Reports
- Auditor Review of Valuation for Financial Reporting

CHECKLIST 5-1: Business Valuation or Real Estate Appraisal?

The following checklist helps determine which discipline—business valuation or real estate appraisal—is the pertinent discipline when valuing an entity.

YES	NO	
		IS THE ENTITY:
❑	❑	A commercial, industrial, or service organization pursuing an economic activity?
❑	❑	An equity interest (e.g., a security in a corporation or partnership interest)?
❑	❑	A fractional interest, minority interest (i.e., less than 100% of the entity)?
❑	❑	Difficult to split up (perhaps because the owners do not have a direct claim on the assets)?
		DOES THE ENTITY:
❑	❑	Derive its revenues from providing goods or services?
❑	❑	Primarily use assets such as machinery, equipment, employee skill, and talent in providing goods or services?
❑	❑	Depend on assets other than or in addition to real estate to generate earnings?
❑	❑	Conduct an economic activity that is more important than the location of the real estate where the economic activity is being conducted?
❑	❑	Likely have a value that fluctuates with conditions in its industry (as opposed to fluctuations in the real estate market)?
		DOES THE ENTITY HAVE:
❑	❑	Intangible assets (e.g., patents, trademarks, copyrights, franchises, licenses, customer lists, employment contracts, noncompete covenants, or goodwill) that the entity uses to generate earnings?
❑	❑	Substantial assets that can be moved?
❑	❑	A variety of tangible and intangible assets that interact to produce economic activity?
❑	❑	Significant operating expenses (e.g., marketing, advertising, research, or transportation)?
❑	❑	Substantial labor expenses?
❑	❑	Management that substantially adds to the profit of the company?

Yes answers in the majority — Business Valuation
No answers in the majority — Real Estate Appraisal
Mix of yes and no answers — May need both disciplines

CHECKLIST 5-2:   Key Information Requirements

Financial

❏ historical and prospective financial on:
  (a) turnover
  (b) contribution
  (c) marketing
  (d) manufacturing/production
  (e) R&D/marketing/capital expenditure
❏ unusual, nonrecurring events
❏ accounting principles and methods
❏ contingent assets/liabilities
❏ details of acquisition of assets
❏ licensing arrangements
❏ serious offers received for the asset

Market Characteristics

❏ product/service awareness
  (a) spontaneous
  (b) prompted
❏ market share/position
❏ consumer loyalty
❏ image/esteem
❏ geographical coverage
❏ extension potential
  (products, markets, channels)
❏ product history and life cycle
❏ buyer purchase criteria
❏ marketing mix
❏ demographics

Industry Structure

❏ structure of industry
❏ nature of competition
❏ barriers to entry
❏ availability of substitutes
❏ bargaining leverage of buyers
❏ availability of supply
❏ distribution arrangements
❏ major industry trends
❏ social, political, regulatory,
  environmental and economic factors

Legal

❏ registered or statutory rights
  (a) categories of goods or services
  (b) jurisdictions
  (c) pending applications
❏ common law or similar rights
  (including assessment of legal
  protection)
❏ duration of property rights
❏ details of licensing arrangements
❏ legal matters outstanding (e.g.,
  infringements)

CHECKLIST 5-3: Valuation Information Request (VIR) General

Business Name: _____

Valuation Date: _____

This is a generalized information request. Some items may not pertain to your company, and some items may not be readily available to you. In such cases, indicate N/A or notify us if other arrangements can be made to obtain the data. Items already provided have been marked with an "X". If you have any questions on the development of this information, please call.

A. Financial Information

_____ 1. Financial statements for fiscal years ending FIVE YEARS (order of preference: audited, reviewed, compiled, and internal).

_____ 2. Interim financial statements for the month-end DATE OF VALUATION and one year prior.

_____ 3. Financial projections, if any, for the current year and the next three years. Include any prepared budgets and/or business plans.

_____ 4. Federal and State Corporate Income Tax Returns and supporting schedules for fiscal years ending FIVE YEARS.

_____ 5. Explanation of significant nonrecurring and/or nonoperating items appearing on the financial statements in any fiscal year if not detailed in footnotes.

_____ 6. Accounts payable aging schedule or summary as of DATE OF VALUATION.

_____ 7. Accounts receivable aging schedule or summary and management's general evaluation of quality and credit risk as of DATE OF VALUATION.

_____ 8. Restatement of inventories and cost of goods sold on a FIFO basis for each of the past five fiscal years if LIFO accounting is used for inventory reporting purposes.

_____ 9. Fixed asset and depreciation schedule as of DATE OF VALUATION.

_____ 10. Amortization schedules of mortgages and notes payable; and terms of bank notes, credit lines, and/or debt agreement(s) as of DATE OF VALUATION.

_____ 11. Current financial statements for any ESOP, profit sharing, pension, or other employee benefit trust at DATE OF VALUATION.

_____ 12. Current level of over (under) funding for any defined benefit plan at DATE OF VALUATION.

_____ 13. Description of any compensation, salaries, dividends, or distributions received by persons not active in the operations of the business, including the year and respective compensation.

_____ 14. Estimated total revenue, gross profit, and net income for the current fiscal year.

_____ 15. Explanation of fluctuations, growth, or decline in the revenue of the business during the past five years.

_____ 16. Explanation of expected failure of the business to meet this year's budget based on the year-to-date financial data, if applicable.

_____ 17. Do you anticipate any significant rate increases in the cost of labor or materials?

_____ 18. Estimate revenues, gross profits, and earnings before interest and tax (EBIT) for the next five years, if revenue growth, gross margins, or net margins are expected to be significantly different as compared to the past five years.

_____ 19. Explanation of expected changes in the amount of capital expenditures during the next five years if expectations differ from those incurred during the past five years, including the anticipated new levels of capital expenditures.

_____ 20. Average borrowing rate for the business and financial ratios that must be maintained to comply with lenders' credit terms.

_____ 21. Description of any assets with stated net book value on the balance sheet that differ significantly from the fair market value that could be realized if the business were liquidated (i.e., appreciated real estate, obsolete inventory or equipment).

_____ 22. Description of any assets owned by the business that are not being used in the operations of the business (i.e., excess land, investments, excess cash, unused equipment, etc.).

B. Products and Markets

_____ 1. List of major products, services, or product lines of the business and copies of marketing materials, including sales brochures, catalogs, or other descriptive sales materials.

_____ 2. Sales and profit contributions analysis by product, product line, service category, customer, subsidiary, and/or location (whichever is applicable).

_____ 3. Unit volume analyses for existing product lines for the past five years.

_____ 4. Description of major products or services added in the last two years (or anticipated) and current expectations as to sales potential.

_____ 5. Description of the features, if any, that distinguish the business's products or services from the competition.

_____ 6. Causes for the cost of products and services supplied to your business to fluctuate and list of alternative suppliers available at similar rates, if any.

_____ 7. Description of new products under development with expectations as to potential.

_____ 8. List of the top ten customers of the business, indicating sales (or sales upon which commissions were earned) and unit volumes for each of the past three fiscal years if customers are consolidated.

_____ 9. Summary of major accounts gained (lost) in the last year indicating actual sales in the current year and beyond.

_____ 10. List of major competitors (full name, location, size, and estimate market share of each).

_____ 11. List of trade association memberships and industry publications of interest to management.

_____ 12. Classification of the business's industry (SIC No. or NAICS No.).

_____ 13. Description of any significant business operations that have been discontinued in recent years or are expected to be discontinued in the future (i.e., sale of facility or business line, closed-out product line, etc.), including date of discontinuation and impact on revenues and profits.

_____ 14. Description of any significant business operations that have been added in recent years or are expected to be added in the near future (i.e., purchase of facility, business acquisition, introduction of new product line, etc.), including date of addition and financial impact.

_____ 15. List of the names of all principal suppliers accounting for over 10% of total purchases.

_____ 16. Summary of terms of any existing purchase agreements with principal suppliers.

_____ 17. Summary of importance of research and development to the success of the business.

_____ 18. Characteristics of customers (i.e., industries served, demographics).

_____ 19. Approximate number of customers that the business has and percentage that are repeat clientele.

_____ 20. Approximate time the average customer has been purchasing from the business.

_____ 21. Description of customers that account for over 10% of annual revenue or gross profit of the business.

_____ 22. Summary of any contractual agreements with customers and/or distributors.

_____ 23. Description of any contracts or agreements with customers, suppliers, or distributors that would be nontransferable if the business were sold.

_____ 24. Number of clients that would discontinue relations with the business if the business were sold, including reasons and the estimated impact on revenues.

_____ 25. Summary of factors that stimulate demand for the business's products or services.

_____ 26. Description of seasonal or cyclical factors, if any.

_____ 27. Reason for increases or decreases of major competitors during the past five years, including their respective market share.

_____ 28. Approximate percentage of the market the subject business holds.

_____ 29. Description of level of difficulty to enter into the market or industry by potential competitors.

_____ 30. Description of the differences of the subject business to its competitors, including price, quality, strengths, and weaknesses.

_____ 31. List any publicly held companies or subsidiaries known to operate in your industry.

_____ 32. Name, address, and phone number of contact at industry organization that assists with market data, if any.

C. Operations

_____ 1. In a paragraph or so, complete this statement: "Our company is in the business of . . ."

_____ 2. Name and description of the operations of all major operating entities, whether divisions, subsidiaries, or departments.

_____ 3. List of the top ten suppliers (or all accounting for 5% or more of total purchases) and the level of purchases in each of the past two years (include total purchases by the business in each year).

_____ 4. List of the product(s) on which the business is single-sourced, or suppliers on which the business is otherwise dependent.

_____ 5. Dividend policy, dividend history, and prospect for future dividends.

_____ 6. Copy of any existing employee stock ownership plan (ESOP).

_____ 7. Copies of all other stock option plans or option agreements, or any other plan providing vested benefits in business stock. Also list number of options granted and to whom, and the stated exercise price(s) and expiration date(s).

_____ 8. Basis for business contributions (contribution policy), contributions in each of the past five years, and projection for future contributions to the ESOP, pension plan, and/or profit-sharing plan.

_____ 9. The most recent projection of emerging ESOP repurchase liability. If no study has been done, list known ESOP liquidity requirements during the next three years (e.g., known retirements during periods).

_____ 10. Copies of any appraisals of the stock of the business made during the last three years.

_____ 11. State(s) and year of incorporation or registration.

_____ 12. Form of ownership (C corporation, S corporation, general partnership, limited partnership, sole proprietorship).

_____ 13. List of the largest ownership interests in the business, including name of owner, percentage of shares held and position with business or inactive in business, total shares authorized, total shares issued, and total shares outstanding.

_____ 14. Description of any unusual stock features (i.e., voting or nonvoting, preferred or convertible, class A and class B).

_____ 15. Description of any restrictions on the sale or transfer of ownership interests (buy-sell agreement, lettered stock option to buy, stock options, etc.).

_____ 16. Description of familial or other relationships between owners.

_____ 17. Description of sales or transfers of any ownership interests in the business in the past five years, including how the price or value was determined.

_____ 18. Description of any bona fide offers to purchase the business during the past five years.

_____ 19. Analysis of adequacy of the current business insurance.

_____ 20. Description of any subsidiaries, joint ventures, or investments of a material nature in other companies.

_____ 21. Description of any services performed for, or by, a related party or business, including services provided, dollar amounts, and nonmonetary benefits, and if transactions are at market rates.

D. Facilities

_____ 1. Location, age, and approximate size of each facility, including business volume by major facility.

_____ 2. Ownership of each facility and other major fixed assets. If leased, include name of lessor and lease terms or agreements. If owned by the business, include:
   (a) date purchased;
   (b) purchase price;
   (c) recent appraisals;
   (d) insurance coverage; and
   (e) book values.

_____ 3. Estimated depreciation of all assets on a straight-line depreciation basis, if accelerated depreciation is used for financial statement purposes.

_____ 4. Copies of any appraisals of real estate or personal property owned by the business.

_____ 5. Copies of any appraisals of any company-owned real property or personal property performed during the last three years.

_____ 6. Comparison of rates of leases to market rates if facilities rented from a related party.

_____ 7. Description of the terms of your real estate lease including date of expiration, anticipated lease rate changes, and whether it is renewable.

_____ 8. Estimate of the cost to relocate business operations, including lost profits from business interruption.

_____ 9. Percentage of total capacity (expressed as percentage of total revenue) of the current business operation.

_____ 10. Description of changes in total operating capacity during the past five years (i.e., physical expansion, technological improvement), including related expenditures.

_____ 11. Based on future expected growth, description of when additional facilities or expansion (if foreseeable) will be needed, including approximate cost.

_____ 12. Approximate current and historical backlog (in revenues) or waiting list (number of customers).

E. Personnel

_____ 1. Current organization chart.

_____ 2. Number of employees (distinguish full-time and part-time) at year end for the last six years, including current employee classifications, general wage scales, and approximate rate.

_____ 3. List all union relationships, including name of union, date of current agreement, and workers and facilities covered.

_____ 4. Number of part-time and full-time business-employed salespersons including compensation arrangements or schedules. If there are none, describe how sales are obtained and by whom.

_____ 5. Description of the management team, including current title, age, length of service, background, annual salary, and bonus for the current year and each of the last two years.

_____ 6. Full names of the board of directors, including occupation of outside members.

_____ 7. Summary of employee turnover (i.e., below average, average or above average?

_____ 8. Is there an adequate supply of labor?

_____ 9. Summary of employee compensation (i.e., below average, average, or above average) compared to your industry.

_____ 10. Description of any significant staffing changes or increases anticipated during the next three to five years.

_____ 11. Description of terms of any contracts with personnel, such as noncompete agreements or employment contracts.

_____ 12. Description of a significant adverse effect(s) on the operating performance of the business, due to the loss of a key employee or manager, including potential revenue losses.

_____ 13. Specify succession of management, if determined.

_____ 14. Description of staff members who would not be retained if your business were sold, including their respective current compensation and position with the business.

F. Corporate Documents and Records

_____ 1. Corporate charter, articles of incorporation, and/or bylaws.

_____ 2. Minutes of board of directors' and shareholders' meetings for the most recent three years (may be reviewed by us on-site).

_____ 3. Summary of major covenants or agreements binding on the business, (e.g., union contracts, capital leases, employment contracts, service contracts, product warranties, etc.).

_____ 4. Description of any pending litigation, including parties involved, date of filing, description and nature of the lawsuit or claim, current status, expected outcome, and financial impact.

_____ 5. List of all subsidiary companies and the percentage ownership in each.

_____ 6. Name of any "related" companies (common ownership, common shareholders, etc.) and brief description of the relationship(s).

_____ 7. Stock ledger.

_____ 8. All closing statements and purchase agreements related to all purchases of the business's stock over the history of the business.

_____ 9. All closing statements and purchase agreements related to all mergers or acquisitions by the business up to the valuation date.

_____ 10. Terms of any offers to purchase the business.

CHECKLIST 5-4: Valuation Information Request (VIR) Accounting Practice

Practice Name: _____

Valuation Date: _____

This is a generalized information request. Some items may not pertain to your accounting firm, and some items may not be readily available to you. In such cases, indicate N/A or notify us if other arrangements can be made to obtain the data. Items already provided have been marked with an "X". If you have any questions on the development of the information, please call.

A. Financial Information

_____ 1. Financial statements for the fiscal years ending FIVE YEARS (order of preference: audited, reviewed, compiled, and internal), including:
   (a) All unusual charges or credits that are not expected to recur;
   (b) All assets that are included in the financial records, but are distinctly not related to the practice of accounting;
   (c) A description of the classes of corporate stock (if more than one);
   (d) A list of ownership of stock at DATE OF VALUATION; and
   (e) A description of any recent transactions in stock. If none, so indicate.

_____ 2. Federal and state corporate income tax returns and supporting schedules for the fiscal years ending FIVE YEARS.

_____ 3. State intangible personal property tax returns and supporting schedules for the fiscal years ending FIVE YEARS.

_____ 4. Any existing buy-sell agreements or other restrictive agreements.

_____ 5. Any existing profit-sharing, pension, or 401(k) plans.

_____ 6. All prior real estate and business appraisals, if any.

_____ 7. An accounts receivable listing as of DATE OF VALUATION, or if not available, as of the most recent date available.

_____ 8. A listing of work-in-process, including fees earned but not billed.

_____ 9. The fee schedule in effect at the valuation date for each accountant on staff, plus each average realization rate (percentage) for the last year.

_____ 10. A fixed asset schedule, including all furniture, fixtures, and equipment utilized in the office. This schedule should include the date of purchase, the original cost, the approximate condition, and the remaining estimated useful life.

_____ 11. For the firm's and your major accounting categories, the three largest total client billings, the grand total billings within the category, and the total number of clients. Client identity is not necessary, and examples of major accounting categories would be tax, auditing, accounting, management, consulting, and other.

B. Documents and Records

_____ 1. Corporate charter, articles of incorporation, and/or bylaws.

_____ 2. Minutes of board of directors' and shareholders' meetings for the most recent three years (may be reviewed by us on-site).

_____ 3. Summary of major covenants or agreements binding on the professional practice (e.g., all contracts or letters of agreement that have been entered for specialty work, capital leases, lease agreements, employment contracts, service contracts, etc.) in existence as of the valuation date.

_____ 4. Description of any pending litigation including parties involved, date of filing, description, and nature of the lawsuit or claim, current status, and expected outcome and financial impact.

_____ 5. Name of any "related" companies or professional associations (common ownership, common shareholders, etc.) and brief description of the relationship(s), including percentage of ownership in each.

_____ 6. Stock ledger.

Disclaimer Excluding Any Warranties: This checklist is designed to provide guidance to analysts, auditors, and management, but is not to be used as a substitute for professional judgment. These procedures must be altered to fit each assignment. The practitioner takes sole responsibility for implementation of this guide. The implied warranties of merchantability and fitness of purpose and all other warranties, whether expressed or implied, are excluded from this transaction and shall not apply to this guide. The Financial Valuation Group shall not be liable for any indirect, special, or consequential damages.

CHECKLIST 5-5: Valuation Information Request (VIR) Bank/Holding Company

Business Name: _____

Valuation Date: _____

This is a generalized information request. Some items may not pertain to your bank/holding company, and some items may not be readily available to you. In such cases, indicate N/A or notify us if other arrangements can be made to obtain the data. Items already provided have been marked with an "X". If you have any questions regarding the development of this information, please call.

A. Financial Statements (Banks Only)

_____ 1. Financial statements for fiscal years ending FIVE YEARS (order of preference: audited, reviewed, compiled, and internal).

_____ 2. Federal and state corporate tax returns (if not consolidated) for fiscal years ending FIVE YEARS at DATE OF VALUATION.

_____ 3. Call reports (include all schedules) as of DATE OF VALUATION.

_____ 4. Uniform bank performance reports as of DATE OF VALUATION.

_____ 5. Internally prepared financial statements. (Audits are sometimes presented in abbreviated form and with supplementary schedules, including copies of auditors' management letters.)

B. Financial Statements (Holding Company if Applicable)

_____ 1. Financial statements for fiscal years ending FIVE YEARS (order of preference: audited, reviewed, compiled, and internal).

_____ 2. Federal and state corporate tax returns (if not consolidated) for fiscal years ending FIVE YEARS at DATE OF VALUATION.

_____ 3. Holding company Form Y-9 filed with Federal Reserve as of DATE OF VALUATION.

_____ 4. Holding company performance reports as of DATE OF VALUATION.

_____ 5. Internally prepared financial statements as of DATE OF VALUATION, including shareholder reports, 10-Ks and 10-Qs (Parent Company Only and Consolidated).

C. Employee Stock Ownership Plan/Trust (If Applicable)

_____ 1. DATE OF VALUATION financial statement (unaudited) or most recent if DATE OF VALUATION statement not yet prepared.

_____ 2. Accountant's report for DATE OF VALUATION.

_____ 3. Name of lender, amount, and terms of debt, if ESOP is leveraged.

D. Other Financial Documents

_____ 1. Bank budget as of DATE OF VALUATION.

_____ 2. Holding company budget as of DATE OF VALUATION.

_____ 3. Any multiyear projection or business plan available for the bank and/or the holding company.

_____ 4. Copies of all documents filed with the SEC or FDIC during YEAR OF VALUATION, if you are a "public reporting company" with the SEC or the FDIC.

_____ 5. Copies of any offering materials prepared in conjunction with any offering of equity or debt securities during YEAR or PRIOR YEAR OF VALUATION.

_____ 6. Directors' examination reports.

_____ 7. Letters from outside auditors.

E. Corporate Documents and Records

_____ 1. Summary shareholder list (for the entity being valued) showing names and number of shares owned, including:
   (a) Directors and officers;
   (b) Employee stock ownership plan; and
   (c) All other 5% (or more) shareholders by name. Indicate if a family controls more than 5% (even though no individual does).

_____ 2. If there is a controlling group of shareholders, please provide:
   (a) The complete list of shareholders with their holdings;
   (b) Copy of any voting trust agreement between the controlling parties;
   (c) Copy of any restrictive legends applicable to the institution's shares; and
   (d) Copy of documentation regarding any hybrid equity securities at either the bank or holding company level, including:
      (i) Stock options;
      (ii) Warrants (to purchase shares); and
      (iii) Other convertible securities (convertible debentures, convertible preferred stock, etc.).

_____ 3. Board of directors' minutes, copies of bank/holding company minutes during YEAR OF VALUATION, or excerpts pertaining to discussions of the following topics:
   (a) Merger with or acquisition by another banking institution;
   (b) Purchase or sale of branch facilities;
   (c) Purchase, sale or creation of nonbank subsidiaries;
   (d) Response to report of regulatory examination;
   (e) Declaration or payment of dividends or establishment of dividend policy;
   (f) Plans to raise capital in any form, including the refinancing of capital notes or holding company debt;
   (g) Plans to renovate existing facilities or to build new facilities;
   (h) Discussions of or approval of any off-balance sheet hedging activities;
   (i) Discussions of nonroutine charges to the allowance for loan losses or provisions to the allowance for loan losses; and
   (j) Business planning or financial projections for YEAR OF VALUATION and beyond.

_____ 4. ESOP Documentation:
   (a) Copy of ESOP document provisions related to repurchase of employee shares specifying obligation to repurchase, terms or repurchase, and other material factors;
   (b) Specify if the holding company has a repurchase option or obligation related to ESOP shares;

    (c) Copy of any ESOP study of its repurchase liability. If there is no study, please list known liquidity requirements for next three years from anticipated retirements or other commitments to repurchase shares;

    (d) Current ESOP contribution policy or basis for determining annual contributions;

    (e) Provide estimated ESOP contribution for LAST THREE YEARS; and

    (f) Accounting treatment of leveraged ESOP if not noted in financial statements.

_____ 5. Documentation of transaction(s) on known stock transactions during the last year(s) in the following form:

    (a) Date;

    (b) Purchaser;

    (c) Seller;

    (d) Price/director/ explanatory; and

    (e) Share officer comments.

F. Banking Facilities

_____ 1. List of all banking branch facilities, indicating for each:

    (a) Branch name/location;

    (b) Actual (or approximate) deposit and loan volumes;

    (c) Whether full service or specific limited services;

    (d) Number of full-time employees at branch;

    (e) Whether facility owned or leased (if lease, from whom on what terms);

    (f) Approximate square footage of the facility;

    (g) Book value of facility on institution's books; and

    (h) Approximate fair market value of the facility.

_____ 2. Improved or unimproved real estate held by the bank for future expansion (or which is otherwise not presently occupied):

    (a) Description;

    (b) Date acquired and acquisition cost; and

    (c) Estimated (or appraised) current fair market value.

G. Other Assets

_____ 1. Current list of equity securities (including convertible and preferred stocks) owned by the bank or holding company as of the DATE OF VALUATION, including:

    (a) Name of security;

    (b) Original (or current carrying) cost; and

    (c) Current market value.

_____ 2. List of all mutual fund investments owned, including:

    (a) Name of fund(s);

    (b) Original cost(s); and

    (c) Current carrying cost and the amount of any equity allowance related to the mutual funds.

_____ 3. Bond portfolio printout summary page(s) detailing book value, market value, weighted average rate, and weighted average maturity by each major category of the bond portfolio:

    (a) U.S. government and agencies;

    (b) Tax-exempt securities; and

    (c) Other securities.

_____   4. Summary of the bank's present investment portfolio positioning strategy (in a paragraph or so).

_____   5. Description of any additional assets that may be considered temporary (debt repossessions) or not directly related to the bank's normal course of business.

H. Data Processing Facilities

_____   1. Description of the current data processing system in use by the bank and discuss its adequacy for the current level of operations.

_____   2. Date an in-house system was implemented, if applicable.

_____   3. Data center, provider and starting date, if applicable.

_____   4. Brief description of any plans for changing data centers or purchasing an in-house system.

I. Nonbank Subsidiaries of the Bank or Bank Holding Company, Whether Controlled or Not

_____   1. Name and description of the business of any operating nonbank subsidiaries.

_____   2. Year-end financials for the subsidiaries, if not in audited statements or in consolidating financial statements.

J. Trust Department Activities

_____   1. Brief description of trust activities, including services rendered, number of employees, assets under management, and revenues for last three years.

_____   2. Summary of future plans for this department.

K. Liquidity and Asset/Attainability Management

_____   1. Brief description of the bank's liquidity policy (or operating practice) including terms of objectives, target ratios, or other terms used to track and monitor liquidity.

_____   2. GAP (asset/liability management) policy.

_____   3. Brief description of the bank's GAP policy.

_____   4. Names and titles of management and board members of ALCO committee (or equivalent)?

_____   5. Recent printout from your asset/liability system or planning model if available, providing:
   (a) Projected balance sheets and income statements over projection horizon GAP reports; and
   (b) A brief statement of the bank's positioning relative to its objectives.

L. Loan Portfolio Information—Determining the adequacy of the allowance for loan losses (i.e., the loan loss reserve)

_____   1. Description of the method used and the frequency of the determination.

_____   2. Copy (or a summary of results) for the most recent determination if a written report is developed.

_____   3. Description of the system or process of loan review in use at the bank.

Lending Policy and Practice

_____ 4. List of the major types of loans routinely made by type and describe typical pricing and maturities for each type.

_____ 5. Copy of the loan policy or summary of the bank's:
   (a) Stated lending limit authorities "effective lending limits in practice policy" for out-of-territory loans, and
   (b) Number and dollar volume of loans outside your CRA (Community Reinvestment Act) territory, including any loan participations purchased.

_____ 6. Summary of the bank's legal and in-house lending limits.

Lending Concentrations

_____ 7. List of all loans of _____% of your lending limit or above. If credits to related borrowers constitute a concentration of 50% of the lending limit or more, include the relationship totals.

_____ 8. Summary of any known industry concentrations or exposures in the bank's loan portfolio.

M. Regulation and Regulatory Compliance

_____ 1. Dates of the two most recent regulatory examinations by appropriate category.

	BANK BY STATE AGENCY	BANK BY FDIC (OCC IF NAT'L BANK)	HOLDING COMPANY BY FEDERAL RESERVE
Most Recent			
Next Most Recent			

_____ 2. Summary of any formal, written agreements with any regulatory body under which the bank and/or the holding company is operating, including:
   (a) Agency;
   (b) Data and type of agreement (memorandum of understanding, cease and desist, other);
   (c) Basic reasons for its issuance;
   (d) General description of its requirements; and
   (e) State of the institution's compliance with the order.

N. Management and the Directorate

_____ 1. Summary of management compensation for the top five officers of the bank and holding company, including:
   (a) Name/title;
   (b) Annual compensation, including bonuses, for YEAR OF VALUATION and ONE YEAR PRIOR; and
   (c) Beneficial stock ownership in bank or bank holding company.

_____ 2. List of senior management (key officers of the bank or holding company), including:
   (a) Name/title/age/years of service with bank;
   (b) Current operating responsibilities;
   (c) Prior jobs with bank;
   (d) Prior banking experience;

(e) Other relevant experience;

(f) If bank carries life insurance on key executives, provide coverage amounts and annual premiums; and

(g) If executive is working under an employment agreement, summarize its terms.

_____ 3. List of board of directors, including:

(a) For Bank: name/board title/age/board tenure in years/occupation;

(b) For Holding company: name/board title/age/board tenure in years/occupation (for significant overlaps between bank and holding company, provide entire list and indicate for each individual whether bank, holding company, or both);

(c) Name and describe membership and functions of major board committees; and

(d) Method of outside board members' compensation.

O. Background and History

_____ 1. For the bank:

(a) Date of formation and name(s) of principal founder(s);

(b) Type of charter;

(c) Approximate dates of acquisitions of other banks or branches since formation;

(d) Name changes, if any, since formation;

(e) Date current control group obtained control, if applicable;

(f) Other significant historical events; and

(g) Copy of written history, if any.

_____ 2. For the holding company:

(a) Date of formation and name(s) of principal founder(s);

(b) Description of process of gaining control of the bank; and

(c) Date control acquired.

P. Competition and the Local Economy

_____ 1. List of major competitors (bank, thrift or credit union). If a market share study exists, provide a copy of the most recent study.

_____ 2. Background information on the economy of your city/county/region (from chamber of commerce and local university economics departments, for example), if available.

CHECKLIST 5-6: Valuation Information Request (VIR)
Eminent Domain

Business Name: _____

Date of Damages: _____

This is a generalized information request. Some items may not pertain to your company, and some items may not be readily available to you. In such cases, indicate N/A or notify us if other arrangements can be made to obtain the data. Items already provided have been marked with an "X". If you have any questions on the development of this information, please call.

A. Financial Information

_____ 1. Financial statements for fiscal years ending FIVE YEARS (order of preference: audited, reviewed, compiled, and internal).
_____ 2. Financial projections for the DAMAGE YEAR and the next three years.
_____ 3. Federal and state corporate income tax returns and supporting schedules for fiscal years ending FIVE YEARS.

B. Products and Markets

_____ 1. Major product services or product lines of the company.
_____ 2. Top ten customers of the company indicating sales and unit volume for each of the past three fiscal years.
_____ 3. Major competitors (full name, location, size, and estimated market share of each).
_____ 4. Trade association memberships and brochures of the company.

C. Operations

_____ 1. In a paragraph or so, complete this statement: "The Company is in the business of …".
_____ 2. List of the top ten suppliers.
_____ 3. Dividend policy, dividend history, and prospects for future dividends.
_____ 4. Copies of any appraisals of the stock of the company made during the last three years.

D. Facilities

_____ 1. Location, age, and approximate size of each facility.
_____ 2. Ownership of each facility and other major fixed assets. If leased, include name of lessor and lease terms or agreements.
_____ 3. Real estate appraisal, including a fair market value of price per square foot.
_____ 4. Copies of appraisals of any company-owned real property or personal property performed during the last three years.

E. Personnel

_____ 1. Current organizational chart.
_____ 2. Number of employees (distinguish between full-time and part-time).

_____ 3. Description of the management team, include current title, age, length of company service, and background.

_____ 4. Full names of the board of directors.

F. Corporate Documents and Records

_____ 1. Corporate charter, articles of incorporation and/or bylaws.

_____ 2. Minutes of board of directors' and shareholders' meetings for the most recent three years.

_____ 3. Stock ledger.

_____ 4. All closing statements and purchase agreements related to all purchases of the company's stock over the history of the company.

_____ 5. All closing statements and purchase agreements related to all mergers or acquisitions by the company up to the valuation date.

G. Engineering Data

_____ 1. Engineering report, including:

   (a) Actual square footage of the take;

   (b) Effect of the take on parking and maneuverability;

   (c) Actual square footage of the building loss due to the taking;

   (d) Suggestions of possible cures, if any; and

   (e) Cost associated to items lost on the property, such as sign, etc.

CHECKLIST 5-7: Valuation Information Request (VIR) ESOP

Business Name: _____

Valuation Date: _____

This is a generalized information request. Some items may not pertain to your company, and some items may not be readily available to you. In such cases, indicate N/A or notify us if other arrangements can be made to obtain the data. Items already provided have been marked with an "X". If you have any questions regarding the development of this information, please call.

_____   1. Name, mailing address, telephone number, and key contact of the trustee(s).

_____   2. Name, mailing address, telephone number, and key contact of the plan administrator(s).

_____   3. Date of plan inception?

_____   4. Description of plan leveraged, if applicable.

_____   5. Amount of annual (or monthly) payments.

_____   6. Summary of any existing plan for the ESOP to acquire a majority of the outstanding stock.

_____   7. Summary of voting rights, including pass-throughs.

_____   8. Individual or entity who votes the unallocated shares.

_____   9. Summary of put option, if any.

_____   10. Summary of right of first refusal, if any.

_____   11. Description of any other restrictive agreements.

_____   12. List of the contribution to the ESOP and dividend amount for the past five years or since inception.

_____   13. List of the total number of shares held by the ESOP.

_____   14. Description of the assets held by the ESOP.

_____   15. Percentage of qualified employees who are vested.

_____   16. Availability of insurance on participants through the plan or company, and percentage of participants covered.

_____   17. Summary of method of "cashing out" participants (i.e., stocks, cash, notes), and method of action.

_____   18. Summary copy of the plan as updated and last plan statement.

CHECKLIST 5-8:   Valuation Information Request (VIR) Gas and Oil Rights

Business Name: _____

Date of Taking: _____

This is a generalized information request. Some items may not pertain to your company, and some items may not be readily available to you. In such cases, indicate N/A or notify us if other arrangements can be made to obtain the data. Items already provided have been marked with an "X". If you have any questions regarding the development of this information, please call.

_____ 1. Financial statements for fiscal years ending FIVE YEARS (order of preference: audited, reviewed, compiled, and internal).

_____ 2. Federal and state corporate income tax returns and supporting schedules for fiscal years ending FIVE YEARS.

_____ 3. Division orders or other documents showing the subject interests, property identification, and legal description for all producing properties.

_____ 4. All reserve studies related to the producing properties.

_____ 5. All remittance advices, canceled checks, and statements from banks and statements from entities controlling distributions related to the oil and gas rights.

_____ 6. Names, addresses, and phone numbers of operators and purchasers related to the producing properties.

_____ 7. Joint interest bills for the past twelve months.

_____ 8. Unit agreements.

_____ 9. Operating agreements.

_____ 10. Field descriptions, including geologic data and well logs, core analyses or studies, pressure data, fluid analyses, drill stem tests, completion reports, gravity information, and other geologic information related to the producing properties.

_____ 11. Proposed drilling activities, timing related to the proposed drilling activities, estimated costs, and other activities proposed.

_____ 12. Gas contracts, gathering and transportation agreements, gas balancing and processing agreements.

_____ 13. Severance and ad valorem tax rates.

_____ 14. Gas BTU content including shrinkage data.

_____ 15. Production histories.

_____ 16. Decline curves and projections.

_____ 17. Future oil contracts.

_____ 18. Posted field prices for oil, gas, condensate, or other minerals or metals.

_____ 19. Amounts of bonuses or delay rentals for nonproducing properties.

CHECKLIST 5-9: Valuation Information Request (VIR) High Tech Business

Business Name: _____

Valuation Date: _____

This is a generalized information request. Some items may not pertain to your company, and some items may not be readily available to you. In such cases, indicate N/A or notify us if other arrangements can be made to obtain the data. Items already provided have been marked with an "X". If you have any questions on the development of this information, please call.

A. Financial Information

_____ 1. Financial statements for fiscal years ending FIVE YEARS, (order of preference: audited, reviewed, compiled, and internal).

_____ 2. Interim financial statements for month-end DATE OF VALUATION and one year prior.

_____ 3. Federal and state corporate income tax returns and supporting schedules for fiscal years ending FIVE YEARS.

_____ 4. Financial projections for the current year and the next five years, including balance sheets, income statements, cash flow statements, identification of any adjustments of assets to fair market value, and assumptions supporting the projections.

_____ 5. Summary of agings of current accounts receivables and payables.

B. Products and Markets

_____ 1. A complete market study, including potential users by market (geographic and service), current and expected competition, and current and expected market share.

_____ 2. Analysis of actual or perceived competition, including discussion of alternative sources of information service or product that would be used if the business did not exist.

_____ 3. Complete Web site statistical analysis.

_____ 4. Copies of any relevant industry studies you have purchased, produced, or obtained.

_____ 5. Description of all strategic alliances and/or partnerships.

_____ 6. Description of and a strength and weaknesses analysis of your information technology infrastructure (software, hardware, bandwidth, etc.).

_____ 7. Copies of sales materials or other promotional literature.

_____ 8. History of company and major competitors.

_____ 9. List of five largest customers and their percentage of total sales (if applicable).

C. Operations

_____ 1. List of all stock options and warrants including owner, date granted, number of shares, option period, and exercise price.

_____ 2. List of all venture funding including investor, date of investment, number of shares, and type of shares (if preferred).

_____ 3. Notification of any discussions held or planned to be held with potential investors, buyers, investment bankers, or underwriters.

_____ 4. Copies of latest two versions of company's business plan.

_____ 5. Copies of all prior appraisals of the company.

_____ 6. List of five major suppliers including amounts paid (if relevant).

D. Facilities

_____ 1. Detailed real property information, including any recent appraisals.

_____ 2. Detailed fixed asset information, including brand, type, age, serial number, and condition of fixed assets (if available).

_____ 3. Addresses and descriptions of all facilities.

E. Personnel

_____ 1. Officers' compensation for last five years.

_____ 2. Detail of company ownership and any recent transactions involving company stock or stock options.

CHECKLIST 5-10: Valuation Information Request (VIR) Law Practice

Practice Name: _____

Valuation Date: _____

This is a generalized information request. Some items may not pertain to your practice, and some items may not be readily available to you. In such cases, indicate N/A or notify us if other arrangements can be made to obtain the data. Items already provided have been marked with an "X". If you have any questions on the development of this information, please call.

A. Financial Information

_____ 1. Financial statements for the fiscal years ending FIVE YEARS (order of preference: audited, reviewed, compiled, and internal), including:
  (a) All unusual charges or credits that are not expected to recur;
  (b) All assets that are included in the financial records, but are distinctly not related to the practice of law;
  (c) A description of the classes of corporate stock (if more than one);
  (d) A list of ownership of stock at DATE OF VALUATION; and
  (e) A description of any recent transactions in stock.

_____ 2. Federal and state corporate income tax returns for the fiscal years ending FIVE YEARS.

_____ 3. State intangible personal property tax returns for the fiscal years ending FIVE YEARS.

_____ 4. Any existing buy-sell agreements or other restrictive agreements.

_____ 5. Any existing profit-sharing, pension, or 401(k) plans.

_____ 6. All prior real estate and business appraisals, if any.

_____ 7. An accounts receivable listing as of DATE OF VALUATION, or if not available, as of the most recent date available.

_____ 8. A listing of work-in-process, including fees earned but not billed.

_____ 9. The fee schedule in effect at the valuation date for each attorney on staff, plus each average realization rate (percentage) for the last year.

_____ 10. A fixed-asset schedule, including all furniture, fixtures, and equipment utilized in the office. This schedule should include the date of purchase, the original cost, the approximate condition, and the remaining estimated useful life.

_____ 11. For the firm's and your major legal categories, provide the three largest total client billings, the grand total billings within the category, and the total number of clients. Client identity is not necessary, and examples of major legal categories would be tax, general litigation, real estate, corporate law, commercial banking, family law, criminal law, and so forth.

B. Documents and Records

_____ 1. Corporate charter, articles of incorporation, and/or bylaws.

_____ 2. Minutes of board of directors' and shareholders' meetings for the most recent three years (may be reviewed by us on-site).

_____ 3. Summary of major covenants or agreements binding on the professional practice (e.g., all contracts or letters of agreement that have been entered for specialty legal work, capital leases, lease agreements, employment contracts, service contracts, etc.) in existence as of the valuation date(s).

_____ 4. Description of any pending litigation including parties involved, date of filing, description and nature of the lawsuit or claim, current status, and expected outcome and financial impact.

_____ 5. Name of any "related" companies or professional associations (common ownership, common shareholders, etc.) and briefly describe the relationship(s). Include percentage of ownership in each.

_____ 6. Stock ledger.

CHECKLIST 5-11:   Valuation Information Request (VIR) Partnership

Partnership Name: _____

Valuation Date: _____

This is a generalized information request. Some items may not pertain to your partnership and some items may not be readily available to you. In such cases, indicate N/A or notify us if other arrangements can be made to obtain the data. Items already provided have been marked with an "X". If you have any questions on the development of this information, please call.

A. Financial Information

_____ 1. Financial statements for fiscal years ending FIVE YEARS (order of preference: audited, reviewed, compiled, and internal).

_____ 2. Interim financial statements as of month-end DATE OF VALUATION and one year prior.

_____ 3. Federal and state income tax returns and supporting schedules for fiscal years ending FIVE YEARS. Include state intangible personal property tax returns.

_____ 4. Explanation of significant nonrecurring and/or nonoperating items appearing on the financial statements or tax returns in any fiscal year if not detailed in footnotes.

_____ 5. Opening balance sheet, if a new partnership, or balance sheet at or near the valuation date.

_____ 6. List of assets owned, if not detailed in (4), including location, age, approximate size of each parcel of real estate, estimated book value, and market value.

_____ 7. Support documentation for fair market values of assets (e.g., real estate appraisals, statements of account for marketable securities, etc.)

B. Operations

_____ 1. In a paragraph or so, complete this statement: "The Partnership is in the business of ..."

_____ 2. Name and description of operations of all major operating entities, whether divisions, subsidiaries, or departments.

_____ 3. Distribution policy, distribution history, and prospect for future distribution.

_____ 4. Trade association memberships and industry publications of interest to management.

_____ 5. Copies of any appraisals of Partnership interests made during the last five years, if any.

C. Documents and Records

_____ 1. Partnership agreement.

_____ 2. Description of any pending litigation including parties involved, date of filing, description and nature of the lawsuit or claim, current status, and expected outcome and financial impact.

_____ 3. List of all subsidiary entities and the percentage ownership in each.

_____ 4. Name of any "related" entities (common ownership, common shareholders or partners, etc.) and briefly describe the relationship(s).

_____ 5. Copies of any appraisals of the stock of the partnership made during the last three years.

D. Other

_____ 1. Current organization chart and ownership schedule.

_____ 2. Number of employees (distinguish full-time and part-time) at year end for the last three years including current employee classifications and compensation.

_____ 3. Description of partners, including age, length of service, background, annual compensation, and distributions of each person for the current year and each of the last two years.

_____ 4. Copies of appraisals of any partnership-owned real property or personal property performed during the last three years.

CHECKLIST 5-12:   Valuation Information Request (VIR) Professional Practice

Professional Practice Name: _____

Valuation Date: _____

This is a generalized information request. Some items may not pertain to your practice, and some items may not be readily available to you. In such cases, indicate N/A or notify us if other arrangements can be made to obtain the data. Items already provided have been marked with an "X". If you have any questions on the development of this information, please call.

A. Financial Information

_____   1. Financial statements for fiscal years ending FIVE YEARS (order of preference: audited, reviewed, compiled, and internal).

_____   2. Interim financial statements as of month-end DATE OF VALUATION and one year prior.

_____   3. Financial projections for the current year and the next three years. Include any prepared budgets and/or business plans.

_____   4. Federal and state corporate income tax returns and supporting schedules for fiscal years ending FIVE YEARS. Include state intangible personal property tax returns.

_____   5. Explanation of significant nonrecurring and/or nonoperating items appearing on the financial statements in any fiscal year if not detailed in footnotes.

_____   6. Accounts payable aging schedule or summary at DATE OF VALUATION.

_____   7. Accounts receivable aging schedule or summary at DATE OF VALUATION.

_____   8. Fixed asset and depreciation schedule at DATE OF VALUATION.

_____   9. Amortization schedules of mortgages and notes payable; and terms of bank notes, credit lines, and/or ESOP debt agreement(s).

_____   10. Current financial statements for the ESOP, profit sharing, pension, or other employee benefit trust.

_____   11. Current level of over (under) funding for any defined benefit plan.

B. Services and Markets

_____   1. List of the major services of the practice and copies of marketing materials, including sales brochures, catalogs, or other descriptive sales materials.

_____   2. Sales and profit contributions analysis by service category.

_____   3. Unit volume analyses for existing services for the past five years.

_____   4. Description of major services added in the last two years (or anticipated) and current expectations as to sales potential.

_____   5. Description of new services under development with expectations as to potential.

_____ 6. List of the top ten customers of the practice, indicating sales (or sales upon which commissions were earned) and unit volumes for each of the past three fiscal years.

_____ 7. Summary of major accounts gained (lost) in the last year indicating actual sales in the current year and beyond.

_____ 8. List of major competitors (full name, location, size, and estimate market share of each).

_____ 9. List of trade associations memberships.

_____ 10. List of industry publications of interest to management.

C. Operations

_____ 1. In a paragraph or so, complete this statement: "The practice is in the business of ..."

_____ 2. Name and description of the operations of all major operating entities, whether divisions, subsidiaries, or departments.

_____ 3. List of the top ten suppliers (or all accounting for 5% or more of total purchases) and the level of purchases in each of the past two years (include total purchases by the practice in each year).

_____ 4. Summary of services on which the practice is single-sourced, or suppliers on which the practice is otherwise dependent.

_____ 5. Dividend policy, dividend history, and prospect for future dividends.

_____ 6. Copy of any existing employee stock ownership plan (ESOP).

_____ 7. Copies of all other stock option plans or option agreements, or any other plan providing vested benefits in practice stock. Also, list number of options granted and to whom, and the stated exercise price(s) and expiration date(s).

_____ 8. Basis for practice contributions (contribution policy), contributions in each of the past five years, and projection for future contributions to the ESOP, pension plan, and/or profit sharing plan.

_____ 9. The most recent projection of emerging ESOP repurchase liability. If no study has been done, list known ESOP liquidity requirements during the next three years (e.g., known retirements during periods).

_____ 10. Copies of any appraisals of the stock of the practice made during the last three years.

D. Facilities

_____ 1. Location, age, and approximate size of each facility, including business volume by major facility.

_____ 2. Ownership of each facility and other major fixed assets. If leased, include name of lessor and lease terms or agreements. If owned by the practice, include date purchased, purchase price, recent appraisals, insurance coverage, and book values.

_____ 3. Estimated depreciation of all assets on a straight-line depreciation basis if accelerated depreciation is used for financial statement purposes.

_____ 4. Copies of appraisals of any real property or personal property owned by the practice.

E. Personnel

_____ 1. Current organization chart.

_____ 2. Number of employees (distinguish full-time and part-time) at year end for the last six years, including current employee classifications, general wage scales, and approximate rate.

_____ 3. List of all union relationships including name of union, date of current agreement, workers and facilities covered.

_____ 4. Number of part-time and full-time practice-employed salespersons, including compensation arrangements or schedules. If there are none, describe how sales are obtained and by whom.

_____ 5. Description of management team, including current title, age, length of practice service, background, annual salary, and bonus of each person for the current year and each of the last two years.

_____ 6. Full names of the board of directors, including occupation for outside members.

F. Corporate Documents and Records

_____ 1. Corporate charter, articles of incorporation, and/or bylaws.

_____ 2. Minutes of board of directors' and shareholders' meetings for the most recent three years (may be reviewed by us on-site).

_____ 3. Summary of major covenants or agreements binding on the practice (e.g., union contracts, capital leases, employment contracts, service contracts, product warranties, etc.).

_____ 4. Description of any pending litigation, including parties involved, date of filing, description and nature of the lawsuit or claim, current status, and expected outcome, and financial impact.

_____ 5. List of all subsidiary companies and the percentage ownership in each.

_____ 6. Name of any "related" companies (common ownership, common shareholders, etc.) and brief description of the relationship(s).

_____ 7. Stock ledger.

_____ 8. All closing statements and purchase agreements related to all purchases of the practice's stock over the history of the practice.

_____ 9. All closing statements and purchase agreements related to all mergers or acquisitions by the practice up to the valuation date.

CHECKLIST 5-13: Valuation Information Request (VIR) Services

Business Name: _____

Valuation Date: _____

This is a generalized information request. Some items may not pertain to your business, and some items may not be readily available to you. In such cases, indicate N/A or notify us if other arrangements can be made to obtain the data. Items already provided have been marked with an "X". If you have any questions on the development of this information, please call.

A. Financial Information

_____ 1. Financial statements for fiscal years ending FIVE YEARS (order of preference: audited, reviewed, compiled, and internal).

_____ 2. Interim financial statements for the month-end DATE OF VALUATION and one year prior.

_____ 3. Financial projections for the current year and the next three years. Include any prepared budgets and/or business plans.

_____ 4. Federal and state corporate income tax returns and supporting schedules for fiscal years ending FIVE YEARS.

_____ 5. Explanation of significant nonrecurring and/or nonoperating items appearing on the financial statements in any fiscal year if not detailed in footnotes.

_____ 6. Accounts payable aging schedule or summary at DATE OF VALUATION.

_____ 7. Accounts receivable aging schedule or summary at DATE OF VALUATION.

_____ 8. Fixed asset and depreciation schedule at DATE OF VALUATION.

_____ 9. Amortization schedules of mortgages and notes payable; and terms of bank notes, credit lines, and/or employee stock ownership plan (ESOP) debt agreement(s).

_____ 10. Current financial statements for any ESOP, profit sharing, pension, or other employee benefit trust at DATE OF VALUATION.

_____ 11. Current level of over (under) funding for any defined benefit plan.

B. Services and Markets

_____ 1. List of the major services of the business and copies of marketing materials, including sales brochures, catalogs, or other descriptive sales materials.

_____ 2. Sales and profit contributions analysis by service category.

_____ 3. Unit volume analyses for existing services for the past five years.

_____ 4. Description of major services added in the last two years (or anticipated) and current expectations as to sales potential.

_____ 5. Description of new services under development with expectations as to potential.

_____ 6. List of the top ten customers of the business, indicating sales (or sales upon which commissions were earned) and unit volumes for each of the past three fiscal years.

_____ 7. Summary of major accounts gained (lost) in the last year indicating actual sales in the current year and beyond.

_____ 8. List of major competitors (full name, location, size, and estimate market share of each).

_____ 9. List of trade associations memberships.

_____ 10. List of industry publications of interest to management.

C. Operations

_____ 1. In a paragraph or so, complete this statement: "The company is in the business of ..."

_____ 2. Name and description of the operations of all major operating entities, whether divisions, subsidiaries, or departments.

_____ 3. List of the top ten suppliers (or all accounting for 5% or more of total purchases) and the level of purchases in each of the past two years (include total purchases by the business in each year).

_____ 4. List of the services on which the business is single-sourced, or suppliers on which the business is otherwise dependent.

_____ 5. Dividend policy, dividend history, and prospect for future dividends.

_____ 6. Copy of any existing employee stock ownership plan.

_____ 7. Copies of all other stock option plans or option agreements, or any other plan providing vested benefits in company stock. Also list number of options granted and to whom, and the stated exercise price(s) and expiration date(s).

_____ 8. Basis for business contributions (contribution policy), contributions in each of the past five years, and projection for future contributions to the ESOP, pension plan, and/or profit-sharing plan.

_____ 9. The most recent projection of emerging ESOP repurchase liability. If no study has been done, list known ESOP liquidity requirements during the next three years (e.g., known retirements during periods).

_____ 10. Copies of any appraisals of the stock of the business made during the last three years.

_____ 11. Copies of any appraisals of the stock of the business made during the last three years.

D. Facilities

_____ 1. Location, age, and approximate size of each facility, including business volume by major facility.

_____ 2. Ownership of each facility and other major fixed assets. If leased, include name of lessor and lease terms or agreements. If owned by the business, include date purchased, purchase price, recent appraisals, insurance coverage, and book values.

_____ 3. Estimated depreciation of all assets on a straight-line depreciation basis, if accelerated depreciation is used for financial statement purposes.

_____ 4. Copies of appraisals of real property or personal property owned by the business.

E. Personnel

_____ 1. Current organization chart.

_____ 2. Number of employees (distinguish full-time and part-time) at year end for the last six years, including current employee classifications, general wage scales, and approximate rate.

_____ 3. List all union relationships, including name of union, date of current agreement, and workers and facilities covered.

_____ 4. Number of part-time and full-time business-employed salespersons including compensation arrangements or schedules. If there are none, describe how sales are obtained and by whom.

_____ 5. Description of management team including current title, age, length of company service, background, annual salary, and bonus of each person for the current year and each of the last two years.

_____ 6. Full names of the board of directors, including occupation for outside members.

F. Corporate Documents and Records

_____ 1. Corporate charter, articles of incorporation, and/or bylaws.

_____ 2. Minutes of board of directors' and shareholders' meetings for the most recent three years (may be reviewed by us on-site).

_____ 3. Summary of major covenants or agreements binding on the business, (e.g., union contracts, capital leases, employment contracts, service contracts, product warranties, etc.).

_____ 4. Description of any pending litigation including parties involved, date of filing, description and nature of the lawsuit or claim, current status, and expected outcome and financial impact.

_____ 5. List all subsidiary companies and the percentage ownership in each.

_____ 6. Name of any "related" companies (common ownership, common shareholders, etc.) and briefly describe the relationship(s).

_____ 7. Stock ledger.

_____ 8. All closing statements and purchase agreements related to all purchases of the business's stock over the history of the business.

_____ 9. All closing statements and purchase agreements related to all mergers or acquisitions by the business up to the valuation date.

CHECKLIST 5-14: Valuation Information Request (VIR) Medical Practice

Practice Name: _____

Valuation Date: _____

This is a generalized information request. Some items may not pertain to your practice, and some items may not be readily available to you. In such cases, indicate N/A or notify us if other arrangements can be made to obtain the data. Items already provided have been marked with an "X". If you have any questions on the development of this information, please call.

A. Financial Information

_____ 1. Financial statements for fiscal years ending FIVE YEARS (order of preference: audited, reviewed, compiled, and internal).

_____ 2. Interim financial statements for the month-end DATE OF VALUATION and one year prior.

_____ 3. Financial projections, if any, for the current year and the next three years. Include any prepared budgets and/or business plans.

_____ 4. Federal and state corporate income tax returns and supporting schedules for fiscal years ending FIVE YEARS.

_____ 5. Additional financial information:
(a) Assets included in the financial records not related to the practice;
(b) A description of the classes of corporate stock (if more than one);
(c) A list of ownership of stock at DATE OF VALUATION; and
(d) A description of any recent transactions in stock. If none, please so indicate.

_____ 6. Copies of buy-sell or other restrictive agreements.

_____ 7. Copies of profit sharing, pension, or 401-K plans.

_____ 8. Copies of any prior real estate and business appraisals, if any.

_____ 9. An accounts receivable listing as of DATE OF VALUATION or the most recent date available.

_____ 10. A fixed-asset schedule, including all furniture, fixtures, and equipment utilized in the office. This schedule should include the date of purchase, original cost, approximate condition, and estimated remaining useful life.

_____ 11. List of inventory and whether it is valued LIFO, FIFO, or specific identification.

B. Other Documents and Records

_____ 1. Corporate charter, articles of incorporation, and/or bylaws.

_____ 2. Minutes of board of directors' and shareholders' meetings for the most recent three years (may be reviewed by us on-site).

_____ 3. Summary of major covenants or agreements binding on the professional practice, such as capital leases, employment contracts, service contracts, etc.

_____ 4. Description of any pending litigation including parties involved, date of filing, description and nature of the lawsuit or claim, current status, and expected outcome and financial impact.

_____ 5. Name of any "related" companies or professional associations (common ownership, common shareholders, etc.) and the relationship(s), including percentage of ownership in each.

_____ 6. Stock ledger.

_____ 7. Leases.

C. Facilities

_____ 1. Location, age, and approximate size of each facility, including business volume by major facility.

_____ 2. Ownership of each facility and other major fixed assets. If leased, include name of lessor and lease terms or agreements. If owned by the practice, include:
(a) Date purchased;
(b) Purchase price;
(c) Recent appraisals;
(d) Insurance coverage; and
(e) Book value.

_____ 3. Estimated depreciation of all assets on a straight-line depreciation basis if accelerated depreciation is used for financial statement purposes.

D. Personnel

_____ 1. Current organization chart.

_____ 2. Number of employees (distinguish full-time and part-time) at year end for the last six years, including current employee classifications, general wage scales, and approximate rate.

_____ 3. Description of the management team including current title, age, length of practice service, background, annual salary, and bonus of each person for the current year and each of the last two years.

_____ 4. Full names of the board of directors, including occupation, for outside members.

CHECKLIST 5-15: Management Interview Operations

Date: _____

Exact Business Name: _____

Address: _____

_____

Phone: _____

Analyst/Interviewer: _____

The objective of this management interview is to provide us with operational information that will aid us in the valuation of your business. We will keep the information confidential. Describe the following to the best of your ability on a separate sheet of paper, with reference to each item number. If some items are not applicable, please indicate N/A.

1. Interviewee(s):

Name	Title
(a) _____	_____
(b) _____	_____
(c) _____	_____
(d) _____	_____

2. Purpose and Objective of the Valuation

   (a) The activity or transaction giving rise to the valuation

3. Other Information Regarding the Transaction

   (a) Number of shares being valued (each class)
   (b) Total number of shares issued (each class)
   (c) Total number of shares outstanding (each class)
   (d) Date of the valuation
   (e) State of incorporation
   (f) Standard of value

4. Name, Address, and Telephone Number of the Business Attorney

5. Name, Address, and Telephone Number of the Business Accountant or Bookkeeper

6. Description of the Business

   (a) Type of business
   (b) Products/services sold

(c) Type of customers/clients
(d) Location of sales/services
(e) Business code (see tax return)
(f) SIC number or NAICS number
(g) Type of industry(s)
(h) Important industry trends
(i) Date business started
(j) Fiscal year-end date
(k) Factors you consider most important to your business's success

7. **History of the Business**

(a) From founding to the present, history including people, date, places, new products, markets, and physical facilities

8. **Ownership**

(a) Shareholder list as of the date of valuation.
(b) Transactions in the common stock and basis for price (parties, dates, shares, and prices).
(c) Offers to purchase the company, if any. Discuss prices, dates, terms, and current status of negotiations.
(d) Prior appraisals.

9. **Management**

(a) Current organizational chart
(b) List of key management personnel with title, length of service, age, and annual compensation

	Name	Title	LOS	Age	Compensation
(1)					
(2)					
(3)					
(4)					
(5)					

(c) Key management positions open at this time
(d) Plans for succession if key man dependency exists
(e) Adverse impact on business if sudden loss or withdrawal of any key employee
(f) Amount and description of key-person life insurance policy, if any

10. **Products/Services**

(a) Business mix
(b) Changes in business mix
(c) New products/services
(d) Development procedure(s) of new products/services
(e) Expected performance of new products/services
(f) Percent of output manufactured by company

(g) Percentage of manufactured products for resale

(h) Proportion of sales that are replacement parts

(i) Note any important differences in profit margins by product-line

11. Markets and the Economy

(a) Market area

(b) Determination of market area by market segment, geography, or customer type

(c) Important characteristics of the relevant economic base (obtain information of local chambers of commerce if needed)

(d) Business sensitivity to economic cycles or seasonal influences

(e) Industry(s) of market concentration

(f) Approximate percentage and total dollar amount of foreign sales, if any

(g) Difference in profit margins of foreign sales to domestic sales, if any

(h) New product lines or services under consideration

12. Customers

(a) Major customers and the annual sales to each

(b) Length of relationships and customer turnover

(c) Company dependency, if any, on small group of large customers or large group of small customers

13. Marketing Strategy

(a) Sales and marketing strategy

(b) Sales procedures

(c) Sales personnel

(d) Basis of sales personnel compensation

(e) Risks of obsolescence or replacement by new or similar products

14. Operations

(a) Corporate organization structure (divisions, departments, etc.)

(b) Flow of operations that produce the product or service

15. Production

(a) Operating leverage of business (high or low level)

(b) Relationship of variable costs and fixed costs to total revenue

(c) Difficulty obtaining liability insurance, if any

(d) Insurance rates

(e) OSHA or EPS concerns in the work environment, if any, including the prospective cost of compliance

(f) Concerns over environmental hazards due to location or previous uses of land or facility

(g) Dependency in the production process on patents, licenses, or other contracts not controlled by the company

(h) Major suppliers and for what production inputs

(i) Raw material suppliers that are manufacturers

(j) Raw material suppliers that are wholesalers
(k) Dependency for critical components of the product or service on any one supplier
(l) Name of union, if any
(m) Status of union contract or future organizing activities
(n) Number of past union strikes
(o) Number of full- and part-time employees
(p) Number of employees by division or department
(q) General experience, skill, and compensation levels of employees

16. **Real Property**

    (a) List of real estate and equipment used by the company including name of owner, affiliated parties (if leased), and market terms (if leased)

Property/Equipment	Owner	Affiliated Party/ Market Terms
(1)		
(2)		
(3)		
(4)		
(5)		

    (b) Size, age, condition, and capacity of the facilities
    (c) Adequacy of facilities or plans for future expansion
    (d) Plant/office facilities, including:
        (1) Owners
        (2) Real estate taxes
        (3) Land
            i. Acreage
            ii. Cost
            iii. Assessed value
            iv. Fair market value, if known
        (4) Buildings
            i. Type of construction
            ii. Age condition
            iii. Location on the property
            iv. Assessed value
            v. Fair market value, if known
            vi. Fire insurance amount
            vii. Square feet
        (5) Machinery and equipment
            i. Description
            ii. Age and condition
            iii. Efficiency utilization (older equipment or state of the art)
            iv. Future plant, machinery, and equipment requirements, including estimated repairs

    (e) Current value of the real estate and equipment

    (f) Appraisals of read estate and equipment, or estimates

17. **Description of the Capital Structure**

    (a) Classes of securities

    (b) Common stock restrictions (such as a buy-sell agreement or charter restrictions), if any

    (c) Preferred stock terms of issue and protective covenants

    (d) Subordinated debt terms of issue and protective covenants

    (e) Outstanding stock options or warrants

    (f) Obtain and attach copies of the option agreement

18. **Other**

    (a) Dividend policy and dividend history

    (b) Anticipated future dividend payments

    (c) Pending litigation and potential impact on the company

    (d) Existing buy-sell or other restrictive agreements

    (e) Prenuptial agreement, if any

    (f) Profit sharing, ESOP, or other retirement plans

    (g) Copy of the ESOP plan, if not already provided

    (h) Copies of provisions related to shareholder liquidity in the plan

    (i) Company's regulators (e.g., public service commissions, bank regulators)

    (j) Copies of regulatory orders, if any

19. **General Outlook (if not covered elsewhere)**

20. **Other Pertinent Information About the Business**

CHECKLIST 5-16:   Management Interview Financial Review

Date: _____

Exact Business Name: _____

Address: _____

_____

Phone: _____

Analyst/Interviewer: _____

The objective of this management interview is to review financial information in the valuation of your business. We will keep the information confidential. Describe the following to the best of your ability on a separate sheet of paper, with reference to each item number. If some items are not applicable, please indicate N/A.

The objective of the interview is not only to identify changes in numbers but also to *ascertain the reasons* for the change.

1. Interviewee(s)

     Name   Title

   (a) _____   _____

   (b) _____   _____

   (c) _____   _____

   (d) _____   _____

2. Financial Statement Review

   (a) Quality of the financial statements
   (b) Reason(s) for qualifications of audited and qualified statements, if applicable
   (c) Consistency of accounting principles of company prepared interim statements with accountant prepared statements

3. Balance Sheet Review

   (a) Approximate total asset book value
   (b) Approximate net book value
   (c) Cash
   (d) Minimum level of cash required to operate the company
   (e) Accounts receivable
      (1) Normal terms of sale
      (2) Comparison of collection period to industry norms and history
      (3) History of bad debts
      (4) Receivables concentration by customer

(f) Inventory
    (1) Accounting method used to calculate inventories
    (2) Trend in level of inventories and turnover rate
    (3) Obsolete inventory and the amount paid for it
(g) Other current assets
    (1) Other current assets
    (2) Current assets not related to the business, if any
(h) Fixed assets
    (1) Major fixed assets
    (2) Depreciation calculations for book and tax purposes
    (3) Capital budget for the coming years
    (4) Types of fixed assets needed in the future
    (5) List of excess assets
(i) Notes receivable
    (1) Names and terms (if due from officers and affiliates, comparison of terms to market rates)
(j) Other assets
    (1) Long-term
(k) Notes payable
    (1) Names and terms of vendors
(l) Accounts payable
    (1) General terms of purchase of goods and services
    (2) Trend in payables and turnover ratios
(m) Taxes payable and deferred taxes
(n) Other accrued expenses
(o) Long-term debt
    (1) Names and terms (if secured, state asset(s) used as security)
(p) Mortgage notes payable
    (1) Terms and collateral
(q) Any contingent liabilities

4. **Income Statement Review**

(a) Approximate annual sales volume
(b) Sales
    (1) Reason for changes in sales over the past five years
    (2) Attribution of growth in sales
        i. unit volume
        ii. inflation
    (3) Comparison of growth rate in sales to other items on the income statement
    (4) Projections for the current year and beyond
    (5) Basis for projections
(c) Costs of goods sold
    (1) Key factors which affect cost of goods sold
    (2) Changes in accounting procedures, if any
(d) Gross profit margin (GPM)
    (1) Changes in GPM for the last five years (price increases, cost increases, inventory write-downs, etc.)

(e) General and administrative expenses
    (1) Major expense items of the company
    (2) Fluctuations in expenses over the last five years
    (3) Nonrecurring expenses included in the totals
(f) Other income/expense
    (1) Sources
(g) Taxes
    (1) Federal tax rate
    (2) State tax rate
(h) Hidden or intangible assets, such as
    (1) Patents
    (2) Favorable leases
    (3) Favorable financing arrangements
    (4) Number of recurring, stable customers
    (5) Employment contracts
    (6) Copyrights
    (7) Long-term customers' contracts
    (8) Trademark
    (9) Unique research and development
    (10) Highly trained staff in place
    (11) Undervalued securities or other investments
(i) Key liabilities
    (1) Commitments for new buildings or machinery
    (2) Long-term loans outstanding and terms

CHECKLIST 5-17   Management Interview
Accounting Practice

Date: _____

Exact Practice Name: _____

Address: _____

_____

Phone: _____

Analyst/Interviewer: _____

The objective of this management interview is to provide us with operational information that will aid us in the valuation of your practice. We will keep the information confidential. Describe the following to the best of your ability on a separate sheet of paper, with reference to each item number. If some items are not applicable, please indicate N/A.

1. Interviewees

Name	Title
(a) _____	_____
(b) _____	_____
(c) _____	_____

2. **Name, Address, and Telephone Number of the Business Attorney**

3. Accountants

   (a) List key personnel with title, and approximate annual compensation (with bonuses listed separately)

	Name	Title	Compensation	Bonus
(1)	_____	_____	_____	_____
(2)	_____	_____	_____	_____
(3)	_____	_____	_____	_____
(4)	_____	_____	_____	_____
(5)	_____	_____	_____	_____

   (b) Abbreviated curriculum vitae of each accountant, including age, education, specialty certification, and unusual experience
   (c) Accountant limitations due to health, if any
   (d) Life insurance in which the practice is the beneficiary
   (e) Typical week for the average partner, including the percentage of time spent in the following areas
       (1) Directly billable
       (2) Administrative
       (3) Promotion
       (4) Civic affairs

4. The Practice

(a) If not correct above, exact name of the practice

(b) Date practice established

(c) Brief history of the development of the practice, including past partners, important dates, previous locations, etc.

(d) Current organizational chart

(e) List the management team including current title, age, length of service, background, annual salary, and bonus of each person for the current year and the last two years

(f) List all personnel (other than accountants and the management team), stating the title/function and compensation of each

(g) List board of directors by name and title, including occupation for outside members

(h) Growth trends, revenue, and operating capacity (billable hours)

(i) Changes in accounting services being considered

(j) Practice sensitivity to seasonal fluctuations (e.g., does the practice have a disproportionate tax practice)

(k) Sales and marketing strategy

(l) Office facilities, including
   (1) Any land owned
      i. Acreage
      ii. Original cost
      iii. Approximate fair market value
   (2) Buildings owned
      i. Age and condition
      ii. Original cost
      iii. Approximate fair market value
      iv. Fire insurance amount
      v. Square feet
   (3) Furniture, fixtures, and equipment (FF&E) (Since the FF&E schedule has been requested in our valuation information request, there will be no need to duplicate the listing here. What is requested is a discussion of the future plans for significant purchases of FF&E.)
   (4) Library
      i. Description by major service and/or groups of works
      ii. Original cost
      iii. Replacement cost
      iv. Unique volumes, if any

5. Other Pertinent Information About the Practice

CHECKLIST 5-18:   Management Interview Insurance Agency

Date: _____

Exact Business Name: _____

Address: _____

_____

Phone: _____

Analyst/Interviewer: _____

The objective of this management interview is to provide us with operational information that will aid us in the valuation of your business. We will keep the information confidential. Describe the following to the best of your ability on a separate sheet of paper, with reference to each item number. If some items are not applicable, please indicate N/A.

1. Interviewee(s)

Name	Title
(a) _____	_____
(b) _____	_____
(c) _____	_____
(d) _____	_____

2. History of the Business

    (a) Brief but complete description of the start-up of business
    (b) Date business started
    (c) Purchases of other businesses during the development of agency

3. Name, Address, and Telephone Number of the Business Attorney

4. Name, Address, and Telephone Number of the Business Accountant or Bookkeeper

5. Owners

    (a) List all owners by class of stock and percentage owned

Name	Class of Stock	Percentage
(1) _____	_____	_____
(2) _____	_____	_____
(3) _____	_____	_____
(4) _____	_____	_____
(5) _____	_____	_____

(b) Job history and experience (i.e., resumes) of the owners
(c) Ages and health of the owners
(d) Recent transactions in the common stock of the company
(e) Ownership and management perquisites

6. Personnel

(a) List all personnel, with title, length of service, age, and annual compensation

	Name	Title	LOS	Age	Compensation
(1)					
(2)					
(3)					
(4)					
(5)					

(b) Number of part-time employees
(c) Describe licenses and designations of key personnel, including the year earned
(d) Adverse impact on business if sudden loss or withdrawal of any key employee
(e) Copies of all noncompete agreements, if any

7. Real Property

(a) Describe the office facilities
(b) Provide a copy of the lease, if applicable

8. Furniture and Equipment

(a) Describe the furniture and equipment
(b) Provide a copy of the lease(s), if applicable
(c) For all owned furniture and equipment, provide a fixed-asset schedule

9. Insurance Carriers

(a) List any EDP terminals owned by insurance carriers that are utilized in the agency
(b) Provide copies of all insurance carrier contracts
(c) List any new carrier contracts that have been applied for
(d) List all carriers that have terminated contracts, the dates terminated, and the amounts and types of coverage formerly provided in the last full year of representation
(e) Provide the amount of the limit to settle claims, if any

10. Book of Business

(a) Describe the amounts of direct billed and agency billed
(b) Describe the amounts of property/casualty, life, and health premiums
(c) Describe the amounts of commercial and personal lines premiums

11. **Policy Holders**

    (a) Attach a list of all policyholders by product line, the original years of coverage, and if applicable, the years of termination, if available

    (b) List the five largest policyholders, the amounts of premium, and descriptions of coverage, including the original issue date

	Issue Date	Premium	Coverage
(1)	_____	_____	_____
(2)	_____	_____	_____
(3)	_____	_____	_____
(4)	_____	_____	_____
(5)	_____	_____	_____

    (c) Provide the amount of written premium and commissions earned by carrier

    (d) Provide the amount of contingency commissions, the applicable carrier, and the year earned

12. **Financial Statements**

    (a) Provide complete financial statements of the business for the last five years

    (b) Provide corporate tax returns for the last five years

    (c) Provide all production reports for the last five years (or all years available)

    (d) Provide all photocopies of any buy-sell or other restrictive agreements

    (e) Describe any hidden assets or liabilities. These would be items or benefits (or liabilities) to the agency that may not have been fully reflected in the financial statements. They would include such things as long-term policyholder contracts, lawsuits, or undervalued securities.

    (f) Describe any extraordinary or highly unusual downturns or upturns to the business

    (g) Describe any unusual or nonrecurring or credits (debits) not evident on the income statements

    (h) List nonoperating assets that are included on recent balance sheets. These would include assets not necessary in the day-to-day operations of the business.

13. **General Outlook (if not covered elsewhere)**

14. **Other Pertinent Information About the Business**

CHECKLIST 5-19:   Management Questionnaire Law Practice

Date: _____

Exact Practice Name: _____

Address: _____

_____

Phone: _____

Analyst/Interviewer: _____

The objective of this management interview is to provide us with operational information that will aid us in the valuation of your practice. We will keep the information confidential. Describe the following to the best of your ability on a separate sheet of paper, with reference to each item number. If some items are not applicable, please indicate N/A.

1. Interviewee(s)

	Name	Title
(a)	_____	_____
(b)	_____	_____
(c)	_____	_____
(d)	_____	_____

2. **Name, Address, and Telephone Number of the Business Accountant or Bookkeeper**

3. **Attorneys**

   (a) List key personnel with title, and approximate annual compensation (with bonuses listed separately)

	Name	Title	Compensation	Bonus
(1)	_____	_____	_____	_____
(2)	_____	_____	_____	_____
(3)	_____	_____	_____	_____
(4)	_____	_____	_____	_____
(5)	_____	_____	_____	_____
(6)	_____	_____	_____	_____
(7)	_____	_____	_____	_____
(8)	_____	_____	_____	_____
(9)	_____	_____	_____	_____
(10)	_____	_____	_____	_____

(b) Provide an abbreviated curriculum vitae of each attorney, including age, education, board certification, and unusual experience

(c) Describe any limitations of each attorney due to health

(d) Describe life insurance in which the firm is the beneficiary

(e) Describe a typical week for the average partner, including the percentage of time spent in the following areas
   (1) Directly billable
   (2) Administrative
   (3) Promotion
   (4) Civic affairs

4. The Practice

(a) If not correct above, exact name of the practice

(b) Provide a brief history of the development of the practice, including date practice was established, past partners, important dates, previous locations, etc.

(c) Provide a current organizational chart. Describe the management team including current title, age, length of service, background, annual salary, and bonus of each person for the current year and the last two years.

(d) Attach a list of all personnel (other than attorneys and the management team) stating the title/function and compensation of each

(e) List board of directors by name and title, including occupation for outside members

(f) Describe the growth trends, revenue, and operating capacity (billable hours)

(g) Describe changes in legal services offered that are being considered

(h) Describe practice responsiveness to seasonal fluctuations (For instance, does the firm have a disproportionate estate practice susceptible to northern residents?)

(i) Describe previous and future marketing and advertising plans

(j) Describe the office facilities including
   (1) Any land owned
      i. Acreage
      ii. Original cost
      iii. Approximate fair market value
   (2) Buildings owned
      i. Age and condition
      ii. Original cost
      iii. Approximate fair market value
      iv. Fire insurance amount
      v. Square feet
   (3) Furniture, fixtures, and equipment (FF&E) (Since the FF&E schedule has been requested in our valuation information request, there will be no need to duplicate the listing here. What is requested is a discussion of the future plans for significant purchases of FF&E.)
   (4) Library
      i. Description by major service and/or groups of works
      ii. Original cost
      iii. Replacement cost
      iv. Unique volumes, if any

5. Other Pertinent Information About the Practice

(a) Any information that will add to (or detract from) the reputation of the practice or any information about the practitioners that will have a similar effect on the valuation.

Disclaimer Excluding Any Warranties: This checklist is designed to provide guidance to analysts, auditors, and management, but is not to be used as a substitute for professional judgment. These procedures must be altered to fit each assignment. The practitioner takes sole responsibility for implementation of this guide. The implied warranties of merchantability and fitness of purpose and all other warranties, whether expressed or implied, are excluded from this transaction and shall not apply to this guide. The Financial Valuation Group shall not be liable for any indirect, special, or consequential damages.

CHECKLIST 5-20: Management Questionnaire Medical Practice

Date: _____

Exact Practice Name: _____

Address: _____

_____

Phone: _____

Analyst/Interviewer: _____

The objective of this management interview is to provide us with operational information that will aid us in the valuation of your practice. We will keep the information confidential. Describe the following to the best of your ability. on a separate sheet of paper, with reference to each item number. If some items are not applicable, please indicate N/A.

1. Interviews:

	Name	Title
(a)	_____	_____
(b)	_____	_____
(c)	_____	_____
(d)	_____	_____

2. Description of the Practice

   (a) Full name of the practice
   (b) Date the practice was established
   (c) Discuss the history of the practice, from founding to present, including past physicians, important dates, past locations, etc.

3. Name, Address, and Telephone Number of the Practice's Attorney(s).

4. Name, Address, and Telephone Number of the Practice's Accountant(s).

5. Physicians

   (a) For all doctors, provide
       (1) Name
       (2) Age
       (3) Education background
       (4) Special license requirements
       (5) Board certification
       (6) Number of years experience

(7) Articles written

(8) Lectures delivered

(a) General health (excellent, good, or poor)

(b) Describe life insurance in which the practice is the beneficiary

(c) Describe the typical work week for each doctor, including

    (1) Average number of patients per day

    (2) Nature of treatment

    (3) Average time per patient/treatment

    (4) Hours worked per day

    (5) Time spent in

        i. Office visits/treatments

        ii. Surgery—hospital

        iii. Surgery—in office

        iv. Administration

        v. Promotion

        vi. Civic affairs

6. Personnel

(a) Provide a current organizational chart

(b) Provide a list of employees, other than physicians, at year-end for last year, including current employee classifications, general wage scales, and approximate rate (distinguish full-time and part-time)

(c) List management personnel with title, length of service, age, and annual compensation (including bonuses) for the current year and past two years

	Name	Title	LOS	Age	Compensation
(1)	_____	_____	____	____	_____
(2)	_____	_____	____	____	_____
(3)	_____	_____	____	____	_____
(4)	_____	_____	____	____	_____
(5)	_____	_____	____	____	_____

(d) List board of directors by name and title, including occupation for outside members

7. The Practice

(a) Type of marketing

    (1) Professional referral

    (2) Patient referral

    (3) Direct mail

    (4) Yellow pages

    (5) Other

(b) Provide list of competition

    (1) Specialized

    (2) General

    (3) Minihospitals

   (c) Discuss growth trends, revenue, and operating capacity
     (1) Past
     (2) Projected
     (3) Limiting factors
     (4) New products/services being considered
     (5) Any recent sales of stock (or interests) or offers to buy (or sell)
     (6) Any comparable sales of similar practices

8. Property and Equipment

   (a) Describe your office facilities
     (1) Square feet
     (2) Number of examining rooms
     (3) Number of operating rooms
     (4) Number of x-ray rooms
     (5) If owned, provide
       i. Age and condition
       ii. Assessed value
       iii. Fair market value, if known
     (6) If leased, provide
       i. Amount of monthly payment
   (b) Discuss specialized equipment
     (1) If owned, provide
       i. Age and condition
       ii. Assessed value
       iii. Fair market value, if known
     (2) If leased, amount of monthly payment
   (c) List and discuss company-owned vehicles
   (d) Describe the library
     (1) Original cost
     (2) Replacement cost
     (3) Unique volumes

9. General Outlook (if not covered elsewhere)

10. Other Pertinent Information About the Practice

Disclaimer Excluding Any Warranties: This checklist is designed to provide guidance to analysts, auditors, and management, but is not to be used as a substitute for professional judgment. These procedures must be altered to fit each assignment. The practitioner takes sole responsibility for implementation of this guide. The implied warranties of merchantability and fitness of purpose and all other warranties, whether expressed or implied, are excluded from this transaction and shall not apply to this guide. The Financial Valuation Group shall not be liable for any indirect, special, or consequential damages.

CHECKLIST 5-21:   Valuation Information Request Copyright

Business Name: _____

Valuation Date: _____

This is a generalized information request. Some items may not pertain to your company, and some items may not be readily available to you. In such cases, indicate N/A or notify us if other arrangements can be made to obtain the data. Items already provided have been marked with an "X". If you have any questions on the development of this information, please call.

A. Copyrights

_____   1. List of all copyrighted registrations.

_____   2. List of works (articles, books, painting, etc.).

_____   3. Identify copyright names that are associated with products and/or services (such as software or report templates).

_____   4. Identify historical sale of products and/or services employing the works for the last five years.

_____   5. Projection of products and/or services that will employ the works for the next five years.

_____   6. Details of licensing transaction(s) (in or out) of any copyrighted works.

CHECKLIST 5-22: Valuation Information Request Customer Relationships

Business Name: _____

Valuation Date: _____

This is a generalized information request. Some items may not pertain to your company, and some items may not be readily available to you. In such cases, please indicate N/A or notify us if other arrangements can be made to obtain the data. Items already provided have been marked with an "X". If you have any questions on the development of this information, please call.

A. Customer Relationships

_____ 1. Customer sales history for the last five years for the top 10 customers.

_____ 2. Complete customer history for the last five years (this would be for lifing).

_____ 3. Financial data representing annual costs for the last five years associated with developing/soliciting new customers.

_____ 4. Schedule of new customers gained in each of the last five years with sales.

_____ 5. For the last five years, number of customers in a given year that failed to purchase in the following year, including those customers' sales for the prior year.

CHECKLIST 5-23:   Valuation Information Request In-Process Research and Development

Business Name: _____

Valuation Date: _____

This is a generalized information request. Some items may not pertain to your company, and some items may not be readily available to you. In such cases, indicate N/A or notify us if other arrangements can be made to obtain the data. Items already provided have been marked with an "X". If you have any questions on the development of this information, please call.

A. In-Process Research and Development

_____ 1. Description of the in-process research and development.

_____ 2. Description of competitive advantages and disadvantages of the in-process research and development.

_____ 3. Description of industry trends and competitive pressures that may affect the useful life of the in-process research and development.

_____ 4. In light of 2 and 3 above, estimate the useful life of the in-process research and development support.

_____ 5. Cost records documenting development of the in-process research and development, including:
(a) Person hours to develop;
(b) Various technical levels of persons working on the assignment;
(c) Pay scales for individuals in 5b; and
(d) Information to determine overhead rate.

_____ 6. In the absence of cost records, estimate effort to create the in-process research and development, including:
(a) Who would work on the assignment (employees and consultants);
(b) Pay rates for individuals in 6a; and
(c) Information to determine overhead rate.

_____ 7. Projection of products and/or services that will employ the in-process research and development for the next five years:
(a) Projection of revenues including licensing income for the life span of the in-process research and development;
(b) Projection of direct expenses associated with producing revenue in 7a; and
(c) Summary of indirect expenses (i.e., overhead).

CHECKLIST 5-24:   Valuation Information Request
Know-How

Business Name: _____

Valuation Date: _____

This is a generalized information request. Some items may not pertain to your company, and some items may not be readily available to you. In such cases, please indicate N/A or notify us if other arrangements can be made to obtain the data. Items already provided have been marked with an "X". If you have any questions on the development of this information, please call.

A. Know-How

_____ 1. Description of know-how, including competitive advantages and disadvantages.

_____ 2. Description of industry trends and competitive pressures that may affect the useful life of the know-how.

_____ 3. In light of 1 and 2 above, estimate the useful life of the know-how.

_____ 4. Products or services that employ the know-how.

_____ 5. Historical cost records documenting development of the know-how, including:
   (a) Person hours to develop;
   (b) Various technical levels of persons working on the assignment;
   (c) Pay scales for individuals in 5b; and
   (d) Information to determine overhead rate.

_____ 6. In the absence of historical cost records, estimate corporate effort to re-create the know-how if it were to be developed from scratch, including:
   (a) Who would work on the assignment (employees and consultants);
   (b) Pay rates for individuals in 6a; and
   (c) Information to determine overhead rate.

_____ 7. Historical sale of products and/or services employing the know-how for the last five years.

_____ 8. Know-how associated with products and/or services:
   (a) Projection of products and/or services that will employ the know-how for the next five years;
   (b) Projection of direct expenses associated with producing revenue in 8a; and
   (c) Obtain or develop indirect expenses (i.e., overhead).

_____ 9. Details of licensing transaction(s) (in or out) of any know-how.

CHECKLIST 5-25: Valuation Information Request Patent

Business Name: _____

Valuation Date: _____

This is a generalized information request. Some items may not pertain to your company, and some items may not be readily available to you. In such cases, indicate N/A or notify us if other arrangements can be made to obtain the data. Items already provided have been marked with an "X". If you have any questions on the development of this information, please call.

A. Patent

_____ 1. Summary of patents held by the company.
_____ 2. Copies of patent applications and patent abstracts.
_____ 3. Distinguish which patents have commercial applications (i.e., are producing or are reasonably forecast to produce revenue in the future).
_____ 4. Historical cost records documenting development of the patent(s):
   (a) Person hours to develop;
   (b) Various technical levels of people working on the assignment;
   (c) Pay scales for individuals in 4b; and
   (d) Information to determine overhead rate.
_____ 5. Identify patents and associated products that now have or are expected to have commercial viability:
   (a) Projection of revenues related to patent over the life of the patent; and
   (b) Projection of direct expenses associated with producing revenue in 5a.
_____ 6. Comment on the possibility of extending patent protection beyond statutory life of patent.
_____ 7. Details of licensing transaction(s) (in or out) of any patents.

CHECKLIST 5-26: Valuation Information Request Software

Business Name: _____

Valuation Date: _____

This is a generalized information request. Some items may not pertain to your company, and some items may not be readily available to you. In such cases, please indicate N/A or notify us if other arrangements can be made to obtain the data. Items already provided have been marked with an "X". If you have any questions on the development of this information, please call.

A. Software

_____ 1. Describe the function of the software.

_____ 2. For Cost Approach:
   (a) If available, provide historical cost records documenting development of the software, including:
      (1) Person hours to develop;
      (2) Various technical levels of people working on the assignment;
      (3) Pay scales for individuals in 2a(2); and
      (4) Information to determine overhead rate.
   (b) In the absence of historical cost records, estimate effort to re-create the software if it were to be developed from scratch, including:
      (1) Who would work on the assignment (employees and consultants);
      (2) Pay rates for individuals in 2b(1); and
      (3) Information to determine overhead rate.

_____ 3. Lifing/Obsolescence:
   (a) Expected useful life at inception and at valuation date (obtain support for estimate);
   (b) Date software was actually placed in use;
   (c) Description of internal development that may extend life;
   (d) Description of internal development of replacement software that might shorten life; and
   (e) Description of external factors that may affect life.

_____ 4. For Income Approach:
   (a) Obtain historical revenues applicable to software;
   (b) Projection of revenues including licensing income for life span of software;
   (c) Projection of direct expenses associated with producing revenue in 4b;
   (d) Obtain or develop indirect expenses (i.e., overhead); and
   (e) Identify expenses, direct and indirect, not associated with acquired software.

CHECKLIST 5-27:   Valuation Information Request Proprietary Processes/Products Technology

Business Name: _____

Valuation Date: _____

This is a generalized information request. Some items may not pertain to your company, and some items may not be readily available to you. In such cases, please indicate N/A or notify us if other arrangements can be made to obtain the data. Items already provided have been marked with an "X". If you have any questions on the development of this information, please call.

A. Proprietary Processes/Products Technology

_____ 1. Description of the proprietary process/product technology.

_____ 2. Description of competitive advantages and disadvantages of the proprietary process/product technology.

_____ 3. Description of industry trends and competitive pressures that may affect the useful life of the proprietary process/product technology.

_____ 4. In light of 2 and 3 above, estimate the useful life of the proprietary process/product technology support.

_____ 5. Historical cost records documenting development of the process/product technology:
   (a) Person hours to develop;
   (b) Various technical levels of people working on the assignment;
   (c) Pay scales for individuals in 5b; and
   (d) Information to determine overhead rate.

_____ 6. In the absence of historical cost records, estimate effort to recreate the process/product technology if it were to be developed from scratch:
   (a) Who would work on the assignment (employees and consultants);
   (b) Pay rates for individuals in 6a; and
   (c) Information to determine overhead rate.

_____ 7. Historical sale of products and/or services employing process/product technology for the last five years.

_____ 8. Projection of products and/or services that employ the process/product technology for the next five years:
   (a) Projection of revenues including licensing income for the life span of process/product technology;
   (b) Projection of direct expenses associated with producing revenue in 8a; and
   (c) Obtain or develop indirect expenses (i.e., overhead).

_____ 9. Details of licensing transaction(s) (in or out) of any technology.

CHECKLIST 5-28:   Valuation Information Request
Trademark/Trade Name

Business Name: _____

Valuation Date: _____

This is a generalized information request. Some items may not pertain to your company, and some items may not be readily available to you. In such cases, please indicate N/A or notify us if other arrangements can be made to obtain the data. Items already provided have been marked with an "X". If you have any questions on the development of this information, please call.

A. Trademark/Trade Name

_____   1. List of all trademark/trade name registrations.
_____   2. List of trademark/trade names that are not registered.
_____   3. Identify trademarks/trade names that are associated with products and/or services.
_____   4. Identify historical sale of products and/or services employing trademarks/trade names for the last five years.
_____   5. Projection of products and/or services that employ the trademarks/trade names for the next five years.
_____   6. Details of licensing transaction(s) (in or out) of any trademarks/trade names.

CHECKLIST 5-29: Procedures for the Valuation of Intangible Assets

The definition of intangible asset should include current and noncurrent assets (excluding financial instruments) that lack physical substance. An intangible asset acquired in a business combination shall be recognized as an asset apart from goodwill if that asset arises from contractual or other legal rights. If an intangible asset does not arise from contractual or other legal rights, it shall be recognized as an asset apart from goodwill only if it is separable—that is, it is capable of being separated or divided from the acquired enterprise and sold, transferred, licensed, rented, or exchanged (regardless of whether there is an intent to do so). For GAAP purposes, an intangible asset that cannot be sold, transferred, licensed, rented, or exchanged individually is considered separable if it can be sold, transferred, licensed, rented, or exchanged with a related contract, asset, or liability. However, the value of an assembled workforce of at will employees acquired in a business combination shall be included in the amount recorded as goodwill regardless of whether it meets the criteria for recognition apart from goodwill.

Complete the following:

1. Determine the standard of value:
   a. Fair market value
   b. Fair value
   c. Investment value
   d. Intrinsic value or fundamental value
   e. _____

2. Purpose of the valuation:

   _____

3. Determine the premise of value:
   a. Value in use, as part of a going concern—this premise contemplates the contributory value to an income-producing enterprise of the intangible asset as part of a mass assemblage of tangible and intangible assets.
   b. Value in place, as part of an assemblage of assets—this premise contemplates that the intangible asset is fully functional, is part of an assemblage of assets that is ready for use but is not currently engaged in the production of income.
   c. Value in exchange, in an orderly disposition—this premise contemplates that the intangible asset will be sold in its current condition, with normal exposure to its appropriate secondary market, but without the contributory value of any associated tangible or intangible assets.
   d. Value in exchange, in a forced liquidation—this premise contemplates that the intangible asset is sold piecemeal, in an auction environment, with an artificially abbreviated exposure to its secondary market.
4. Specific identification and recognizable description of the intangible asset.
5. Categorize the intangible asset:
   a. Marketing-related
   b. Customer-related
   c. Artistic-related
   d. Contract-based
   e. Technology-based

6. List the intangible assets eligible for appraisal.

_____

_____

_____

_____

7. Describe fully the intangible asset identified. Attach necessary contracts, drawings, patents, listings, and so on, to fully identify the intangible asset.
8. Describe the legal existence and protection associated with the intangible asset.
9. Explain restrictions of the transferability of ownership.
10. Describe the susceptibility of the asset being destroyed.
11. Describe the inception of the intangible asset (attach a list providing start dates for all customer or client lists).
12. Explain to what degree the revenue associated with these intangible assets is due to the day-to-day efforts of the owner.
13. Provide isolated financial results directly related to the asset, such as:
    a. Historical cost to create the asset
    b. Annual cost to maintain the asset
    c. Specific cash flow related to the asset
14. Description of the history of the asset, including year(s) created.
15. Provide all contracts or agreements related to the asset.
16. Provide all strategic, marketing and business plans related to the asset.
17. Provide all market or industry surveys or studies related to the asset.
18. Describe the competitive environment related to the asset.
19. Describe the general economic environment related to the asset.
20. Describe the specific industry environment related to the asset.
21. Provide all previous valuation reports related to the asset.
22. Provide all financial projections including unit sales.
23. Provide all budgets/forecasts related to the asset.
24. Determine associated cost of capital related directly to the asset.
25. Describe the product life cycle.
26. Describe the stage of the life cycle of the asset.
27. Determine valuation approach:
    a. Cost approach
    b. Market approach
    c. Income approach

Cost Approach

The cost approach is based on the principle of substitution. A prudent investor would not pay more for an intangible asset than it would cost to replace that intangible asset with a ready-made comparable substitute. Some intangible assets likely to be valued using the cost approach include computer software, automated databases, technical drawings and documentation, blueprints and engineering drawings, laboratory notebooks, technical libraries, chemical formulations, food and other product recipes, and so on.

28. Determine the appropriate cost method.
    a. Reproduction cost—the cost at current prices to construct an exact duplicate or replica of the subject intangible asset. This duplicate would be created using the same materials, standards, design, layout, and quality of workmanship used to create the original intangible asset.
    b. Replacement cost—the cost to create at current prices an asset having equal utility to the intangible asset. Replacement cost utilizes modern methods and standards, state-of-the-art design and layout, and the highest available quality of workmanship.
29. Determine the appropriate adjustment for obsolescence:
    a. Physical deterioration—the reduction from cost due to physical wear and tear resulting from continued use.
    b. Functional obsolescence—the reduction due to the inability to perform the function or yield the periodic utility for which the asset was originally designed.
    c. Technological obsolescence—the reduction due to improvements in technology that make an asset less than an ideal replacement for itself, generally resulting in improvements in design or engineering technology and resulting in greater standardized measure of utility production.
    d. Economic obsolescence—the reduction due to the effects, events or conditions that are not controlled by, and thus external to, the current use or condition of the subject asset.
30. Reproduction cost new:
    a. Determine the number of employees involved in creating the intangible asset.
    b. Categorize the employees in 30a by salary level.
    c. Capture the associated employer cost related to each hour of salary level in 30b.
    d. Determine the number of hours per employee salary level utilized to develop the asset.
    e. Extend the number of hours per salary level by the salary and associated employer cost for an estimate of reproduction costs new.
31. Replacement cost:
    a. Adjust reproduction cost new for associated deterioration or obsolescence.
    b. Compare net result of reproduction cost with replacement cost new.
32. Complete the cost approach analysis.

Market Approach

The market approach compares the subject intangible asset with similar or comparable intangible assets that have been sold or listed for sale in the appropriate primary or secondary market. Correlations must be extrapolated.

33. Determine the market served by the guideline or comparable asset.
34. Complete a primary and secondary market search for similar guideline assets, including an analysis of available public data specific to royalty rates and intellectual property transactions.
35. Determine the historical return on the investment earned by the subject intangible asset.

36. Determine the income-generating capacity of the subject intangible asset.
37. Determine the expected prospective return on the investment earned by the guideline asset.
38. Determine the expected prospective return by the subject intangible asset.
39. Determine the historical age and expected remaining useful life of the guideline or comparable intangible asset.
40. Determine the historical age and the remaining useful life of the subject intangible asset.
41. Analyze the terms of the sale of the guideline or the comparable intangible asset including:
    a. The time of the sale
    b. The price paid
    c. The payout terms
    d. Other related terms (including special seller financing and earn-out agreement, noncompete agreement, and so on)
42. Determine the degree of adjustment necessary to the guideline or comparable intangible asset related to:
    a. Physical deterioration
    b. Functional obsolescence
    c. Technological obsolescence
    d. Economic obsolescence
43. Determine the degree of adjustment necessary to the subject intangible asset related to:
    a. Physical deterioration
    b. Functional obsolescence
    c. Technological obsolescence
    d. Economic obsolescence
44. Complete extrapolation of market approach correlation.

Income Approach

45. Determine the economic income related to the identified intangible asset for the following:
    a. Net income before tax
    b. Net income after tax
    c. Net operating income
    d. Gross rental income
    e. Gross royalty or license income (actual or hypothetical if a relief from royalties method is employed, in which case should include an analysis of available public data specific to royalty rates and intellectual property transactions)
    f. Gross or operating cash flow
    g. Net or free cash flow
46. Determine the direct cost associated with maintaining the identified intangible asset. These costs should include cost of operating the asset, storing the asset (facilities), and managing a return from the asset (staff expenses). Pay particular attention to any anticipated unusual costs (such as renewing a patent).

47. Determine specific cash flow to the intangible asset by taking an economic return on contributory assets that are part of the initial cash flow stream. Contributory assets include:
    a. Working capital
    b. Fixed assets
    c. Other intangible assets
48. Determine an appropriate discount rate reflecting a fair return on the investment by considering:
    a. The opportunity cost of capital
    b. The term period of the investment (including consideration of the expected remaining life of the subject intangible asset)
    c. The systematic risk of the investment
    d. The unsystematic risk of the investment
    e. The time value of money
    f. Growth (utilized for computing terminal value)
49. Obtain the necessary data to complete the actuarial retirement rate methodology including:
    a. Inception dates for all active files
    b. Inception dates and retirement dates for all inactive files comprising the subject intangible asset (five-year history desirable)
50. In absence of hard data for no. 49, obtain management's representations as to:
    a. Average age of all active files
    b. Average remaining life of all active files
    c. Estimate the number of visits per file
51. Complete the actuarial retirement rate methodology by:
    a. Observing the data
    b. Determine the curve fitting using appropriate statistical tools:
       - S curve
       - O curve
       - L curve
       - R curve
52. Match the actuarial retirement rate curve with the actual data.
53. Determine the probable life curve.
54. Determine the remaining useful life and survivorship percentages.
55. Apply the survivorship percentages to the discounted cash flow.
56. Complete income approach methodology.

Relief from Royalties Method

57. Determine attributes that make the licensed product unique.
58. Describe competitive advantages of the licensed product including the scope and remaining life of any patents related to the products.
59. Analyze the markets in which the licensee will sell the licensed products, including:
    a. Market size
    b. Growth rates
    c. Extent of competition
    d. Recent developments

60. Determine the degree of complexity in the sale of the licensed product.
61. Determine the extent of customization in customer-specific applications. (Royalty rates are generally inversely related to the level of complexity and licensee customization.)
62. Determine the size of the licensed territory, including any restrictions or exclusivity. (Exclusivity is directly correlated to higher royalty rates.)
63. Determine the length of the initial license term and provisions for renewal. (Royalty rates will increase if the provisions for renewal are favorable for licensing.)
64. Assess the provisions for termination. (The conditions for unilateral license termination generally protect the licensor from a material breach committed by the licensee. These terms should be identified.)
65. Describe the minimum royalty rate if any.
66. Analyze the licensee's ability to assign the license to a third party, either directly or indirectly (for instance through the purchase of stock ownership).
67. Describe the licensor's presence within its own markets.
68. Describe the licensor's financial viability.
69. Describe the licensor's size and market share.
70. Describe the licensor's depth of senior management and stability.
71. Describe the licensor's depth of technical knowledge.
72. Describe the licensor's business plan related to the licensed products, including R&D funding and market analysis.
73. Describe extent and timeliness the licensor offers to support the licensee, including:
    a. Technical product advice
    b. Assisting the licensee with sales
    c. Assisting the licensee with marketing efforts in the defined territory
74. Determine the licensee's available profit percentage available for the royalty dependent on the following:
    a. Available profitability as compared with the industry
    b. The nature of the long-term competitive advantage of the product
    c. The degree the license terms are favorable to the licensee
    d. The degree of support and market share offered by the licensor
    e. The degree of any noncash value offered by the licensee to the licensor
    f. The degree the licensee is required to purchase certain components used in the manufacturing of licensed products from the licensor (mandatory supply arrangement)
    g. The degree of foreign exchange risk borne by either the licensee or the licensor (the risk of future devaluation)

CHECKLIST 5-30:   Checklist for Business Valuations— Royalty Factors

Business Name: _____

Valuation Date: _____

Litigation Date: _____

This checklist has been developed for the purpose of providing a convenient method of assuring that the royalty rate chosen is adequately supported. The analyst should check in the appropriate space below to indicate receipt of necessary data and completion of each phase of the analysis.

❏   1. The royalties received by the patentee for the licensing of the patent in suit, proving or tending to prove an established royalty.

❏   2. The rates paid by the licensee for the use of other patents comparable to the patent in suit.

❏   3. The nature and scope of the license (exclusive or nonexclusive, restricted or nonrestricted) in terms of territory or with respect to whom the manufactured product may be sold.

❏   4. The licensor's established policy and marketing program to maintain his or her patent monopoly by not licensing others to use the invention or by granting licenses under special conditions designed to preserve that monopoly.

❏   5. The commercial relationship between the licensor and licensee, such as whether they are competitors in the same territory in the same line of business, or whether they are inventor and promoter.

❏   6. The effect of selling the patented specialty in promoting sales of other products of the licensee; the existing value of the invention to the licensor as a generator of sales of his or her nonpatented items; and the extent of such derivative or convoyed sales.

❏   7. The duration of the patent and the term of the license.

❏   8. The established profitability of the product made under the patent; its commercial success; and its current popularity.

❏   9. The utility and advantages of the patent property over the old modes or devices, if any, that had been used for working out similar results.

❏ 10. The nature of the patented invention; the character of the commercial embodiment of it as owned and produced by the licensor; and the benefits to those who have used the invention.

❏ 11. The extent to which the infringer has made use of the invention; and any evidence probative of the value of that use.

❏ 12. The portion of the profit or of the selling price that may be customary in the particular business or in comparable businesses to allow for the use of the invention or analogous inventions.

❑ 13. The portion of the realizable profit that should be credited to the invention as distinguished from nonpatented elements, the manufacturing process, business risks, or significant features or improvements added by the infringer.[1]

❑ 14. The opinion testimony of qualified experts.

❑ 15. The amount that a licensor (such as the patentee) and licensee (such as the infringer) would have agreed upon (at the time the infringement began) if both had been reasonably and voluntarily trying to reach an agreement; that is, the amount that a prudent licensee—who desired, as a business proposition, to obtain a license to manufacture and sell a particular article embodying the patented invention—would have been willing to pay as a royalty and yet be able to make a reasonable profit and which amount would have been acceptable by a prudent patentee who was willing to grant a license.[2]

Disclaimer Excluding Any Warranties: This checklist is designed to provide guidance to analysts, auditors, and management, but is not to be used as a substitute for professional judgment. These procedures must be altered to fit each assignment. The practitioner takes sole responsibility for implementation of this guide. The implied warranties of merchantability and fitness of purpose and all other warranties, whether expressed or implied, are excluded from this transaction and shall not apply to this guide. The Financial Valuation Group shall not be liable for any indirect, special, or consequential damages.

---

[1] Business appraisers may wish to compare Georgia-Pacific (318 Federal Supplement 1116 [1970]) Factor 13 to traditional excess-earnings approaches.
[2] Compare to business appraisal concept of "fair market value."

CHECKLIST 5-31: Management Interview Patent Valuation

Date: _____

Exact Company Name: _____

Address: _____

_____

Phone: _____

Interviewer: _____

The objective of this management interview is to provide us with information that will aid us in the valuation of your business. We will keep the information confidential. Describe the following to the best of your ability on a separate sheet of paper, with reference to each item number. If some items are not applicable, please indicate N/A.

1. List of patents to be valued including copy of complete application.
2. Descriptions of the products and processes encompassed by the patents.
3. Describe how the patent will be utilized in a products(s).
4. Describe the firm's R&D facilities.
5. Identify the portion of time spent on R&D by each member of the group.
6. Describe what the company has done to exploit the patent and the result.
7. Describe the marketplace for the patent, including potential uses, current uses, size of market, etc.
8. If there are competing patents, identify market share for each.
9. Market studies performed related to the patent.
10. Summary of how the lack of additional registrations will affect the size of the marketplace for the products and the market penetration in other parts of the world.
11. Defensability of the patent.
12. Reasons patent was not registered in additional countries.
13. Actual, threatened, or potential litigation involving the patent.
14. Estimated time until the patent becomes technically obsolete.
15. Alternatives (real or perceived) for the patents for potential users.
16. Summary of how the patent benefits the user.
17. Estimate cost to upgrade technology for necessary enhancements to keep it competitive.
18. List untapped uses of the patent.
19. Terms of license agreement(s) (past, present, or future) of patent, if any.
20. Price at which the patent has ever been (or planned to be) offered for sale.
21. Provide copies of value opinions by internal or external parties, if any.
22. If the company is gifting the patent, explain why the company wants to get rid of the patent and reasons for development.

23. Explain why the tax benefit of a charitable donation is more valuable to the company than exploiting the patent.

CHECKLIST 5-32: Revenue Ruling 59-60

Revenue Ruling 59-60 contains a wealth of information. It has also stood the test of time and is often quoted in valuation situations, whether tax, divorce, litigation, ESOPs, etc. However, many analysts feel that it is poorly organized and hard to follow.

This valuation checklist has been created to assist in a quick review of the key points as well as for the practical application of this ruling to an actual valuation. The primary information concerning discounts and premiums is highlighted by an asterisk (*).

A. Purpose

❑   Estate tax
❑   Gift tax
❑   Income tax (as amplified by R.R. 65-192)
❑ * Value of closely held corporations
❑ * Value of thinly traded stock
❑   Value of other business entities such as partnerships, proprietorships, etc. (as amplified by R.R. 65-192)

B. Background Definitions

Dates of valuation
❑ Date of death
❑ Alternate date (6 months after date of death)

Definition of fair market value
❑ "…the price at which the property would change hands between a willing buyer and a willing seller when the former is not under any compulsion to buy and the latter is not under any compulsion to sell, both parties having reasonable knowledge of relevant facts."
❑ "…the hypothetical buyer and seller are assumed to be able, as well as willing, to trade and to be well informed about the property and concerning the market for such property."

C. Approach to Valuation

❑ Facts and circumstances
❑ No general formula applicable
❑ Wide difference of opinion as to fair market value
❑ Valuation is not an exact science
   ❑ Sound valuation
      ❑ Relevant facts
      ❑ Common sense
      ❑ Informed judgment
      ❑ Reasonableness
❑ Future outlook
   ❑ Value varies as general economic conditions change
   ❑ Optimism vs. pessimism

❏ Uncertainty as to the stability or continuity of future income
❏ Risk of loss of earnings and value
❏ Highly speculative value to very uncertain future prospects
❏ Valuation is a prophecy as to the future.
❏ Use of guideline public companies

D. **Factors to Consider**

The nature of the business and the history of the enterprise from its inception
❏ Past stability or instability
❏ Growth or lack of growth
❏ * Diversity or lack of diversity of its operations
❏ * Degree of risk in the business
❏ Study of gross and net income
❏ * Dividends history
❏ Nature of the business
❏ Products or services
❏ Operating and investment assets
❏ * Capital structure
❏ Plant facilities
❏ Sales records
❏ * Management
❏ Due regard for recent significant changes
❏ Events of the past that are unlikely to recur in the future should be discounted.
❏ Value has a close relation to future expectancy.
❏ Recent events are of greatest help in predicting the future.

The economic outlook in general and the condition and outlook of the specific industry in particular
❏ Current and prospective economic conditions
❏ National economy
❏ Industry or industries
❏ More or less successful than its competitors; stable with competitors
❏ Ability of industry to compete with other industries
❏ Prospective competition
❏ Price trends in the markets for commodities and securities
❏ * Possible effects of a key person or thin management/lack of succession
❏ Effect of the loss of the manager on the future expectancy of the business
❏ * Key person life insurance could be partially offsetting.

The book value of the stock and the financial condition of the business
❏ Two historical fiscal year-end balance sheets
❏ Balance sheet as of the end of the month preceding the valuation date
❏ * Liquid position (ratio of current assets to current liabilities)
❏ Gross and net book value of principal classes of fixed assets
❏ Working capital
❏ Long-term indebtedness
❏ * Capital structure
❏ Net worth

❏ * Nonoperating assets such as investments in securities and real estate should be revalued on the basis of their market price.

❏ Generally, nonoperating assets command lower rate of return.

❏ Acquisitions of production facilities or subsidiaries

❏ Improvements in financial position

❏ * Recapitalizations

❏ * Changes in capital structure

❏ * Classes of stock

❏ * Examine charter or certificate of incorporation to examine the rights and privileges of the various stock issues including

    ❏ Voting powers

    ❏ Preference as to dividends

    ❏ Preference as to assets in the event of liquidation

The earning capacity of the company

❏ Preferably five or more years of detailed profit-and-loss statements

❏ Gross income by principal items

❏ Principle deductions from gross income

    ❏ Operating expenses

    ❏ Interest and other expense on each item of long-term debt

    ❏ Depreciation and depletion

    ❏ * Officers' salaries in total if reasonable and in detail if they appear excessive

    ❏ Contributions based on nature of business and its community position

    ❏ Taxes

❏ * Net income available for dividends

❏ * Rates and amounts of dividends paid on each class of stock

❏ Remaining amount carried to surplus

❏ Adjustments to, and reconciliation with, surplus as stated on the balance sheet

❏ Separate recurrent from nonrecurrent items of income and expense.

❏ * Distinguish between operating income and investment income.

❏ Ascertain whether any line of business is operating consistently at a loss and might be abandoned with benefit to the company.

❏ * Percentage of earnings retained for business expansion should be noted when dividend-paying capacity is considered.

❏ Since potential future income is a major factor in many valuations, all information concerning past income that will be helpful in predicting the future should be secured.

❏ Prior earnings records are usually the most reliable guide as to future earnings expectancy.

❏ The use of arbitrary five- or ten-year averages without regard to current trends or future prospects will not produce a realistic valuation.

❏ If a record of progressively increasing or decreasing net income is found, then greater weight may be accorded the most recent years' profits in estimating earning power.

❏ Look at margins and percentages of sales to assess risk

    ❏ Consumption of raw materials and supplies for manufacturers, processors, and fabricators

- ❑ Cost of purchased merchandise for merchants
- ❑ Utility services
- ❑ Insurance
- ❑ Taxes
- ❑ Depreciation and depletion
- ❑ Interest

The dividend-paying capacity
- ❑ * Primary consideration to dividend-paying capacity rather than dividends actually paid
- ❑ * Recognition of the necessity of retaining a reasonable portion of profits to meet competition
- ❑ * When valuing a controlling interest, the dividend factor is not a material element, since the payment of such dividends is discretionary with the controlling stockholders.
- ❑ * The individual or group in control can substitute salaries and bonuses for dividends, thus reducing net income and understating the dividend-paying capacity of the company.
- ❑ * Dividends are a less reliable factor for valuation.

Whether the enterprise has goodwill or other intangible value
- ❑ Goodwill is based on earning capacity.
- ❑ Goodwill value is based upon the excess of net earnings over and above a fair return on the net tangible assets.
- ❑ Factors to consider to support intangible value
  - ❑ Prestige and renown of the business
  - ❑ Trade or brand name
  - ❑ Record of success over a prolonged period in a particular locality
- ❑ In some instances, it may not be possible to make a separate valuation of tangible and intangible assets.
- ❑ Intangible value can be measured by the amount that the value of the tangible assets exceeds the net book value of such assets.

Sales of the stock and the size of the block of stock to be valued
- ❑ Prior sales should be arm's length.
- ❑ Forced or distressed sales do not reflect fair market value.
- ❑ Isolated sales in small amounts may not control as a measure of value.
- ❑ * Blockage is not an issue since the stock is not publicly traded.
- ❑ * The size of the block of stock is a relevant factor.
- ❑ * A minority interest in an unlisted corporation's stock is more difficult to sell than a similar block of listed stock.
- ❑ * Control of a corporation, either actual or in effect, may justify a higher value for a specific block of stock since it is an added element of value.

The market price of stocks of corporations engaged in the same or a similar line of business having their stocks actively traded in a free and open market, either on an exchange or over the counter
- ❑ * Must be evidence of an active free public market for the stock as of the valuation date to be used as a comparable company
- ❑ Use only comparable companies.

❏   The lines of business should be the same or similar.

❏   A comparable with one or more issues of preferred stock, bonds, or debentures in addition to its common stock should not be considered to be directly comparable to one having only common stock outstanding.

❏   A comparable with a declining business and decreasing markets is not comparable to one with a record of current progress and market expansion.

E. Weight to Be Accorded Various Factors

❏   Certain factors carry more weight than others because of the nature of the company's business.

❏   Earnings may be the most important criterion of value in some cases, whereas asset value will receive primary consideration in others.

❏   Primary consideration to earnings when valuing stocks of companies that sell products or services to the public

❏   Greatest weight to the assets underlying the security to be valued for investment or holding-type companies

❏   Closely held investment or real estate holding company

   ❏   Value is closely related to the value of the assets underlying the stock.

   ❏   The appraiser should determine the fair market values of the assets of the company.

   ❏ *   Operating expenses of such a company and the cost of liquidating it, if any, merit consideration.

   ❏   The market values of the assets give due weight to potential earnings and dividends of the particular items of property underlying the stock, capitalized at rates deemed proper by the investing public at the valuation date.

   ❏   Adjusted net worth should be accorded greater weight in valuing the stock of a closely held investment or real estate holding company, whether or not family owned, than any of the other customary yardsticks of appraisal, such as earnings and dividend-paying capacity.

F. Capitalization Rates

❏   It is necessary to capitalize the average or current results at some appropriate rate.

❏   One of the most difficult problems in valuation

❏   That there is no ready or simple solution will become apparent by a cursory check of the rates of return and dividend yields in terms of the selling price of corporate shares listed on the major exchanges.

❏   Wide variations will be found even for companies in the same industry.

❏   The ratio will also fluctuate from year to year depending on economic conditions.

❏   No standard tables of capitalization rates applicable to closely held corporations can be formulated.

❏   Important factors to consider

   ❏   Nature of the business

   ❏   Risk

   ❏   Stability or irregularity of earnings

G. Average of Factors

❏   Valuations cannot be made on the basis of a prescribed formula.

❏   There is no means whereby the various applicable factors in a particular case can be assigned mathematical weights in deriving the fair market value.

❏   No useful purpose is served by taking an average of several factors (e.g., book value, capitalized earnings, and capitalized dividends) and basing the valuation on the result.

❏   Such a process excludes active consideration of other pertinent factors, and the end result cannot be supported by a realistic application of the significant facts in the case except by mere chance.

H. Restrictive Agreements

❏ *   Where shares of stock were acquired by a decedent subject to an option reserved by the issuing corporation to repurchase at a certain price, the option price is usually accepted as the fair market value for estate tax purposes.

❏ *   The option price is not determinative of fair market value for gift tax purposes.

❏ *   Where the option, or buy and sell agreement, is the result of voluntary action by the stockholders and is binding during the life as well as at the death of the stockholders, such agreement may or may not, depending on the circumstances of each case, fix the value for estate tax purposes.

❏ *   Such agreements are a factor to be considered, with other relevant factors, in determining fair market value.

❏ *   Where the stockholder is free to dispose of his or her shares during life and the option is to become effective only upon his or her death, the fair market value is not limited to the option price.

❏ *   Determine whether the agreement represents a bona fide business arrangement or is a device to pass the decedent's shares for less than an adequate and full consideration in money or money's worth
   ❏   Relationship of the parties
   ❏   Relative number of shares held by the decedent
   ❏   Other material facts

CHECKLIST 5-33:   Revenue Ruling 77-287

Revenue Ruling 77-287 deals with the valuation of restricted securities. These types of securities are also referred to as unregistered securities, investment letter stock, control stock, or private placement stock. A thorough understanding of this revenue ruling will also assist in determining DLOM in closely held companies.

This valuation checklist has been created to assist in a quick review of the key points as well as for the practical application of this ruling to an actual valuation.

A. Purpose

❏ Amplifies Revenue Ruling 59-60
❏ Valuation of securities that cannot be immediately resold because they are restricted from resale pursuant to federal securities laws.

B. Nature of the Problem

❏ Valuation of stock that has not been registered for public trading when the issuing company has stock of the same class that is actively traded in the securities markets
❏ Determine the difference between the fair market value of the registered actively traded shares versus the unregistered shares of the same company.
❏ Encountered in estate and gift tax as well as when unregistered shares are issued in exchange for assets or the stock of an acquired company

C. Background and Definitions

❏ Restricted securities cannot lawfully be distributed to the general public until a registration statement relating to the corporation underlying the securities has been filed, and has also become effective under the rules of the SEC and Federal securities laws.
❏ Restricted securities
   Defined in Rule 144 as "securities acquired directly or indirectly from the issuer thereof, or from an affiliate of such issuer, in a transaction or chain of transactions not involving any public offering."
❏ Unregistered securities
   Securities where a registration statement, providing full disclosure by the issuing corporation, has not been filed with the SEC pursuant to the Securities Act of 1933. The registration statement provides the prospective investor with a factual basis to make an investment decision.
❏ Investment letter stock
   Also called letter stock. Shares of stock issued without SEC registration. The stock is subject to resale and transfer restrictions set forth in a letter agreement requested by the issuer and signed by the buyer. Such stock may be found in the hands of individual or institutional investors.
❏ Control stock
   The stock is held by an officer, director, or other person close to corporate management. These people are subject to certain requirements pursuant to SEC rules upon resale of shares they own in such corporations.

❏ Private placement stock

    The stock has been placed with an institution or other investor who will presumably hold it for a long period and ultimately arrange to have the stock registered if it is to be offered to the general public. This stock may or may not be subject to a letter agreement. Private placements are exempted from the registration and prospectus provisions of the Securities Act of 1933.

❏ Exempted securities

    Expressly excluded from the registration provisions of the Securities Act of 1933 and the distribution provisions of the Securities Exchange Act of 1934.

❏ Exempted transactions

    Certain sales or distributions that do not involve a public offering and are excluded from the registration and prospectus provisions of the 1933 and 1934 acts. It is unnecessary for issuers to go through the registration process.

D. Securities Industry Practice in Valuing Restricted Securities

❏ Investment company valuation practices
  ❏ Open-end investment companies must publish the valuation of their portfolios on a regular basis.
  ❏ Many own restricted and unrestricted securities of the same companies
  ❏ Valuation methods
    ❏ Market price of unrestricted publicly traded stock less a constant percentage discount based on purchase discount
    ❏ Market price of unrestricted publicly traded stock less a constant percentage discount different from purchase discount
    ❏ Market price of unrestricted publicly traded stock less a discount amortized over a fixed period
    ❏ Market price of the unrestricted publicly traded stock
    ❏ Cost of the restricted stock until it is registered
  ❏ The SEC stated that there are no automatic formulas.
  ❏ The SEC has determined that it is the responsibility of the board of directors of the particular investment company to determine the "fair value" of each issue of restricted securities in good faith.
❏ *Institutional Investors Study*
  ❏ SEC undertook an analysis of the purchases, sales, and holding of securities by financial institutions.
  ❏ Published in March 1971
  ❏ Includes an analysis of restricted securities
  ❏ Period of study is January 1, 1966 through June 30, 1969
  ❏ Characteristics of the restricted securities purchasers and issuers
  ❏ The size of transactions in both dollars and shares
  ❏ Marketability discounts on different trading markets
  ❏ Resale provisions
  ❏ The amount of discount allowed for restricted securities from the freely traded public price of the unrestricted securities was generally related to the following factors

Earnings

❏ Earnings and sales have significant influence on the size of the disounts
❏ Earnings patterns rather than sales patterns determine the degree of risk of an investment.

Sales

❏ The dollar amount of sales of the issuers' securities also has a major influence on the amount of discounts.
❏ Generally, companies with the lowest dollar amount of sales during the period accounted for most of the transactions involving the highest discounts while they accounted for the lowest number that involved the lowest discounts.

Trading market

❏ Higher discounts for over-the-counter, followed by the American Stock Exchange, then the New York Stock Exchange

Resale agreement provisions

❏ The discount from market price provides the main incentive for a potential buyer to acquire restricted securities.
❏ Two factors important in judging the opportunity cost of freezing funds in a restricted security.
  ❏ The risk that the underlying value of the stock will change in a way that, absent the restrictive provisions, would have prompted a sale.
  ❏ The risk that the contemplated means of legally disposing the stock may not materialize.
❏ Seller may be relieved of the expenses of registration and public distribution as well as the risk that the market will adversely change before the offering is completed.
❏ Buyer and seller bargaining strengths influence the discount.
❏ Most common provisions are as follows
  ❏ Option for piggyback rights to register restricted stock with the next registration statement, if any, filed by the issuer with the SEC
  ❏ Option to require registration at the seller's expense
  ❏ Option to require registration, but only at the buyer's own expense
  ❏ A right to receive continuous disclosure of information about the issuer from the seller
  ❏ A right to select one or more directors of the issuer
  ❏ An option to purchase additional shares of the issuer's stock
  ❏ A provision given the buyer the right to have a greater voice in operations of the issuer, if the issuer does not meet previously agreed upon operating standards.
❏ Institutional buyers often obtain these rights from sellers of restricted stocks.
❏ The more rights a buyer can acquire, the lower the buyer's risk, thus the lower the buyer's discount.
❏ Small buyers may not be able to negotiate the large discounts or the rights and options that the volume buyers are able to negotiate.

Summary

- ❏ A variety of methods have been used by the securities industry to value restricted securities.
- ❏ The SEC rejects all automatic or mechanical solutions to the valuation of restricted securities.
- ❏ The SEC prefers to rely on good-faith valuations by the board of directors of each company.
- ❏ The study made by the SEC found that restricted securities generally are issued at a discount from the market value of freely traded securities.

E. Facts and Circumstances Material to the Valuation of Restricted Securities

- ❏ Often a company's stock cannot be traded because of securities statutes as in the case of investment letter restrictions.
- ❏ Stock may also be restricted from trading because of a corporate charter restriction or a trust agreement restriction.
- ❏ The following documents and facts, when used in conjunction with those discussed in Section IV of Revenue Ruling 59-60, will be useful in the valuation of restricted securities
  - ❏ A copy of any declaration of trust agreement or any other agreements relating to the shares of restricted stock
  - ❏ A copy of any documents showing any offers to buy or sell or indications of interest in buying or selling the restricted shares
  - ❏ The latest prospectus of the company
  - ❏ Three to five years of annual reports
  - ❏ Trading prices and trading volume and the related class of traded securities one month preceding the valuation date
  - ❏ The relationship of the parties to the agreements concerning the restricted stocks, such as whether they are members of the immediate family or perhaps whether they are officers or directors of the company
  - ❏ Whether the interest being valued represents a majority or minority ownership

F. Weighing Facts and Circumstances Material to Restricted Stock Valuation

- ❏ Depending on the circumstances of each case, certain factors may carry more weight than others.
- ❏ Earnings, net assets, and net sales must be given primary consideration.
- ❏ In some cases one element may be more important than others.
- ❏ For manufacturing, producing, or distributing companies primary weight must be accorded earnings and net sales.
- ❏ For investment or holding companies, primary weight must be given to the net assets.
- ❏ Careful review of resale provisions found in restricted agreements
- ❏ The two elements of time and expense should be reflected in a discount.
- ❏ The longer the buyer of the shares must wait to liquidate the shares, the greater the discount.
- ❏ If the provisions make it necessary for the buyer to bear the expense of registration, the greater the discount.

❑ If the provisions of the restricted stock agreement make it possible for the buyer to piggyback shares of the next offering, the discount would be smaller.

❑ The relative negotiating strengths of the buyer and seller of restricted stock

❑ A tight money situation may cause a buyer to have the greater balance of negotiating strength.

❑ In some cases the relative strengths may tend to cancel each other out.

❑ The market experience of freely tradable securities of the same class as restricted securities is also significant.

❑ Whether the shares are privately held or publicly traded

❑ Securities traded on a public market generally are worth more to investors than those that are not traded on a public market.

❑ The type of public market in which the unrestricted securities are traded is to be given consideration.

CHECKLIST 5-34:   Revenue Ruling 93-12

The IRS revoked Revenue Ruling 81-253, which applied family attribution to determine control when valuing minority interests in closely held companies. Since Revenue Ruling 81-253 was issued, the IRS lost a majority of the court cases concerning this issue.

Revenue Ruling 93-12 states that a minority discount on transferred stock to a family member will not be challenged solely because the transferred interest, when aggregated with interest held by family members, will be part of a controlling interest. This ruling arose from a gift tax case.

This valuation checklist has been created to assist in a quick review of the key points as well as for the practical application of this ruling to an actual valuation.

A. Issue

❏ If a donor transfers shares in a corporation to each of the donor's children, is the factor of corporate control in the family to be considered in valuing each transferred interest?

B. Facts

❏ Taxpayer owned all the shares of stock of a corporation.
❏ Taxpayer made simultaneous gifts of 20% blocks of stock to each of five children.

C. Law and Analysis

❏ The value of the property at the date of the gift shall be considered the amount of the gift.
❏ The value of the property is the price at which the property would change hands between a willing buyer and a willing seller, neither being under any compulsion to buy or to sell, and both having reasonable knowledge of relevant facts.
❏ Fair market value on the date of the gift.
❏ The degree of control of the business being represented by the block of stock to be valued is among the factors to be considered.
❏ Revenue Ruling 81-253, 1981-1C.B. 187 holds that, ordinarily, no minority shareholder discount is allowed with respect to transfers of shares of stock between family members if, based on a composite of the family members' interests at the time of the transfer, control (either majority voting control or de facto control through family relationships) of the corporation exists in the family unit.
❏ Revenue Ruling 81-253 states that the Service will not follow the decision in the 1981 case *Est. of Bright* v. *United States*.
❏ In *Bright* the court allowed a 27.5% interest to be valued as a minority interest, even though the shares were to be held by the decedent's surviving spouse.
❏ There is mention of *Propstra* v. *United States* (1982), *Est. of Andrews* v. *Comm* (1982), and *Est. of Lee* v. *Comm* (1978). These cases held that the corporations' share owned by other family members cannot be attributed to

an individual family member for determining whether the individual family member's share should be valued as a controlling interest of the corporation.

❏ The Service has concluded, in the case of a corporation with a single class of stock, notwithstanding the family relationship of the donor, the donee, and other shareholders, the shares of other family members will not be aggregated with the transferred shares to determine whether the transferred shares should be valued as part of a controlling interest.

❏ The five 20% interests that were gifted should be valued without regard to the family relationship of the parties.

D. Holding

❏ If a donor transfers shares in a corporation to each of the donor's children, the factor of corporate control in the family is not considered in valuing each transferred interest.

❏ The Service will follow *Bright, Propstra, Andrews,* and *Lee* in not assuming that all voting power held by family members may be aggregated as part of a controlling interest.

❏ A minority discount will not be disallowed solely because a transferred interest, when aggregated with interests held by family members, will be part of a controlling interest.

❏ This will be the case whether the donor held 100% or some lesser percentage of the stock immediately before the gift.

E. Effect on Other Documents

❏ Revenue Ruling 81-253 is revoked.

CHECKLIST 5-35: Review Checklist
General

Business Name: _____

Valuation Date: _____

Premise of Value: _____

This work program checklist has been developed for the purpose of providing a convenient method of establishing that the necessary review procedures have been completed, thus assuring the work papers adequately support valuation conclusions. The reviewer should check in the appropriate space below to indicate completion of the various phases of review.

- ❏ Check that the scope of the work has been unrestricted. If the scope has been restricted, sufficient data must be available to support the valuation conclusion. Such restrictions should be clearly stated in the reports.
- ❏ Check that the valuation standard and premise of value being considered have been properly defined:
    - ❏ If the valuation concerns a business enterprise or equity interest, consider any buy-sell agreements, investment letter stock restrictions, restrictive corporate charter or partnership agreement clauses, and any similar features or factors that may have an influence on value.
    - ❏ If the valuation concerns assets, consider whether the assets are:
        - ❏ valued independently; or
        - ❏ valued as parts of a going concern.
    - ❏ If the valuation concerns equity interests in a business enterprise, consider whether the interests are valued on a majority or minority basis, and document the appropriate adjustments.
    - ❏ If the equity interest is valued on a majority basis, investigate and document the possibility that the business enterprise may have a higher value in liquidation than for continued operation as a going concern. If liquidation is the indicated basis of valuation, any real estate or personal property to be liquidated must be valued under the appropriate standard.
- ❏ Review all work programs for completeness, including:
    - ❏ Valuation information request
    - ❏ Management interview notes
- ❏ Check the source data, management interview, and site visit, and objectively document:
    - ❏ The nature and history of the business
    - ❏ Financial and economic conditions affecting the business enterprise, its industry, and the general economy
    - ❏ Past results, current operations, and future prospects of the business enterprise, including a thorough analysis of tax returns or financial statement information
    - ❏ Past sales of capital stock or partnership interests in the business enterprise being valued
    - ❏ Sales of similar businesses or capital stock of publicly held similar businesses

- ❏ Prices, terms, and conditions affecting past sales of similar business assets
- ❏ Physical condition, remaining life expectancy, and functional and economic utility or obsolescence of assets
- ❏ Review selected financial data by agreeing the report to the source documents, including:
  - ❏ Most current stockholders equity
  - ❏ Most current net income
  - ❏ Most current sales
  - ❏ Most current shares of stock at the valuation date
- ❏ Verify the guideline company's selection criteria are clearly defined and acceptable. Review and assure the subject company is sufficiently comparable to each guideline company, specifically noting strengths and weaknesses in the following areas:
  - ❏ Business operations (SIC/NAICS)
  - ❏ Product or services similarity
  - ❏ Method of marketing (internal sales, external brokers, etc.)
  - ❏ Advantages or disadvantages of patents, copyrights, or trademarks
  - ❏ Advantages or disadvantages of intangible assets
  - ❏ Size (specify revenue, total assets, earnings, etc.)
  - ❏ Financial risk comparability (liquidity, activity, leverage, performance)
  - ❏ Years in business
  - ❏ Depth of management
  - ❏ Other factors (unions, geographic diversification, etc.)
- ❏ Explain why companies that survived the first cut were omitted.
- ❏ Verify that adjustments were made to the selected guideline company financial data before valuation ratios (such as LIFO/FIFO, depreciation, etc.) were computed.
- ❏ Trace the guideline company stock prices to the source data, assuring adherence to the valuation date. Stock prices might be specific to a specific date, a 10-day average, a 30-day average, or some other, but should be explained.
- ❏ Assure a satisfactory explanation as to the valuation multiples elected (priced earnings, price to book, invested capital to EBIT, etc.).
- ❏ Verify adequate documentation of the weighting of the multiple indicators in order to arrive at the market approach indication of value. This weighting may be specific percentages or a blended judgment within the array.
- ❏ If the guideline company public price method is used and, based on the adjustments in your assignment, this method produces a minority, marketable value indicator, verify there is adequate documentation to adjust for:
  - ❏ Control interest (if necessary)
  - ❏ Closely held interest
- ❏ If the merger and acquisition transaction method (external transactions) was used, and if this method based on the facts of the assignment produces a control, marketable indicator, verify there is adequate documentation to reflect the necessary adjustments for:
  - ❏ Minority interest
  - ❏ Closely held interest
- ❏ Review the fair market value calculations necessary to compute preferred stock value, and specifically trace market yields to underlying source documents.

❑ Assure an adequate explanation as to the election of the rating of the preferred stock elected for the subject company.

❑ If internal transactions are utilized, trace the following to source documents:
  ❑ Prices
  ❑ Terms
  ❑ Conditions

❑ Review selected computations extending through price for the market approach including preferred stock.

❑ Review the fair market value calculations necessary to compute preferred stock value and other classes of stock, if any.

❑ Review each selected guideline company financial data as of the valuation date by agreeing or tracing the information in the draft valuation report to the original source documents, including:
  ❑ Revenues
  ❑ Net income
  ❑ Total assets
  ❑ Equity
  ❑ Shares outstanding
  ❑ Other terms specific to value drivers (such as debt for invested capital, interest and taxes for an EBIT computation, etc.)

❑ Review the subject company financial performance and its placement within the guideline group, specifically related to critical financial ratios such as liquidity, performance, activity, and leverage ratios. The election of specific ratios within these categories will be different for each assignment.

❑ Review the market price for each guideline company and the computation of market multiples. Verify the data indicated in the report correlates to source documents.

❑ Check that the selection of the discount for lack of marketability, if any, is appropriate.

❑ Check the appropriateness of the adjustment for control premium or minority discount.

❑ Check that all work papers serve a valuation purpose and are completed properly. This includes:
  ❑ The search for guideline company transactions should be clearly documented.
  ❑ Guideline company financial results should be adjusted properly for accounting consistency.
  ❑ All adjustments necessary to develop an economic balance sheet should be supported by adequate documentation.
  ❑ All adjustments to earnings should be adequately documented. This includes substantiation of nonrecurring items.
  ❑ Projections should have reasonable assumptions supported by events such as new customer contracts.
  ❑ The derivation of the discount or capitalization rate as of the valuation date should be detailed.

❑ Review the draft report for grammar and technical consistency. Each valuation report issued must have the following sections:
  ❑ Title page

❏ Transmittal letter
❏ Certification of appraiser(s)
❏ Index
❏ Valuation summary
❏ A description of the subject being valued
❏ A clear definition of the value estimated
❏ A statement of the objectives of the valuation including the valuation date
❏ A clear statement of the scope of the valuation
❏ A description and explanation of the information considered and the valuation methodology utilized
❏ A statement of contingent and limiting conditions (including hypothetical, fractional, or preliminary labeling)
❏ Inclusion of curriculum vitae for all analysts involved on the assignment
❏ Check that generally accepted accounting principles, including the Uniform Standards of Professional Appraisal Practice, have been observed.

Disclaimer Excluding Any Warranties: This checklist is designed to provide guidance to analysts, auditors, and management, but is not to be used as a substitute for professional judgment. These procedures must be altered to fit each assignment. The practitioner takes sole responsibility for implementation of this guide. The implied warranties of merchantability and fitness of purpose and all other warranties, whether expressed or implied, are excluded from this transaction and shall not apply to this guide. The Financial Valuation Group shall not be liable for any indirect, special, or consequential damages.

CHECKLIST: 5-36: Review Checklist
Eminent Domain

Business Name: _____

Date of Taking: _____

Premise of Taking: _____

This work program checklist has been developed for the purpose of providing a convenient method of establishing that the necessary procedures have been completed, thus assuring the work papers adequately support valuation conclusions in an eminent domain valuation. The reviewer should check in the appropriate space below to indicate completion of the various phases of review.

- ❑ Check that the scope of the work has been unrestricted.
- ❑ Obtain and review information gathered during the initial stages of this engagement, including a copy of the right-of-way map and any related memos or notes.
- ❑ Coordinate an initial meeting with the business owner and perform the following procedures:
  - ❑ Verify the history of the business and determine its qualifications for business damages. (The business, not necessarily the same owner, has been at that location for a minimum of four years as of the date of taking; there is a partial taking of property that affects the business on the remainder; the business has been damaged as a result of the take of property, with due consideration given to any limitation on access to and from the business.)
  - ❑ Discuss the taking with the business owner and determine the general effect to the business.
  - ❑ Obtain a general understanding of the business, and ownership in detail.
  - ❑ Determine the future plans the owner has for the business. Document in detail.
  - ❑ Obtain copies of required financial information (normally this would include the prior five years of tax returns and financial statements, building leases, and current financial information since the latest year end).
  - ❑ Obtain necessary operational information.
  - ❑ Document in detail this discussion in your work papers. Send a letter to client providing a summary of this discussion.
  - ❑ As determined necessary, coordinate efforts with other experts, including:
    - ❑ Real estate appraisers
    - ❑ Engineers
    - ❑ Customer surveys
    - ❑ Marketing/site research
    - ❑ Other
- ❑ Analyze financial data and calculate projections based on historical information. The resultant projections should represent the expected revenues and expenses for the business in the foreseeable future, adjusted for nonrecurring items, owner salaries, use of facilities, and equipment.

- ❑ Review and verify the material consistency with reports submitted by other experts, including:
  - ❑ Real estate appraisers
  - ❑ Engineers
  - ❑ Customer surveys
  - ❑ Marketing/site research
  - ❑ Other
- ❑ Using the financial projections and any other information obtained, including the operational data if applicable, determine the preliminary effect of the taking on the business. This analysis should include any possible reductions in revenues (and gross profits), savings from reduced expenses, required increases in expenses, and other costs to mitigate damages.
- ❑ If it appears economically unfeasible to continue in operation at the present location, consider a relocation of the business. This analysis would normally include an understanding of the customer base, the competitive nature of the business, the market rent situation, and any other pertinent factors.
- ❑ In conjunction with the previous steps, calculate the value of the business.
- ❑ Conclude business damages as limited to the lesser of:
  - ❑ Actual damage
  - ❑ Relocation
  - ❑ Value of the business
- ❑ Document thoroughly the assumptions and information sources used.
- ❑ Prepare the business damage report.
- ❑ Review the report draft, and make any necessary changes.
- ❑ Make arrangements to have the business owner and other pertinent parties review the report draft.
- ❑ Incorporate agreed-upon changes from all reviewers into the final report.
- ❑ Review the final report and make sure all initials are obtained on a report control sheet.
- ❑ Coordinate with time and billing personnel to ensure a detailed printout will be available of total time. Have a standard detailed billing prepared.
- ❑ If necessary, prepare a representation letter and have it signed by the business owner.
- ❑ Deliver appropriate copies of the report and billing.
- ❑ Review work paper file to make sure all work papers are complete and support the final report.

CHECKLIST 5-37: Review Checklist Contemporaneous

Business Name: _____

Project Manager: _____

Reviewer Name: _____

Valuation Date: _____ Due Date: _____

Premise of Value: _____ Fee Budget: _____

Each item on this checklist is to be reviewed contemporaneously with the development of the assignment. As the project manager completes the major section of the appraisal, that portion of the assignment must be forwarded to the partner in charge of that assignment for the partner's immediate review.

Completed   Reviewed

❏   ❏   **Planning:** The planning stage includes the review and acceptance of the representation and engagement letter, identifying the **valuation issues** in consultation with the project manager, determining the **file organization** and sections, and establishing **target dates** for key elements of the assignment, including the target report release date.

❏   ❏   **Data Received:** The partner in charge, in consultation with the project manager, must determine that the minimum necessary data have been received. If not, there should be some acceptable means for **follow-up** and gathering of the necessary data. This step may be complicated by the lack of a cooperative client. This step is satisfied when the VIR is satisfied.

❏   ❏   **Financial Statement Input:** The financial statement input must be traced to the financial statement spreads. Further, the project manager's financial analysis of the company must be performed. This step requires the **verification** of the accuracy of the **mechanical input** of the financial data, and, more importantly, the contemporaneous **agreement** with the partner regarding the **financial interpretation** of the data.

❏   ❏   **Market Search and Selection:** The acceptance of the **guideline companies** must be determined.

❏   ❏   **Guideline Companies Input and Ratios:** The financial data input of the guideline companies must be traced for **mechanical accuracy.** The financial ratios for the **peer group** should be analyzed with final determination of the **pricing ratios** made. **Finalize value indication.**

Completed   Reviewed

❏   ❏   **Asset-Based Approach:** Determine **assets and liabilities** to be restated. Obtain **appraisals** performed by other appraisers. Obtain **client representations,** etc. Finalize **value indication.**

❏   ❏   **Income Approach:** Develop the **discount rate** and/or **capitalization rate. Normalize the financial statements.** Develop **ongoing earnings base** and/or projections. Finalize value indication.

❏   ❏   **Conclusion Issues/Valuation Adjustments** (e.g., **control premium, discount for lack of marketability,** etc.): The determination of the **final conclusion** should be made with particular attention to underlying predicate information such as outside appraisals for **asset-based approach** adjustments and/or discount rate development for the **income approach.**

❏   ❏   **Allocation of Intangible Assets:** The **actuarial retirement rate methodology** must be verified as follows:

Number of active customers
Number of inactive customers
Development of angle adds
Determination of the average age of the active customers
Statistical verification of the selection of the lifing curve
Determination of the remaining useful life
Application of the discounted cash flow methodology

❏   ❏   **Report Narrative:** The **draft** of the report should be reviewed. All sections of the draft should be completed in **final form** including necessary exhibits and graphs before submission to the partner in charge.

Prepare draft report
Review draft report
Make changes necessary for final issuance
Review final report/review checklist

CHECKLIST 5-38: Review Checklist
Compliance with the Uniform
Standards of Professional Appraisal
Practice (USPAP)

The following checklist assists valuation analysts to ensure their work is in compliance with USPAP. All NO answers should be explained.

YES	NO	
❏	❏	Has the scope of the work been unrestricted?
❏	❏	If the scope has been restricted, is there sufficient data to support a valuation conclusion?
❏	❏	Has the valuation premise been defined?
❏	❏	Has value been defined?
❏	❏	Have all buy-sell agreements been considered?
❏	❏	Have all investment letter stock restrictions been considered?
❏	❏	Have all restrictive corporate charter or partnership agreement clauses been considered?
❏	❏	If the interest being valued is majority, has a control premium been properly considered?
❏	❏	If the interest being valued is minority, has a minority discount been properly considered?
❏	❏	Has the expert/financial analyst visited the site?
❏	❏	Has the nature and history of the business been fully considered?
❏	❏	Have financial and economic conditions affecting the business been considered?
❏	❏	Have general industry conditions been considered?
❏	❏	Have general economic conditions been considered?
❏	❏	Has there been a thorough analysis of tax returns and/or financial statements reflecting: (a) Past results (b) Current operations (c) Future prospects
❏	❏	Has consideration been given to past sales of capital stock or partnership interest?
❏	❏	Has consideration been given to the sales of similar entire businesses, including: (a) Prices (b) Terms (c) Conditions
❏	❏	Has consideration been given to the trading of capital stock of publicly held companies that are similar?

<u>YES</u>   <u>NO</u>

❑   ❑   Has consideration been given to past sales of the business's individual assets, including:
(a) Prices
(b) Terms
(c) Conditions

❑   ❑   Has consideration been given to the physical condition of individual assets?

❑   ❑   Have all deviations from generally accepted accounting principles been documented as reasonable?

❑   ❑   Have the Uniform Standards of Professional Appraisal Practice been observed?

Disclaimer Excluding Any Warranties: This checklist is designed to provide guidance to analysts, auditors, and management, but is not to be used as a substitute for professional judgment. These procedures must be altered to fit each assignment. The practitioner takes sole responsibility for implementation of this guide. The implied warranties of merchantability and fitness of purpose and all other warranties, whether expressed or implied, are excluded from this transaction and shall not apply to this guide. The Financial Valuation Group shall not be liable for any indirect, special, or consequential damages.

CHECKLIST 5-39:   Appraisal Review

Check YES if the item described has been adequately considered and reflected in the report (or is not applicable). Check NO if the item should have been considered but was not. All NO items should be clarified by the responsible analyst.

YES	NO	
		Description of the valuation subject and purpose
❑	❑	Party retaining the analyst
❑	❑	Interest being valued
❑	❑	Form of organization (C/S corporation, partnership)
❑	❑	State of legal incorporation or registration
❑	❑	Legal rights and restrictions of ownership, if not obvious
❑	❑	Value characteristics and physical condition, if applicable
❑	❑	Description of classes of ownership and distribution of each
❑	❑	Purpose(s) of the valuation
❑	❑	Standard and premise of value with statutory references
❑	❑	Meaning attached to the standard of value used
❑	❑	Date(s) for which the value applies
❑	❑	Statement of contingent and limiting conditions to which the valuation conclusions are subject (including limitations on the use of hypothetical, fractional, and preliminary appraisals)
		Analyst qualifications and independence
❑	❑	Transmittal letter with signatures of responsible parties and inclusion of dissenting opinions
❑	❑	Statement of the analyst's independence (nonconflict of interest)
❑	❑	Analyst made a physical inspection and/or visited with management and conducted an interview at the subject's location
❑	❑	Analyst conducted a telephone interview with management
		Overall appearance of the report
❑	❑	Grammar and diction
❑	❑	Ambiguous vs. well-defined terminology
❑	❑	Spelling and typographical errors
❑	❑	Completeness
❑	❑	Layout, organization, and overall appearance
❑	❑	Reasonable balance between "soft" (boiler-plate) and "hard" analysis
❑	❑	Clear sources of information verifiable by the reader

YES	NO	
		Qualitative factors about the business
❏	❏	Nature and history of the enterprise since inception
❏	❏	Products and services, and business mix
❏	❏	Industries, markets, and customers served
❏	❏	Competitors and the competitive environment
❏	❏	Description of facilities
❏	❏	Flow of operations (discuss vendors if applicable)
❏	❏	Description of management and key personnel
❏	❏	Organizational structure (including subsidiaries and affiliates)
❏	❏	Related parties and entities and extent of relationships
❏	❏	Economic conditions and outlook for the industry
		Financial position and performance
❏	❏	Adequate discussion of assets, liabilities, liquidity, and leverage
❏	❏	Book value and financial condition
❏	❏	Existence of goodwill or other intangible value
❏	❏	Adequate discussion of financial performance (revenue and profit margins, including historical, current, and expected future levels) and nonrecurring or extraordinary items
❏	❏	Earning capacity
❏	❏	Dividend-paying capacity, history, and prospects
		Valuation methodology(ies)
❏	❏	Description and explanation of the appraisals method(s) used
❏	❏	Proper support and justification of approaches used
❏	❏	Reasonable, well-documented financial statement adjustments
❏	❏	Sales of stock and the size of the block to be valued
❏	❏	Market prices of similar companies traded publicly
❏	❏	Clear criteria and selection procedures of guideline companies, if used, and sufficient explanation if not used
❏	❏	Clear and convincing connection between historical and projected performance, if projections are utilized and/or otherwise explained
❏	❏	Reasonable and appropriate capitalization rate/factor, if alternate method is used
❏	❏	Considered all factors relevant to the methodologies used
❏	❏	Proper use of valuation discounts and/or premiums
❏	❏	Appropriate consideration of the marketability of the securities

<u>YES</u>   <u>NO</u>

Final analysis

❑   ❑   Clear statement of the valuation conclusion(s)

❑   ❑   Logic and reasonableness of conclusion(s)

❑   ❑   Proper support and justification of conclusion(s)

❑   ❑   Description of steps taken that can be recreated by the reader

❑   ❑   Reconciliation of valuation method and approach

CHECKLIST 5-40: Nonanalyst's Guide to Reviewing Business Valuation Reports

Check if the item is reflected in the report.

YES   NO

Are the following clearly stated?

❏ ❏ Specific definition of what is being appraised (1)

❏ ❏ Purpose of appraisal (1)

❏ ❏ Date of valuation (1)

❏ ❏ Date of report preparation (1)

❏ ❏ Standard of value, including reference to statutes if a statutory standard is applicable (1)

Are the following adequately described to give you a basic knowledge of:

❏ ❏ Form of ownership (corporate, partnership, etc.) (2)

❏ ❏ History of the company (1)

❏ ❏ Major assets, both tangible and intangible (goodwill, patents, etc.) (1)

❏ ❏ Products or services (1)

❏ ❏ Markets or customers (1)

❏ ❏ Competition (1)

❏ ❏ Management (2)

❏ ❏ Who owns the company

❏ ❏ How the company is capitalized

❏ ❏ Outlook for the economy, industry, and company (1)

❏ ❏ Past transactional evidence of value (sale of stock, etc.) (1)

❏ ❏ Sensitivity to seasonal or cyclical factors (2)

❏ ❏ State of incorporation

❏ ❏ Sources of information (2)

Financial analysis (1):

❏ ❏ Is there a discussion of the firm's financial statements? (2)

❏ ❏ Are there exhibits summarizing balance sheets and income statements for a sufficient period of time? (2)

❏ ❏ Are adjustments made to the financial statements explained? (2)

❏ ❏ Are company financial statements compared to those of its industry? (2)

❏ ❏ If discounted future earnings or cash flows are used, are the appropriate statements summarized and key assumptions included? (2)

<u>YES</u>   <u>NO</u>

Valuation methodology and report:

❑   ❑   Are the methods used identified and the reasons for their selection discussed? (1)

❑   ❑   Are the steps followed in the application of the method(s) understandable, and do they lead you to the value conclusion? (1)

❑   ❑   When applicable, are sales of similar businesses or capital stock of publicly traded similar businesses used for comparison? (3)

❑   ❑   Does the report explain how any discounts, capitalization rates, or valuation multiples were determined or used? (2)

❑   ❑   Is the terminology used in the report defined so that it is understandable?

❑   ❑   Does the report identify the analysts and have the analysts signed the report? (1)

❑   ❑   Does the report contain the statement of certification signed by the analyst? (1)

Does the analyst's statement of qualifications present relevant qualifications for this appraisal?

❑   ❑   Education

❑   ❑   Technical training

❑   ❑   Professional designations

❑   ❑   Professional appraisal organization memberships and activities

❑   ❑   Type and years of experience

❑   ❑   Does the report contain a statement of confidentiality? (2)

Does the report contain a statement of assumptions and limiting conditions (1), regarding

❑   ❑   Conflicts of interest (2)

❑   ❑   Reliance on data and information supplied by others without verification (2)

❑   ❑   The valuation only being valid for the valuation date and stated purpose (2)

Reviewer's judgment:

❑   ❑   Does the report, in your opinion, cover all the material factors that affect the value of the business? (2)

❑   ❑   Is the value conclusion reasonable, as a result of all the factors presented in the report?

Note:

(1) Specifically mentioned in the Appraisal Foundation's Uniform Standards of Professional Appraisal Practice, the American Society of Appraisers' Business Valuation Standards and American Institute of CPAs Practice Aid 93-3.

(2) Specifically mentioned only by American Society of Appraisers.

(3) Specifically mentioned only by the Appraisal Foundation.

Disclaimer Excluding Any Warranties: This checklist is designed to provide guidance to analysts, auditors, and management, but is not to be used as a substitute for professional judgment. These procedures must be altered to fit each assignment. The practitioner takes sole responsibility for implementation of this guide. The implied warranties of merchantability and fitness of purpose and all other warranties, whether expressed or implied, are excluded from this transaction and shall not apply to this guide. The Financial Valuation Group shall not be liable for any indirect, special, or consequential damages.

CHECKLIST 5-41: Auditor Review of Valuation
for Financial Reporting

Client Name: _____ Reviewer: _____

Date of Value: _____ Valuation Type: _____

Each item on this checklist is to be reviewed progressively by the responsible auditor and by category as the analyst completes the engagement. Scheduling this progressive review of the valuation engagement will eliminate surprises at the end of the engagement, which could cause a delay in issuing the audit. This checklist does not replace the valuation audit program, but is intended to facilitate communication between the analysts and the auditors concerning key valuation issues as the valuation progresses. When completed, this review checklist will ensure the auditor has completed critical steps in the audit program.

COMPLETED

Analyst Qualifications

❑ Does the analyst have specialized training in business valuation and intangible assets?

❑ Does the analyst hold the appropriate professional designations in business valuation, e.g., CPA/ABV, ASA, CBA, CVA?

❑ Can the analyst adequately discuss FASB Statements of Financial Accounting Standards (SFAS) Nos. 121, 131, 141, 142, 144, and Financial Accounting Concepts Statement No. 7, and the AICPA's best practices guide on *In-Process Research and Development*?

❑ Does the analyst have adequate experience in valuing intangible assets?

❑ Does the analyst meet the qualifications for a valuation specialist per FASB's SFAS No. 73?

Industry and Company Risks

❑ Does the analyst understand your perception of the industry's business and financial risks applicable to the company?

❑ Does the analyst understand your perception of the company's business and financial risks?

❑ If the analyst is not familiar with the industry's business and financial risks, did they adequately communicate how they would obtain sufficient relevant knowledge about the industry's business and financial risks?

Company Projections

❑ Did the analyst perform a mathematical check of the company projections?

❑ If so, did they find any mathematical errors?

COMPLETED

- ❑ Can the analyst adequately explain how they tested the underlying assumptions?
- ❑ Does the analyst have a list of the assumptions that required additional analysis or support?
- ❑ Does the analyst's risk analysis of the underlying assumptions correspond with your analysis of the underlying assumptions?
- ❑ If not, can you reconcile the differences?

Guideline Companies Selected

- ❑ Can the analyst adequately explain the process used in selecting the guideline companies?
- ❑ Does the analyst have a list of considered but excluded companies?
- ❑ Are all the guideline companies in the same industry?
- ❑ If not, can the analyst explain why the guideline companies have the same investment risk characteristics as the subject company?
- ❑ Do you agree that the selected guideline companies appear appropriate?

Discount Rate Development

- ❑ Did the analyst use the capital asset pricing model?
- ❑ Did the analyst use the build-up method as a fundamental analysis?
- ❑ Did the analyst use the weighted average cost capital?
- ❑ If so, does the equity portion match either the capital asset pricing model or the build-up method?
- ❑ If so, can the analyst justify the selection of the interest rate used?
- ❑ If so, is the tax rate used in determining the after-tax interest rate appropriate for the subject company?
- ❑ If so, can the analyst justify the weighting between the equity and the debt portions of the weighted average cost capital model?
- ❑ Does the analyst have supporting documentation for the input items in the various discount rate development models?

Economic Adjustments

- ❑ Has the company or analyst identified all the appropriate nonrecurring economic events or costs?
- ❑ Can the analyst justify any other economic adjustments made to the income statements?
- ❑ If using an adjusted balance sheet method, did the analyst provide appropriate documentation for the economic adjustments made to the balance sheet?

COMPLETED

Allocation of Income to Identifiable Intangible Assets

❏   Has the analyst made a list of identifiable intangible assets applicable to the subject company?

❏   Does the schedule of income allocation have appropriate supporting documentation?

❏   Does the schedule of income allocation reconcile to total company income?

❏   Are there any reasons to disagree with the income allocation schedule?

❏   If so, have these issues been discussed with the analyst?

Royalty Rates

❏   Does the analyst have a list of royalty rates applicable to each identifiable intangible asset?

❏   Were the royalty rates derived from a royalty rate survey?

❏   If so, did the analyst present any analysis related to the quality or the survey?

❏   Did the analyst use the 25% rule in determining the royalty rate?

❏   Were the royalty rates derived from a study of actual licensing transactions?

❏   Can the analyst adequately explain the selection process used in determining the guideline licensing transaction?

❏   Can the analyst explain any adjustments to the guideline royalty rate transactions?